Includes More Than 300 Raw Food Recipes

# RAWESOMELY VEGAN!

## THE ULTIMATE RAW VEGAN RECIPE BOOK

## Mike Snyder

President of TheRawDiet.com and coauthor of
*The Everything® Raw Food Recipe Book*

**A**dams media

AVON, MASSACHUSETTS

Published by
Adams Media, a division of F+W Media, Inc.
57 Littlefield Street, Avon, MA 02322. U.S.A.
*www.adamsmedia.com*

ISBN-10: 1-4405-2900-0
ISBN-13: 978-1-4405-2900-9
eISBN-10: 1-4405-3207-9
eISBN-13: 978-1-4405-3207-8

Printed in the United States of America.

10   9   8   7   6   5   4   3   2   1

**Library of Congress Cataloging-in-Publication Data**
is available from the publisher.

This publication is designed to provide accurate and authoritative information with regard to the subject matter covered. It is sold with the understanding that the publisher is not engaged in rendering legal, accounting, or other professional advice. If legal advice or other expert assistance is required, the services of a competent professional person should be sought.

—From a *Declaration of Principles* jointly adopted by a Committee of the American Bar Association and a Committee of Publishers and Associations

Many of the designations used by manufacturers and sellers to distinguish their product are claimed as trademarks. Where those designations appear in this book and Adams Media was aware of a trademark claim, the designations have been printed with initial capital letters.

Contains original recipes and photographs contributed by Sayward Rebhal.

Contains material adapted and abridged from *The Everything® Raw Food Recipe Book* by Mike Snyder with Nancy Faass, MSW, MPH, and Lorena Novak Bull, RD, copyright © 2010 by F+W Media, Inc., ISBN 10: 1-4405-0011-8, ISBN 13: 978-1-4405-0011-4; *The Everything® Vegan Cookbook* by Jolinda Hackett with Lorena Novak Bull, RD, copyright © 2010 by F+W Media, Inc., ISBN 10: 1-4405-0216-1, ISBN 13: 978-1-4405-0216-3; *The Everything® Juicing Book* by Carole Jacobs and Chef Patrice Johnson, with Nicole Cormier, RD, copyright © 2010 by F+W Media, Inc., ISBN 10: 1-4405-0326-5, ISBN 13: 978-1-4405-0326-9; *The Everything® Superfoods Book* by Delia Quigley, CNC, with Brierley E. Wright, RD, copyright © 2008 by F+W Media, Inc., ISBN 10: 1-59869-682-3, ISBN 13: 978-1-59869-682-0; *The Everything® Salad Book* by Aysha Schurman, copyright © 2011 by F+W Media, Inc., ISBN 10: 1-4405-2207-3, ISBN 13: 978-1-4405-2207-9; and *The Everything® Soup Cookbook* by B.J. Hanson, copyright © 2002 by F+W Media, Inc., ISBN 10: 1-58062-556-8, ISBN 13: 978-1-58062-556-2.

This book is intended as general information only, and should not be used to diagnose or treat any health condition. In light of the complex, individual, and specific nature of health problems, this book is not intended to replace professional medical advice. The ideas, procedures, and suggestions in this book are intended to supplement, not replace, the advice of a trained medical professional. Consult your physician before adopting any of the suggestions in this book, as well as about any condition that may require diagnosis or medical attention. The author and publisher disclaim any liability arising directly or indirectly from the use of this book.

fabric © iStockphoto/ranplett
fruits and vegetables © iStockphoto/nicoolay

*This book is available at quantity discounts for bulk purchases.*
*For information, please call 1-800-289-0963.*

# Contents

## CHAPTER 5

# Smoothies | 45

## CHAPTER 6

# Breaking the Fast | 59

## CHAPTER 7

# Step Into Salads | 85

## CHAPTER 8

# Soups for All Seasons | 111

## CHAPTER 12

# Mix and Match for the Main Event | 193

# Introduction

If you don't do dull, conventional, mundane meals . . . .

If you'd rather go hungry than go unhealthy . . . .

If your food is fresh, mouthwatering, stereotype-shattering, and enviable in every way . . .

If you're raw vegan because you're driven by *passion*, baby . . .

. . . then it's about time you had a cookbook that could keep up.

You already know the rules of the game: the food is never heated above 118°F, and it's cruelty-free in every way. Whether it's whole, blended, juiced, chopped, infused, fermented, soaked, sprouted, sun-dried, marinated, frozen, extracted, or dehydrated, it's as vital as it was when it was picked from the ground. Still vibrating with its essential *life*.

You know the rewards, as well. You've left animal exploitation behind and you're treating your body to valuable enzymes, easily assimilated nutrients, beneficial bacteria, and unaltered proteins. Forget the processed junk and the grocery aisle garbage. You're free and clear from almost everything that irritates, aggravates, and agitates. The food you choose keeps you energized, satisfied, and feeling fabulous!

And now you've found the book that accompanies your lifestyle: *Rawesomely Vegan*. A recipe collection that's up to your standards—no ifs, ands, or buts; no fillers; and no fake stuff. A manual to meet all your needs, to leave all other cookbooks behind. A compendium that inspires you to push farther into your *rawesome* success.

Contained in these pages you'll find an all-encompassing arsenal of more than 300 radical, raw vegan recipes for any and every occasion. You'll be satisfied from dawn to dusk, from your simple solo dinner plate to your fabulous fancy party platter. With unique flavor combinations featured in unexpected ways, your palate will always be piqued and you'll never need to look elsewhere.

You'll hit each morning running with invigorating starters like the *Energizer Bunny Breakfast Shake* or the *Orchid's Kiss Vanilla Clotted Cream*. Lunches are luxurious with decadent soups and delicious salads, plus plenty of easy, on-the-go gourmet. And clean food made quick means you don't give up good health while you keep pace in the fast lane of life, and with exciting dinner entrées such as *NoLo's Jazzie Jammin' Beans and Rice*, or the *Fanciful Fennel Sprout Croquettes*, you'll never run low on substance or style. Round these out with creative juice blends, smoothies, dips, breads, appetizers, and of course, those delectable raw desserts, and this is truly your one-stop-shop for a life that's worth eating!

Living *rawesomely* means taking a playful approach towards life and diet. There's no getting bogged down in dogma and there's nobody keeping score. It's just you, empowered in your own wealth of wellness, progressing in your own groovy process. What an awesome, *rawesome* ride! Enjoy!

# PART 1

# Keep It Rawesome!

Before you dive into the more than 300 amazing recipes contained within these pages, it's a good idea to take a step back, take an excited deep breath, and take stock. Your kitchen is your workroom, your laboratory, and your art studio. You need it to be well-stocked and running efficiently! The info you'll learn in this part will help you get your bearings—because even a seasoned raw chef can use some back-to-school basics every once in a while. So here you'll find a quick refresher on pantry staples and ways to store and use them, a review of the most important gadgets and gizmos as well as some pro tricks for how to get by without them, a series of helpful tips and tricks for making your food as delicious—and as doable—as possible, and finally, some strategies for long-term success in living a raw vegan lifestyle. So read on to uncover your treasure map to the land of rawesome!

# Chapter 1
# Stocking Your Raw Kitchen

Living the raw lifestyle is fabulous and fun, and it can make you feel on top of the world. But, as you know, getting to the top can be a tough trek, and staying there can sometimes be even harder. Modern life is not designed to support healthy choices, which can make rockin' your rawsome diet difficult. Thankfully, you can stock your kitchen in whatever way you want—and, with a proper set-up that turns food prep into pure pleasure, your raw inspiration will always remain at your fingertips.

In this chapter, you'll find a profile of each performer that plays a key role in a raw pro kitchen. Chances are that you may be good friends with a lot of these foods already, but if not, you don't necessarily need to rustle them all up immediately. If you purchase a few each time you visit the market, you'll be well on your way to building a pretty amazing raw vegan pantry.

## Fresh Produce

Fresh fruits and vegetables are the cornerstone of your healthy lifestyle, and they most likely make up the majority of what you eat. But not all produce is created equal! There are certain fruits and vegetables that, for various reasons, are especially high in chemical contamination. These include fruits with a high surface to volume ratio, like berries, cherries, or grapes; fruits and veggies with edible skins, like apples, carrots, bell peppers, peaches, pears, or nectarines; and leafy vegetables like kale, lettuce, and celery.

These foods should be purchased strictly organic or not at all. Why organic? Well, in essence, organic foods are grown without toxic pesticides and herbicides, are free of artificial fertilizers, free of sewage contamination, free of any genetic modification or genetically modified ingredients, and have never been irradiated.

Conversely, there are a few selections that are safer to buy conventional, if you must. These include thick-skinned fruits such as citrus, melons, or avocados; tropical fruits such as kiwi, mango, papaya, or pineapple; root veggies like sweet potatoes and onions; and the following low-spray crops: asparagus, broccoli, cabbage, eggplant, sweet corn, sweet peas, and tomatoes. While you should buy organic whenever possible to ensure that you're eating the cleanest produce possible, if you need to pinch pennies or if your local store doesn't have a wide selection of organic produce, then these fruits and veggies are where you should make your concessions.

In addition, *where* you buy your produce is just as important as *what* you're eating and it's best to buy as seasonally and as locally as possible, by shopping at farmers' markets or at independent grocers. Buying locally and in season means you'll be getting the freshest, healthiest food available, straight from the farm to your table—often in the same day! Food that's grown far away is picked before it's ripe and shipped for days or even weeks before it reaches the store shelves. All of this is reflected in the lower nutrient content, so for the most vitamin- and mineral-rich produce, keep it local and keep it seasonal.

## Freshen Up

You want to eat the freshest foods possible, but sometimes it's hard to make sure that what you're putting on your table is at its peak. To be sure your food is as fresh as possible and to ensure that you're getting the healthiest and most flavorful fruits and veggies available, it's best to hit the produce aisle frequently throughout the week. Remember that nutrients begin to degrade as soon as an item is picked, so the fresher the better! However, it's not always easy to make it to the store, and if you live a busy life—as you probably do—there are few tips for maximizing pizzazz in those precious plant foods.

Store countertop fruits, like apples and avocados, out of direct sunlight. They should be kept cool (not cold), so make sure your kitchen is well ventilated. Tomatoes should always be kept on the countertop—never in the fridge.

Store refrigerated fruits and vegetables in crisper bins, but separately; keeping fruits in one bin, and veggies in another, will help to prevent accelerated ripening. Place each item or group of items in a perforated plastic bag. Put greens and other tender veggies in the high-humidity crisper. The low-humidity crisper is for hardier items like broccoli or beets.

Store fresh herbs in water. Snip the ends and stand them in a glass, like a bouquet of flowers. Then cover them with a plastic bag and keep them in the fridge. If you're sure to follow these rawesome tips, you guarantee yourself the freshest, more delicious food ever!

## Sea Vegetables

Sea vegetables include seaweed and algae, which comprise a unique group of highly mineralized foods. Foods from this group are rich in calcium, iodine, and iron among other countless critical trace minerals. Iodine is a rare but important mineral, and iodine deficiency is the number one cause of preventable intellectual disability.

There are a lot of creative ways to incorporate sea vegetables into your diet, but they can be a bit of an acquired taste so be prepared to experiment and to try a few varieties. Begin by sampling the recipes provided in this book, and then have fun branching out and exploring with your own creations.

The sea vegetables that you'll want to stock in your kitchen include:

- arame
- dulse
- kelp
- kelp noodles
- Irish moss
- nori (untoasted)
- sea lettuce
- sea spaghetti
- wakame

Keep in mind that, since these items come from the ocean, they are subject to environmental pollution. Always purchase your products from legitimate providers, and aim to buy organic.

## Nuts

Nuts, as you likely know, are the dairy of the raw world—a strange sentiment, but it's absolutely true! They add creaminess, richness, depth, and satiety to a recipe. And, in addition to being versatile and energy dense, they're a good source of protein, and many of them even contain calcium.

Each type of nut has its own impressive nutrient profile, and each boasts its own assortment of benefits, but the three that play the most central role in raw cuisine are almonds, cashews, and walnuts, which are the most versatile and budget-friendly. Almonds are exceptionally high in protein, and they provide a solid source of calcium. Cashews contain high levels of both iron and zinc. And walnuts are rich in essential omega-3 fatty acids, as well as the essential amino acid tryptophan.

*Really Raw?*
Many nuts are falsely labeled as "raw" when they are, in fact, pasteurized. For example, a law requires that all domestically grown, commercially sold almonds undergo pasteurization. "Really Raw" almonds, cashews, and other nuts can be secured from online sources.

Other delicious nutty options include:

- Brazil nuts: a great source of selenium
- hazelnuts: an excellent source of vitamin E
- macadamia nuts: a rare source of the omega fat palmitoleic acid
- pecans: high in zinc
- pine nuts: a great source of manganese

In addition to the benefits mentioned above, all nuts are rich in heart-healthy fats that can contribute to weight loss and lowered cholesterol.

A well-stocked pantry should include a wide variety of both nuts and seeds and you can buy in bulk to cut costs. To make sure your supply doesn't go rancid, you can store overstock in the fridge or freezer (packaged in an airtight container, they'll last about four months in the refrigerator and longer in the freezer). As always, organic is optimal.

## Seeds

Seeds are another power player that you should make sure you have stocked in your rawesome pantry. They are vitamin- and mineral-rich, and tend to be less expensive than their nutty counterparts.

Flaxseed has amazing binding properties along with an impressive nutrient profile, which makes it the cornerstone of countless raw recipes, and an essential part of unbaking. Flaxseed is very high in fiber and is a great source of ALA (alpha-linolenic acid), which is a plant-based form of omega-3 fatty acid.

Some other exceptionally rawesome seeds include:

- chia: a stellar source of calcium and omega-3s
- hempseed: a complete protein and another great source of essential omega-3 fatty acids
- pumpkin: high in iron and zinc
- sesame: very high in calcium and iron
- sunflower: a great source of vitamin E and thiamine

As with nuts, you can buy seeds in bulk to cut costs and store your overstock in the fridge or freezer to ensure freshness. As always, organic is the way to go.

## Grains and Legumes

Grains and especially legumes are excellent sources of amino acids, and they can play an important role in a well-rounded raw diet. Grains are very high in fiber and provide easy access to extra protein, which can be sparse in some raw vegan diets. They're also rich in minerals like zinc and iron, and many of the B-vitamins such as thiamine, riboflavin, pyridoxine, and folic acid. Commonly used grains include:

- amaranth
- barley

- buckwheat
- kamut
- millet
- oats (hulless only)
- quinoa
- rye
- spelt
- wheat berries
- wild rice

Legumes are high in protein, low in fat, and are especially high in the essential amino acid lysine. It's important to make sure you get an adequate amount of all nine essential amino acids, and that's why including legumes (and grains) in your rawesome repertoire is such an important and healthy habit for a sustainable raw vegan lifestyle. The varieties of legumes that you want to stock up on include:

- adzuki
- alfalfa
- black-eyed peas
- clover
- garbanzo beans
- lentils
- mung beans
- peas

Improperly prepared legumes can be hard to digest because we lack the proper enzymes to completely break them down, but soaking and sprouting them before eating—or uncooking!—with them will make them edible in their raw state. The same is true of seeds.

## Soaking Seeds: the Why and the How

As you start to make the recipes in Part 2, you'll notice that many of them call for the soaking of seeds, grains, and legumes before you get down to business. (To make this process easier to understand, in this section "seeds" refers to all seeds, nuts, grains, and legumes.) Why? Well, to start with, soaking seeds softens their texture. The practice allows for cashews to become whippable, for almonds to become "milkable," and for crunchy buckwheat to become a completely blendable breakfast. In this way, soaking is employed as a purely aesthetic agent.

Remember that all seeds are dormant, waiting for an opportunity to grow. Inside of them is everything they need to create life—the blueprint and building blocks to assemble an entire plant. In order to maintain stability in this suspended state, they have evolved protection mechanisms that keep them safe.

Dormancy is accomplished via suppression of enzymatic activity. But the chemicals involved in this process can also inhibit our own enzymes, interfering with healthy digestion, and these compounds can bind to precious minerals like calcium, iron, magnesium, and zinc and actually leech these nutrients from our bodies. Eating too many improperly prepared seeds can lead to mineral deficiency and may contribute to poor bone density.

Soaking seeds initiates germination. Beginning this process causes a biochemical change and a rapid cell division. Enzyme inhibitors release their hold and the proteins, vitamins, minerals, and essential fatty acids begin to multiply. Suddenly the nutrients are bioavailable, and the seeds become more digestible.

Seeds can be soaked in a glass container using fresh filtered water. Simply immerse the seeds in plenty of water, keeping in mind that they will expand as they soak. Cover the container with a loose lid or a dish towel. Soaking times will vary by seed; refer to the Soaking and Sprouting Chart on the next page.

## Sprouting Seeds: the Why and the How

For many seeds (again, "seeds" includes nuts, grains, and legumes), sprouting is the step that follows soaking. Sprouts are some of the healthiest foods on the whole planet. Why? Because germination initiates the production of vitamin C and increases carotene, vitamin E, and many B vitamins. Living sprouts contain an abundance of enzymes that aid in digestion and other metabolic functions, which is why sprouting, much like soaking, helps to prevent the digestive discomfort that's often associated with legumes. Sprouting also causes the protein content of the seed to go through the roof (to 35 to 50 percent protein in the seed), while fat percentage drops, and complex carbohydrates begin breaking down into simple glucose for easy incorporation into the body. Sprouting can turn a seed from an acid-forming food—a food that lowers blood pH—into an alkalinizing food—a food that increases pH.

# Soaking and Sprouting Chart

| Food | Soaking Time | Sprouting Time |
|------|-------------|----------------|
| Alfalfa | 5 hours | 5 days |
| Almonds | 8 to 12 hours | Do not sprout |
| Barley | 6 to 8 hours | 5 to 7 days |
| Broccoli | 6 to 12 hours | 3 days |
| Buckwheat | 15 to 45 minutes | 24 hours |
| Cabbage | 8 to 12 hours | 3 days |
| Chickpeas/Garbanzo Beans | 8 to 12 hours | 1 to 2 days |
| Cloves | 5 hours | 5 days |
| Dulse (sea vegetable) | 5 minutes | Do not sprout |
| Fenugreek | 6 hours | 5 days |
| Flaxseed | 6 to 8 hours | Do not sprout |
| Hempseed | Do not soak | Do not sprout |
| Lentils | 8 to 12 hours | 2 days |
| Macadamia Nuts | Do not soak | Do not sprout |
| Mustard | 5 hours | 5 days |
| Oats, Unhulled | 15 to 45 minutes | 1 to 3 days |
| Pecans | 1 to 2 hours | Do not sprout |
| Pine Nuts | Do not soak | Do not sprout |
| Pistachios | Do not soak | Do not sprout |
| Pumpkin Seeds, Green | 4 hours | 24 hours |
| Quinoa | 3 hours | 24 hours |
| Radish | 6 hours | 5 days |
| Raisins | 1 to 3 hours | Do not sprout |
| Rye | 6 to 8 hours | 5 to 7 days |
| Sesame Seeds | 4 to 6 hours | Do not sprout |
| Sun-Dried Tomatoes | 3 to 4 hours | Do not sprout |
| Sunflower Seeds | 4 to 6 hours | 24 hours |
| Wakame (sea vegetable) | 2 hours | Do not sprout |
| Walnuts | 1 to 2 hours | Do not sprout |
| Wheat | 6 to 8 hours | 5 to 7 days |
| *Leafy Green Sprouts* | | |
| Buckwheat, Unhulled | 6 hours | 7 days |
| Sunflower Seeds, Unhulled | 8 hours | 7 days |
| Wheatgrass | 8 to 12 hours | 7 days |

Sprouting is also inexpensive and easy. Begin by soaking your seeds according to the Soaking and Sprouting Chart outlined in the previous section. When the soak is complete, rinse your seeds and place them in a sprouting bag or glass jar with a mesh lid or cloth (something that breathes). Simply leave them out on the counter and rinse them carefully every 6–8 hours. The sprout time will vary by species; refer to the chart for details.

Use your sprouts in juices or smoothies, atop salads, blended into pâtés, or in any of the many recipes that feature them in the following pages. However, keep in mind that not all seeds actually need to sprout. For example, grains and legumes should be allowed to germinate completely in order to realize their full nourishing potential, but most nuts, on the other hand, can be eaten right after a simple soak.

## Fermented Foods

If you're stocking your totally rawesome pantry, you want to make sure that you have plenty of raw fermented foods on hand, such as:

- kefir
- kimchee
- kombucha
- kvass
- sauerkraut
- water kefir
- yogurt

Fermentation is a naturally occuring process where wild microorganisms like yeast, mold, and bacteria convert sugar into lactic acid. The process of fermentation can be used to preserve foods, but it can also do some super healthy things for you. Like what, you ask? Well, fermented foods facilitate digestion by helping to break down other foods, by contributing important digestive enzymes, and by colonizing the intestines and colon with essential beneficial bacteria. Fermentation also increases the nutrient content of the food. For example, sauerkraut has four times as much available vitamin C as plain cabbage.

Fermented foods can be purchased in health food stores and specialty markets, and are widely available online, but to make sure the foods you're eating are organic and healthy, you can make your own fermented foods by following the recipes found throughout this book.

## Superfoods

A "superfood" is simply a plant—often one that's precious or "exotic"—that has a disproportionately high number of nutrients. There are many "common" foods that are super, like avocados, blueberries, walnuts, and kale, but of course raw foodists are referring to a specifically designated group of highly prized products. Examples of some important superfoods include:

- Greens Powders: chlorella (green algae), marine phytoplankton, spirulina (cyanobacteria), wheat grass, and wild blue-green algae.
- Super Fruits: acaí, coconuts, goji berries, Incan berries, mulberries, and noni.
- Super Pods and Powders: cacao, maca, and mesquite.
- Super Mushrooms: chaga, maitaki, reishi, and shiitake.
- Super Seeds: chia and hemp.

Superfoods can be fun and are undeniably nutrient-rich, which can help to expedite healing and rebuilding. They also offer diversity, excitement, opportunity for exploration and experimentation, and even a bit of mysticism!

## Oils, Vinegars, and Other Flavor Makers

Since you're already living an all-raw lifestyle, you've likely noticed than many traditional condiments are no longer on the table, but you don't have to let tasteless foods hold you hostage. Yes, most common oils are heated or heavily processed, but there's a delicious and healthier raw counterpart for anything you feel you're missing out on. To that end, when you're stocking your kitchen, make sure you have a few premium oils in your pantry. Coconut oil (and sometimes coconut butter) is cold-pressed and remains solid at room temperature. Some liquid oils you want to have in stock include cold-pressed olive and hempseed oils—which both have their own distinct flavors—and flaxseed oil, which is more neutral.

In addition to the flavor that oils brings to a recipe, when you're designing a dish to please your palate, adding acidity or a tangy taste, is pretty important. Many raw foods taste acidic but actually have an alkalinizing effect in the body, like citrus. For example, lemon juice is technically an acid, but in the body it raises blood pH, like all beneficial alkalinizing foods. You'll want to make sure to always have lemon juice on hand. It's raw. It's vegan. And it's imperative to have if you're making dressings, dips, and marinades.

Another way of adding acidic flavor is vinegar. The most commonly used raw vinegar is unpasteurized apple-cider vinegar, which is fermented and contains live active cultures. Another option is coconut vinegar, which has a sweeter quality reminiscent of rice-wine vinegar. Coconut vinegar appears in many recipes in Part 2, but if you can't get your hands on it, you can always substitute apple-cider vinegar.

You also want to add just the right amount of saltiness to your dishes. For meals that need some extra salt added in, nama shoyu, the only raw soy sauce, is perfect to have in stock. An alternative to nama shoyu, for those who may be soy- or gluten-free, is coconut aminos, a fermented product made from coconut palm sap, which has a salty flavor similar to soy sauce.

## Herbs and Spices

The entire plant world is at your disposal, so take full advantage of that kaleidoscope of flavors! Many herbs, like basil, cilantro, parsley, mint, and chives, are widely available in their fresh form. And they're also easy to grow on a windowsill in your very own kitchen. Direct from pot to plate—now that's living food!

Dried herbs and spices are also available, and they open the doorway to many new exotic flavor combinations. However, while some of these are naturally sundried, others are cooked or chemically processed. A lot of raw foodists overlook this, because although the flavors herbs and spices bring to your food is big, the actual quantity that you're using is infinitesimal. But if staying strictly raw is important to you, you can find "guaranteed raw" sources available online.

# Raw Vegan Sweeteners

These days there are a lot of options for sweetening up your favorite treats, and you should make sure you have some sweeteners on hand when you need them. Fill your pantry with some of the most popular sweeteners, including:

- **Agave Syrup:** The syrup is made from desert plants grown in Mexico—the same plants used for making tequila—and ranges in color from clear to dark amber. Agave is mostly fructose, or fruit sugar, and is very sweet, so recipes using agave require less overall sweetener.
- **Coconut Nectar:** This liquid sweetener is made from sap collected from coconut blossoms and, like other undistilled sweeteners, it contains a number of nutritious trace minerals.
- **Coconut Sugar:** Evaporating coconut sap at low temperatures creates this dark and rich sugar that will probably remind you of brown sugar. Coconut sugar is less sweet than the liquid sweeteners, so you may need to use more of it to get the sweetness you're looking for.
- **Dates:** This fruit can be used in its whole form or it can be soaked and blended with water to create a paste. Dates are rich in iron and have the benefit of being a whole-food. Plums, currants, and raisins can all be used in this way.
- **Fruits, Pods, and Roots:** Lucuma (a fruit), carob (a pod), and yacon (a root) are powders that add both sweetness and their own rawesome flavor to a dish. Due to their strong, unique tastes, these ingredients are usually incorporated as part of an overall flavor profile and aren't simply added for sweetness.

Each of these sweeteners allows you to create amazing, mind-blowing, and totally healthy raw desserts to feed your soul—and maybe your friends!—through your raw vegan journey. Sweets that are actually good for you? Man, it sure does pay to live *rawesome*!

As you familiarize yourself with the delicious recipes in Part 2, you'll have plenty of opportunities to get used to each of these inspiring foods. If you buy a few things at a time, you'll find that you have a fully stocked pantry to pull from in no time at all!

*Chapter 2*

# Raw Kitchen Equipment

You already know that you don't have to be a trained professional chef to enjoy the beauty and the benefits of eating live foods—and you don't need access to a gourmet kitchen, either. However, to make sure your rawesome dishes are out-of-this-world delicious, it can be helpful to work with the right tools. It's a fact that by using the proper equipment, you'll elevate the taste of your foods to new heights—and you'll definitely notice the superior quality of the meals you produce. But, if you don't have all the appliances discussed in this chapter, don't worry about it!

Here you'll also learn how to create amazing dishes without having to buy every single gadget ever made. The good thing is that, with a little ingenuity and a little bit of diligence, you *can* make the most out of your raw ambitions. Your taste buds will thank you!

## Food Processor

A food processor is a small machine that's meant to *process* food. In other words, it can slice and dice, chop and blend, shred and knead, and grind and whip. It can mill nuts into butters, purée fruit into smoothies, make dips and pâtés, grate various veggies, and cream soaked cashews. Most models come with multiple blades to achieve these various functions, and if you only have one appliance in your kitchen, a food processor should be it.

# Juicer

A juicer is a special device designed to extract as much of the liquid as possible from fruits and vegetables. There are three types of juicers: masticating, centrifugal, and twin gear. Masticating juicers work by grinding and "chewing up" the produce, literally squeezing out the juice. This results in less oxidative damage, the exposure to oxygen that degrades some nutrients, which equals a more nutritious juice. But these juicers also tend to heat up if overworked, which can be a problem for raw foodists.

Centrifugal juicers use a high-speed spinning grinder to part the juice from the pulp. They're faster than masticating juicers, but the juice is of lower quality. However, centrifugal juicers tend to be much less expensive and can provide an easy gateway into juicing if you really haven't gotten into it before.

Finally, there are the higher-end twin-gear juicers, also called triturating juicers, which work slowly and efficiently using high-power compression. They make the best quality juice of the highest nutritive caliber and cause virtually no oxidative damage. They also produce very little foam, which is a nice bonus—after all, who wants foam airing out their juice!—and can also make baby foods, nut butters, sorbets, and more.

## How to Make Juice Without a Juicer

Even though you don't need a juicer to make fresh, healthy juices, you will need either a blender, an immersion blender, or a food processor, along with some sort of fine strainer. A sprouting bag/nut milk bag is your best bet, but a metal mesh sieve or a few pieces of cheesecloth will work as well.

To get juiced, first, chop up all your produce (see Chapter 4 for recipes) and place the pieces in your blender or food processor (or a big bowl if using an immersion blender). Add 1 cup of water then process everything thoroughly, adding more water if needed.

Then line a large bowl with the sprouting bag, cheesecloth, or mesh strainer. Pour the entire mixture through the bag/cloth/strainer into the bowl. Use your hands to squeeze all of the liquid out of the pulp. You'll end up with a big bowl of strained produce juice.

Transfer juice to a tall glass and enjoy immediately. Why wait?

Refrigerate or freeze the pulp to use in crackers, burgers, cookies, or any other treat you wish. If you don't want to save your pulp, it makes great compost.

## Wheatgrass Juicer

Most standard masticating or centrifugal juicers will not accommodate wheatgrass, because its fibers make it difficult to break down. The good news is that a simple hand-cranked juicer can be purchased relatively inexpensively. If you drink a lot of wheatgrass, the money you'll save by preparing it at home will quickly pay for the cost of this special investment.

## How to Make a Wheatgrass Shot Without a Wheatgrass Juicer

If you don't have a wheatgrass juicer, you can use a blender to make wheatgrass shots, in much the same way as you can make juice without a juicer.

Just trim 1 cup loosely packed wheatgrass, using the entire blade cut from the base. This will be about ¼ of a standard-sized tray of wheatgrass. Cut the blades into 1" pieces and place them in a blender with ¼ cup of water. Blend on high until completely liquified. Then pour the blender contents through a sprouting bag or mesh strainer, using your hands to extract all the juice. Transfer to a shot glass and serve immediately.

*Passionate* **Pairings** If you're looking for something to spice up your wheatgrass shot, know that wheatgrass goes down nicely with a slice of lemon or lime.

# High-Speed Blender

High-speed blenders are powerful machines that can do so much more than just make a smoothie! They'll grind your greens (including stems, which your food processor can't handle) into silky smoothness, pulverize nuts into powders, and then further into butters, grind grains to make flour, whip oil into aioli, and beat cashews into a feather-light fluff. Standard blenders have a fraction of the power and cannot compare to high-speed blenders. And, as you know, for serious raw foodists, high-speed blenders are practically a way of life.

There are two competing brands of high-speed blenders, and the raw foods community is squarely divided into two (friendly) factions. It's the Vitamix-ers versus the Blendtec-ers.

The Vitamix is the original bad boy, while the Blendtec is new-school cool. Both are absolutely phenomenal. The Vitamix has a two-horsepower motor and variable speed control. The Blendtec boasts a three-horsepower motor and offers preprogrammed settings. Vitamix weighs more and is taller. Blendtec has a shorter warranty and is louder. The Vitamix comes with a tamper that many people find very helpful. The Blendtec offers a larger carafe size, which certainly has its benefits. Both are BPA-free. Either way you go, you are guaranteed to absolutely fall in love with your blender—and that's a love that lasts!

# Dehydrator

Dehydrators may not be essential for those living the raw life, but they sure do make it more interesting! In a dehydrator you can "bake"—or unbake, if you will—raw breads and crackers, cookies and muffins, granola and fruit leathers, and so much more. A dehydrator opens up so many possibilities and provides a whole new spectrum of textures and sensations that can calm any cravings that you have for unhealthy cooked foods. There's a lot that you can do without a dehydrator, but if you enjoy preparing foods and experimenting in the kitchen, you'll eventually want to include one of these in your raw repertory.

Dehydrators do their work by slowly extracting moisture at a very low temperature. This can impart a cooked appearance, but the healthful raw benefits remain intact. It's generally accepted that Excalibur brand dehydrators stand a head above the rest. In fact, there isn't much competition. It may be tempting to pick up a cheaper, smaller model, but the second-tier dehydrators can pose a number of problems, like uneven heating, unpredictable dry times, improper ventilation, and inadequate space. Don't wait to upgrade; start outright with a quality model. You'll be glad you did.

### How to Dehydrate Without a Dehydrator

The truth is that there's just no reliable way to dehydrate food without an actual dehydrator; you just don't have enough control over the variables to absolutely guarantee the correct temperature. However, take some time to play around with your oven and see what you can figure out.

Set your oven to the very lowest setting. Often there is a warming function; if there is, use that. Spread your food on a glass or metal tray and place it in the oven, leaving the door ajar. Place a fan in front of the door and turn it on low, pointed inside. This will keep the air circulating for even heat distribution.

And that's your rawesome makeshift dehydrator! It can be hard to measure the temperature, so keep an eye on the food and be aware that the drying time will vary. Don't rely on the time given in the original recipe! Keep in mind that every oven, kitchen, and location will be different so this may take some trial and error, but if you keep at it, you'll figure out what works for you.

## Spiralizer

A spiralizer is a helpful, hand-operated gadget that turns zucchini, beets, or other solid vegetables into "pasta." As a matter of fact, it turns it into the most beautiful, delicious, and healthy pasta you've ever eaten! Spiralizers are relatively cheap and are easy to use. They're also fun, and they add an air of professional preparation to any homemade presentation. Truth be told, they're a bit of a rock star in a raw foods kitchen.

## Mandoline

A mandoline is another little manual mechanism, but this one is used to slice vegetables into paper thin strips and uniform shapes. Mandolines are often used to make veggie chips, lasagna "noodles," ravioli "wrappers," and other such specialties. If you have a mandoline, you can get by without a spiralizer, but why would you want to?

### How to Make Pasta Without a Spiralizer or Mandoline

Raw noodles are a super fun, super fast meal to whip up on a busy weeknight. A spiralizer or a mandoline certainly comes in handy, but don't let the lack of one stop you from enjoying awesome pasta! You can also almost as easily carve up your zucchinis the good old-fashioned way.

Wash the zucchini (or summer squash, beet, etc.) and carefully start to peel it using a standard potato peeler. Take care to keep each strip as long as possible. Rotate the zucchini as you go. Once the entire zucchini is peeled, stack the strips 3–4 high and use a small sharp paring knife to slice the noodles lengthwise, long and skinny, like spaghetti. This can be a bit time-consuming, but it makes for a very elegant presentation. If you'd rather, you can leave the strips as is, more like a broad pappardelle pasta. Toss with your favorite sauce and enjoy!

## Additional Aids

In addition to all the fancy-schmancy appliances we've discussed, there are some other basics that you need to have in your rawesome kitchen. Assuming that you already have the basics—like measuring cups and spoons, mixing bowls, sharp knives, and a cutting board—these are the tools that will make your raw preparation especially easy-breezy:

- **Citrus Juicer:** Also called a hand juicer or a manual juicer. Juicing citrus by hand is easier, faster, and less messy than using an electric juicer. Choose porcelain or stainless steel over a plastic model.
- **Coffee or Spice Grinder:** An electric coffee grinder is perfect for making flax meal or for processing nuts and spices, and it makes it easy to process nuts, seeds, and grains into perfectly powdery pastry flours. Flaxseed, quinoa, and millet do especially well in this sort of setup. However, you'll want to use a food processor to grind larger, softer nuts like almonds, cashews, or walnuts, which will form a fine powder before they relax and release their oils. You may want to have more than one coffee or spice grinder—one for flaxseed and nuts and another for herbs and spices, which will release flavor that will stay on the grinder. If you don't want to buy an electric grinder, a hand-cranked spice grinder works just as well.
- **Garlic Press:** For fine mincing garlic or ginger; try to use a metal one since plastic can leach toxins into food.
- **Long-Handled Silicon Spatula:** For extracting every last delicious drop from your food processor or blender!

- **Microplane:** A microplane is a type of miniature hand-held grater, made for zesting citrus or grating spices. It's shape and size make it much more efficient than a traditional lemon zester.
- **Offset Spatula:** A long, flat, blunt metal blade, this tool is a blessing when working with thick batters. Great for leveling cheesecakes and excellent for spreading cracker or bread dough onto dehydrator sheets.
- **Vegetable Peeler:** If you don't have a spiralizer or mandoline, you'll at least want to have a good, sharp veggie peeler. This can be used in a pinch to make zucchini noodles, and is also great for cleaning and prepping all types of produce.
- **Salad Spinner:** For quickly and easily drying greens. You don't want extra water in your salad dressings, after all!
- **Sprouting Bag/Nut Milk Bag:** You can use these bags for sprouting seeds (see Chapter 1 for more info) and for making nut milk, but also for filtering juice, rinsing small grains, or for straining and hardening cheeses. This is another cheap purchase that's a kitchen powerhouse.
- **Sushi Mat:** Also called a bamboo mat, this is simply a square mat made of bamboo that's used to help properly form sushi rolls. It's very handy if you do a lot of homemade rolls.

If all of this nifty equipment seems intimidating, either instructionally or financially, remember that none of it is really necessary. The fun and fancy stuff certainly helps, but you can get along without it. Now read ahead for some great tips on how else to get along on your rawesome way.

*Chapter 3*

# Strategies for Success

You already know that being raw vegan feels pretty amazing. You're healthy, excited, and have chosen a path to the dinner table that takes animal cruelty and processed foods completely out of the equation! But that doesn't mean that living the rawesome lifestyle is always easy—or inexpensive. So, to keep you on the straight and narrow, here in this chapter you'll learn how to save some money and how to ensure that you'll stay raw for the long haul.

## Take Your Checks to the Bank

As you know, the unfortunate truth is that processed foods are alarmingly cheap, while fresh fruits and veggies seem expensive by comparison. Unhealthy items like meat and dairy and GM soy and feed crop corn are all subsidized by the government, which drives the prices artificially low. What a pity, then, that the foods that truly *feed* us are the ones we have to pay full price for. But never fear! Savvy raw foodists like yourself can keep themselves very well fed while staying on a tight budget. Use these tips for proper planning, and all that you'll need to account for is your steady stream of enthusiasm.

## Buy in Bulk

Chances are that there are types of foods that you use in recipes all the time like nuts, seeds, dried fruits, and powders. In cases like these, you can save a ton of money by buying in bulk. Check your local health food store or scout around online for the best deals. Once you've brought home these large quantities of food, make sure they stay fresh by storing them safely in the freezer.

### Carve Out Some Kitchen Time

Take some time, whenever you have it (on the weekends, late at night, or first thing in the morning), and learn a new raw prep technique each week. Maybe you'll practice how to roll nori wraps, or how to make zucchini noodles. As you master each new method, you'll be able to more easily integrate them into your busy life. Try for one new skill each week.

## Buy on Sale

Shop your local grocery stores and produce markets and keep a keen eye out for sales. If you can snap up a lot of something for very little money, then you can easily process it (clean and cut it) and store it in the freezer. This is especially useful for fruit (bananas, berries, etc.), some vegetables (peppers, garlic, ginger), and greens (tubs of fresh baby spinach freeze very well, and are perfect this way for smoothies).

## Buy from Your Local Farmers' Market

If you have a farmers' market or local equivalent, buying direct from the grower is an invaluable advantage. Not only will you save money by cutting out the middle man, but you'll get to see exactly where your food comes from! You'll also be eating seasonally and locally, which is as healthy as it is eco-friendly.

### Take Home Some Green

To get the best deals at your local farmers' market, go late, right before the market closes. Vendors are usually willing to negotiate—or may just want to unload their produce—right before they head back to the farm.

## Replace Nuts with Sunflower Seeds

Sunflower seeds are nutritional powerhouses and cost a fraction of the price of most nuts. Their flavor is relatively neutral, so in many recipes you can replace the pricier nuts with the cost-effective sun seeds. This works best in pâtés and dips as opposed to rich desserts, but play around a bit and you'll get the feel for it.

### Replace Dates with Raisins

In the same vein, raisins (or prunes) are much cheaper than dates, but you'll barely notice a difference when you work them into a rawesomely delicious recipe. This switcheroo works best in pie crusts and blended recipes, like dressings. Again, you'll get the feel for it with just a bit of practice.

### Don't Waste!

So many people just throw stuff out, but why toss something in the trash—or compost bin—that you can use later? Juice pulp can be made into fruity treats or savory crackers. Nut pulp transforms into sweet cookies or hearty breads. Leftover blended soups can become the base of a great salad dressing (just add a little lemon juice or vinegar), and pâté remains can form the foundation of a rich raw soup. Just get creative and use those leftovers!

### Grow Your Own Sprouts and/or Garden

There is nothing cheaper—or more satisfying!—than growing your own food. Sprouting is easy and quick, and gardening is richly rewarding. Even apartment dwellers can plant boxes on their patios or put pots on a windowsill. A single basil plant goes a long way. Give it a try!

## Keep Your Passion Alive

It's pretty easy, especially when life gets rushed, to end up in a raw rut. You eat the same foods all the time. You get bored. It happens to everyone! And when this happens you may find yourself resorting to snacking on simple foods like whole fruit, cut veggies, and plain nuts. And those things are great! But if you're going to live raw vegan, you need to keep your passion as alive as the food you're eating.

### Texture and Variety

Eating a variety of textures will help to keep you stimulated and enthusiastic about your diet. You don't want to burn out! So try to keep your textural bases covered by always having a variety of snacks on hand. A bag of granola, a few energy bars, and some raw crackers in the cupboard can make all the difference when you're under stress. It's also great to keep some dips and spreads, maybe a raw cheese, and sprouts, ready to go in the fridge.

## Eat Warm Foods

Especially in the colder climates and darker months, when you're craving comfort food and everything seems cold, a warming meal is so important to keep you on the raw path. You can use your dehydrator or the warming setting on your oven (keep a thermometer handy) to gently raise the temperature of a dinner or a drink—or just to enjoy warm chocolate chip cookies!

## Make Extra Food and Store It for Later

Don't ever get caught with a craving while unprepared. If you find yourself starving while out running errands, unable to access any healthy raw foods, well . . . that's when slip-ups happen. To avoid this scenario, it's important to make sure you always have a stash that includes a selection of goodies. Keep some in your purse, your glove box, your bike basket, and anywhere else that may come in handy. You can make your snacks ahead of time in big batches, and keep your freezer full of your favorite familiar treats.

## Keep Your Protein Up

Protein will help you stay fuller for longer, so you'll be less likely to get caught hungry and unprepared. Especially if you're active, try putting protein powders in your smoothies, sprouts in your salads/soups, and seeds sprinkled on everything. Nuts are a good source of protein, but they can be heavier on digestion and high in calories, so they may not work as a regular protein source for everyone. Grains like quinoa, oats, and buckwheat are much lighter and offer a complete source of protein.

With a little forethought and a little practice, you'll have no trouble at all keeping your raw passion burning bright. And the longer you go, the greater you'll glow, as you continue to cultivate your incredible health and wellness that springs forth from deep inside. It all starts with amazing food, so what are you waiting for? Let's get uncooking!

# PART 2

# Rawesome Recipes!

Every lifestyle comes with its own ups and downs, and there are healthier and less healthy options within every dietary model. But raw veganism provides the ideal framework for a healthy, vibrant, and totally rawesome life! The fiber, antioxidants, and bountiful micronutrients found in fresh fruits and vegetables are undeniably beneficial. And conversely, the cholesterol, channel-clogging fats, and cooked carcinogens present in animal-based proteins are detrimental to health and wellness. Period!

By definition, raw vegans partake of unrefined, nutrient-dense ingredients while omitting most common additives, allergens, and irritants. When you eat food in its uncooked form, you maximize its nutritional impact while minimizing your body's work load. Rich with enzymes that aid in digestion, unadulterated and unprocessed raw food—*real* food—is a bright and brilliant beam of light in our society's dark sea of dis-ease. When you eat only the purest foods available, your body is allowed to focus on the important work of renewal and repair—so let's keep that process going with the delicious recipes that you'll find in this part! Uncook on!

*Chapter 4*

# Juices

Freshly pressed. Frothy and fantastic. Overflowing with nutrients.

That's what you should think when you see a gorgeous glass of produce juice—a juice squeezed from real fresh fruits and vegetables. These fruits and vegetables are the cornerstone of an optimal diet, but most people fall short of reaching their adequate daily intake. That's why produce juice, made fresh to order every day, is an easy way to take you over the edge from flirting with your good health to full-on seizing your supreme potential!

Produce juice is the quickest and most convenient way to get a super shot of concentrated nutrition. All the vitality that living fruits and vegetables hold within them—the vitamins, minerals, antioxidants, and phytochemicals—are parted from the plant fibers that would otherwise bind them, which means they can be instantly absorbed and almost effortlessly assimilated into your body. These nutrients make for powerful medicine, and as you're about to see, produce juice is the perfect elixir for spot-treating common ailments as well as maintaining overall wellness. So drink up! Every one of your rawesome cells will thank you as they take in that glorious life-giving green goodness.

## The "Easy Green" Template

How long would it take you to chew an entire medium cucumber and four long celery stalks? A long time, right? You'd fill your tummy with bulky food, but you'd barely gain any energy (calories). But juicing your food allows you to consume more produce, and thus more nutrients, without feeling too full too fast. The recipes in this section are a great way of getting to know your good friend, Green Juice. Follow them to the letter or use them as a loose guideline. Whichever way you slice it, just make sure you juice it up!

# Original Sin Gets Juiced

*This juice is a great, effortless way to get more healthy greens to your life. Try starting this recipe out with two kale leaves, and slowly build your tolerance for the bitter greens. Before you know it you'll be adding four leaves, or five—or even more!*

YIELDS 1½ CUPS

2–5 kale leaves
1 medium cucumber
4 stalks celery
1 green apple, cored

1. Juice the kale first.
2. Juice the rest of the ingredients.
3. Stir and serve immediately.

# Spicy Sour

*Fiery fresh with a bit of kick, this refreshing beverage makes a great mocktail! Ginger stokes the digestive fires, so this can be a nice choice to serve before a rich meal. Garnish with a twisted lemon—it's beautiful and delicious to boot!*

YIELDS 1 CUP

1 medium cucumber
4 stalks celery
1" knob of ginger, unpeeled if organic
Juice from 1 lemon

1. Juice the cucumber, celery, and ginger in a juicer.
2. Juice the lemon by hand.
3. Stir together and serve immediately.

# Spicy Sweet

*Carrot and ginger is a classic combination and calls to mind a hearty autumn soup. If you find yourself craving warmth in the cooler months, this sweet drink may be just what you need! You can fake the feeling of hot foods by eating warming foods instead. The ginger in this recipe will heat you up from the inside out.*

YIELDS 1½ CUPS

1 medium cucumber

4 stalks celery

1" knob of ginger, unpeeled if organic

2 medium carrots

1. Juice all ingredients.
2. Stir and serve immediately.

# The Eyes Have It!

*Did your mother ever tell you to eat your carrots for strong eyesight? She was a smart lady! Vitamin A is a major player in healthy vision, and carrots are bursting with this nutritious, delicious vitamin!*

YIELDS 1½ CUPS

2 cups baby spinach

1 medium cucumber

4 stalks celery

2 medium carrots

1. Juice the spinach first.
2. Juice the rest of the ingredients.
3. Stir and serve immediately.

## Juice for Detoxification

Juice fasting—or juice feasting as it's often called these days—is an age-old healing modality that's been implemented by many cultures in many parts of the world. Many fruits and vegetables are natural detoxifiers, and the recipes in this section put that powerful produce to good use.

# Extra Enzymes Extraordinaire!

*Papayas contain an incredible enzyme, called papain, which promotes healthy digestion. Papain will not only ease the symptoms of colitis, but it has actually been shown to protect the stomach from ulcers! Drink up!*

YIELDS 1¼ CUPS

2 small or 1 large papaya
1 cup strawberries, hull intact

1. Juice both ingredients.
2. Stir and serve immediately.

# Sweet 'n' Mellow

*Zucchini makes a nutritious substitute for cucumber in any green juice recipe. In this recipe, the focus is on zucchini as a liver lover, with its vitamin C, lutein, and sodium. Each of these will help clear out your lackluster liver!*

YIELDS 1 CUP

1 medium green zucchini
3 medium carrots
2 red apples, cored

1. Juice all the ingredients.
2. Stir and serve immediately.

# Orange You Glad You Beet Those Toxins Out?

*Beets are incredibly nutrient rich, but beet juice tastes best when paired with a sweeter, lighter companion. Here the beets combine with vitamin-strong OJ for extra immune support. Yum!*

YIELDS ¾ CUP

1 beet, greens removed

2 oranges

1. Juice the beet in a juicer.

2. Juice the oranges by hand.

3. Stir together and serve immediately.

# A Glass of Sass

*Your gallbladder is a small organ that helps to process fats, and it acts as a receptacle for bile produced in the liver. Dark leafy greens are classic detoxifiers, and they can help clean out any back-up that may accrue there. The wide variety of greens in this recipe provide a powerful, multipronged approach for blasting your gallbladder!*

YIELDS 1 QUART

1 whole bunch spinach

1 medium cucumber

½ bunch celery, leaves intact

1 small bunch parsley

½" knob of ginger, unpeeled if organic

2 apples, cored

½ lime, peeled

½ lemon, peeled

1. Juice all of the ingredients in the order listed.

2. Stir and serve immediately.

---

### Curly Versus Flat-Leaf Parsley

Parsley is the most popular herb in the entire world. There are two predominant types that are widely available: one with curly leaves, and one with flat leaves. The flat-leaf varietal, often called Italian parsley, has a stronger flavor. Curly-leafed parsley is largely ornamental and is often used as a garnish.

## Juice for Weight Management

Juicing is great for managing weight. After all, keeping yourself extremely well-nourished will help to stave off unnecessary hunger pangs—and the snacking that often comes with them—which may have been your body's way of calling out for "more minerals!" Juicing provides maximum nutrition in exchange for minimal calories, almost no fat, and no processed excess at all. This makes it an excellent method for steady, sustained, and healthy weight loss.

# Party in the Cabbage Patch

*You've probably heard of the "cabbage soup diet," because cabbage has long been known to facilitate weight loss. This is because the nutrient-per-calorie ratio in cabbage and other cruciferous veggies is extremely high, which allows your body to function at a high level with fewer calories, which in turn causes the body to respond by discarding extra pounds. Nothing wrong with that!*

YIELDS 1½ CUPS

½ head of green cabbage
2 tangerines

1. Juice the cabbage in a juicer.
2. Juice the tangerines by hand.
3. Stir together and serve immediately.

# Spring in a Glass

*Asparagus and carrots are both low in calories and high in nutrients like vitamins and minerals. Asparagus is a natural diuretic, which will help to reduce bloating and puffiness. It's also high in vitamin E, which plays an essential role in metabolizing fats.*

YIELDS ¾ CUP

1 cup asparagus
3 medium carrots

1. Juice all ingredients.
2. Stir and serve immediately.

# Slim Down Solution

*This is a totally diuretic drink, ready for direct infusion into your body. The spinach is rich in micronutrients that nourish and heal, without adding any calories or fat. The lemon is alkalinizing and detoxifying, and celery juice contains electrolytes that help to maintain homeostasis. So drink up—and shrink down.*

YIELDS ¾ CUP

1 red apple, cored
1 celery stalk
¼ lemon, unpeeled
1 cup baby spinach

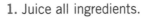

1. Juice all ingredients.
2. Stir and serve immediately.

### Vitamins and Minerals for Weight Loss

All fresh produce will help with weight loss when it displaces other, unhealthy foods. However, there are a few star players in the fat-burning fruits and veggies. Vitamin C, vitamin E, and pantothenic acid all help to regulate metabolism, so look for asparagus, broccoli, kale, spinach, and watercress. Fat-fighting minerals include chromium, magnesium, and zinc, which are found in cabbage, carrots, garlic, lettuce, parsley, and spinach.

# Drinking Dessert

*An important aspect of managing healthy weight loss is being prepared to combat cravings for sweets and other high-calorie foods. And that's where this juice comes in: it tastes just like an apple pie in a glass, and is sure to satisfy any sweet tooth that rears its ugly head.*

YIELDS ¾ CUP

1 sweet apple, cored
1 medium sweet potato, peeled
¼ teaspoon cinnamon
Pinch nutmeg

1. Juice apple and sweet potato.
2. Add spices.
3. Stir and serve immediately.

## Juice to Improve Energy

Produce juice provides the most amazing energy with none of the peaks and valleys and awful artificial jitters that are associated with caffeine and other chemical stimulants. Instead, this type of pure, deep-down enthusiasm comes from the easily accessed natural fuel: glucose. And when you drink down one of these rawesomly delicious juices, each one of your cells gets a super injection of strength for sustained, slow-burning stamina. So get going!

# Citrus-Powered Energy

*This juice is packed with simple and complex sugars, carbohydrates, and vitamin C, which provide a mega dose of energy—both instant and sustained. Vitamin C contributes to increased iron absorption, and iron is a powerful promoter of stamina and endurance. This citrus cooler packs a serious punch!*

YIELDS 1½ CUPS

2 oranges
½ pink grapefruit
½ lemon

1. Juice all ingredients by hand.
2. Stir together and serve immediately.

# Popeye Picker-Upper

*Watercress is a super spicy cousin in the mustard family, but in this juice it's balanced beautifully by the sweetness from the apple. Watercress is often recommended as a veggie that will help to fight anemia. So bring the fight!*

YIELDS ¾ CUP

1 apple, cored
1 cup spinach leaves
1 handful of watercress

1. Juice all ingredients.
2. Stir and serve immediately.

# Bye-Bye Red-Eye

*Calcium and magnesium are both known to promote sleep, which is just what you need in order to regain your momentum when you're on the go. Luckily, cauliflower provides plenty of these amazing minerals. In addition, lettuces like the romaine found in this recipe have a sedative effect that will send you off to dreamland. Just don't miss your departure!*

YIELDS 1¼ CUPS

**4 romaine leaves**
**3 medium carrots**
**½ cup cauliflower**
**½ lemon, peeled**

1. Juice all ingredients in the order listed.
2. Stir and serve immediately.

---

### Pith Power

Pith is the name for the white, spongy tissue that's sandwiched between the outer peel and the inner fruit. Grapefruit pith tends to be bitter, and also tends to be extra thick. However, this soft tissue is more nutritious than even the flesh, with its fiber, pectin, and bioflavonoids, which are powerful disease-fighting antioxidants. Given that it packs such potent nutrient power, it might just be worth your while to leave the pith intact.

---

# Flower Power

*Studies have shown that most sufferers can improve their chronic fatigue syndrome by consuming more fresh produce, getting enough sleep and exercise, and staying hydrated. For sleep and exercise you're on your own, but for the rest: juice! Here, the B vitamins offer an instant pickup, and the magnesium from the cauliflower is a powerhouse when it comes to energizing nutrients.*

YIELDS 1 CUP

**2 beet greens leaves**
**1 cup cauliflower**
**4 medium broccoli spears**

1. Juice all ingredients in the order listed.
2. Stir and serve immediately.

## Juice to Reverse Aging

Some of the most important instruments in the battle for longevity are those unassuming compounds we call antioxidants. These powerful plant-based fountains of youth are responsible for finding and destroying the free radicals that wreak havoc on your health. Many antioxidants are actually the pigments responsible for creating such incredible colors in the produce aisle. So drink the rainbow down while you toast to your good health and long life!

# Fountain of Youth Cocktail

*Berries are some of the best sources of antioxidants, due to their high surface-to-volume ratio that ensures a relatively high proportion of pigmented skin. This blend combines both raspberries and blackberries for maximum antioxidant load, and adds a little ginger to stoke your internal fire, and keep it burning bright into infinity.*

YIELDS ¾ CUP

¼" knob of ginger, unpeeled if organic
1 pint blackberries
1 pint raspberries
½ lemon

1. Juice the ginger and then the berries in a juicer.
2. Juice the lemon by hand.
3. Stir together and serve immediately.

# A Beeting Heart

*Beets are rich in fiber, phytochemicals, and many minerals, and cantaloupe is a great source of vitamins A and C, and potassium. Cantaloupe also contains myo-inositol, a lipid that can help prevent the hardening of arteries. So drink to heart health! Cheers!*

YIELDS 1½ CUPS

½ cantaloupe melon, peeled
2 medium carrots
1 beet, greens removed

1. Juice all ingredients.
2. Stir and serve immediately.

# Liquid Ambrosia

*Vitamin C is both an essential nutrient and a powerful antioxidant. Antioxidants are substances—found primarily in plants—that neutralize free radicals. What does that mean? It means they combat the destructive molecules that break down collagen and elastin. Free radicals cause wrinkles, and antioxidents prevent them!*

YIELDS 1 CUP

**1 pomegranate fruit**
**2 small oranges**

1. Slice open the pomegranate and scoop out the seeds using a spoon.
2. Juice the pomegranate seeds in a juicer.
3. Juice the oranges by hand.
4. Stir together and serve immediately.

### Food and Medicine

You know that food is powerful medicine, but what about actual pharmaceutical medication? Some studies indicate that the compounds present in grapefruits and pomegranates can influence the way that some drugs are metabolized in the body—either increasing or decreasing their effectiveness. If you take presciption drugs, you may want to steer clear of these two powerful fruits.

# The Green Monster

*Small flats of wheatgrass can be purchased at health food stores and produce markets. You can also buy the seeds to grow the grass yourself. Making wheatgrass at home is incredibly cost-effective if the alternative is buying shots at a juice bar.*

YIELDS 1¼ CUPS

**1 cup wheatgrass**
**1 celery stalk with leaves**
**1 handful spinach leaves**
**2 kale leaves**
**½ lemon, peeled**

1. Prepare wheatgrass shot in a wheatgrass juicer or blender (see Chapter 2).
2. Juice all remaining ingredients.
3. Stir together and serve immediately.

## Juice for What Ails You

Produce juice, like so many other natural remedies, can be used to specifically address a whole lot of what ails you. Here you'll find a handful of recipes that target a few common conditions.

# South of the Blender

*This spicy juice is overflowing with vitamin C, one of nature's most potent infection-fighters. You'll also find allium compounds, contributed by the garlic and onions, which can help lower blood pressure with their bioflavonoid antioxidants.*

YIELDS 1¼ CUPS

1 cucumber
½ lime, peeled
1 clove garlic
1 green onion
½ jalapeño pepper, seeded (optional)
1 avocado, pitted and peeled

1. Juice all ingredients except avocado.
2. Transfer to a blender and process with the avocado.
3. Serve immediately.

# Breathe Easy Vegetable Blend

*Beween the jalapeño and the bell pepper, this is one fearsome beverage! Balanced with just enough sweet from the carrots, it's still a delight to drink it down. But the kick is just the thing you'll need to keep those airways nice and cleared. So take a deep breath, and ommmmmm!*

YIELDS 1 CUP

3 medium carrots
1 red bell pepper
1 jalapeño pepper, seeded

1. Juice all ingredients.
2. Stir and serve immediately.

# The Attention Grabber

*This focus-forming elixir is helpful for staying on task and keeping a sharp mind, thanks to the carrots and mangos that provide selenium and beta-carotene. Sufficient selenium is an anti-anxiety remedy, and beta-carotene detoxifies and heals.*

YIELDS 1 CUP

**3 medium carrots**
**1 mango, pitted and peeled**

1. Juice all ingredients.
2. Stir and serve immediately.

### Carrots Are Wellness Warriors!

Carrots may be about as mainstream as produce gets, but they're anything but mundane. These candy-colored root veggies are filled to the brim and overflowing with vitamins and minerals—everything from vitamins A, B, C, E, and K, to calcium, phosphorous, potassium, sodium, and other trace minerals. On top of that, carrots are loaded with incredible cancer-fighting antioxidants, like beta-carotene and selenium.

# Soothe Your Melon

*Ginger has an antihistimine and anti-inflammatory action. It will prevent blood vessels from swelling at the beginning of a migraine, and instantly relieves nerves of pressure. Drink this juice at the very first sign of a migraine, and the first sign may very well be the last sign.*

YIELDS ¾ CUP

**½ cantaloupe melon, peeled**
**¼" knob of ginger, unpeeled if organic**
**½ lemon**

1. Juice melon and ginger in a juicer.
2. Juice the lemon by hand.
3. Stir together and serve immediately.

# "Hear Me Out" Blend

*Tinnitus is a condition with an unknown cause; however, we do know that it can be triggered by medications, toxins, nutritional deficiencies, and medical conditions affecting the jaw. To alleviate tinnitus, look for vitamins A, B, and E, and the mineral zinc. Chlorine, found concentrated in green beans, is also excellent for combating this condition.*

YIELDS 1 CUP

3 medium carrots
1 cup French green beans

1. Juice all ingredients.
2. Stir and serve immediately.

# Cran-Apple Crusher

*Study after study shows that cranberries are effective in preventing urinary tract infections. In fact, they are equally as effective as antibiotics, but they're a whole lot cheaper! They're a whole lot healthier too, and in this juice, they sure do taste great. Now that's delicious disease prevention!*

YIELDS 1 CUP

1¼ cup cranberries (fresh or frozen)
2 red apples, cored

1. Juice all ingredients.
2. Stir and serve immediately.

### Cranberries Can Be Hard to Find

Cranberries are an uncommon food and they're very sour, which means finding raw, unsweetened options can become a challenge. The best thing to do is to buy up a bundle when they're in season in the fall and freeze or dehydrate them yourself to last the rest of the year. You can also find raw dried, unsweetened cranberries online.

# Thanksgiving Special

*Inflammation is your body's way of responding to infection, toxins, or injury, in order to prevent foreign organisms from entering. Beta-cryptoxanthin, a dietary carotenoid found in winter squashes such as butternut, is a first line of defense in the fight against inflammation. But the best part is, this juice is so cravable that you'll want to drink it every day—an easy way to keep inflammation at bay!*

YIELDS 1¼ CUP

2 crisp apples, cored

½ butternut squash, peeled, seeded, and sliced

1 teaspoon pumpkin pie spice

1. Juice apples and butternut squash.
2. Stir in spice and serve immediately.

# Bloody Mary, Quite Contrary

*This spicy tomato mocktail is just the thing to clear out your nasal passage and leave you breathing easy. The radishes have a nice fire, a mild flavor with a peppery finish. Radishes are a relative of mustard and are usually available year round.*

YIELDS ¾ CUP

2 tomatoes

4 radishes, greens removed

1. Juice all ingredients.
2. Stir and serve immediately.

### Radical Radishes: More Than a Garnish

Though radishes are often relegated to the lowly status of simple garnish, they're actually an incredibly healthy food! Each miniature red root contains vitamin C, iron, magnesium, and potassium. Radish juice opens the sinuses, aids digestion, and can help to clear up skin.

# Savor the Flavor

*Garlic is one of the oldest domesticated plants and one of the absolute healthi-est foods you can consume. Numerous studies credit garlic with fighting stomach, colon, bladder, and skin cancers. Eat one to three cloves per day for a therapeutic dose—an amount that's easily met by adding the bulbs to your juice!*

YIELDS 1 CUP

3 Roma tomatoes

2 red apples, cored

1 clove garlic

1 stalk parsley

1. Juice the tomatoes, apples, and garlic.

2. Stir with the parsley stalk and leave it as a garnish.

3. Serve immediately.

# Belle (Pepper) of the Ball

*This juice is a warrior that fights both osteoarthritis and rheumatoid arthritis. The collection of diverse antioxidant pigments present in the three colors of bell peppers make a powerful defense against inflammation and disease. Turmeric contains curcumin, one of the most effective inflammation fighters. However, you may need to use it regularly for up to two months before you see results—so keep on drinking, and don't give up!*

YIELDS 1½ CUPS

½ green bell pepper

½ yellow bell pepper

½ red bell pepper

1 celery stalk with leaves

½ cucumber

1 teaspoon turmeric

1. Juice all the produce.

2. Stir in the turmeric and serve immediately.

## Chapter 5

# Smoothies

Smoothies hold the title as the top raw transitional food. They're simple to shop for and quick to whip up, they're easily incorporated into any sort of schedule, and they're effortlessly adaptable to suit your specific tastes. Replacing your standard breakfast (or lunch) with a big beautiful smoothie brimming with enzymes, vitamins, and minerals is a great way to make raw foods taste their best! Easy on the body and easy on the schedule—now that's a winning blend!

Another awsome attribute of these cravable, curative smoothies is their ability to "hide" healthy foods and supplements. A pure fruit smoothie is full of antioxidants and phytochemicals all on its own, and that's always a rawesome choice. But, you can also add in mineral-rich greens, which assimilate into the fruity flavor and become almost undetectable to the tongue. Protein powders, green powders, microalgae, superfoods—all of these nutrient-packed items partner perfectly with a smoothie. But either way, a la carte or a la mode, a smoothie is a super way to celebrate a perfectly rawesome day!

## The "Easy Green" Template

There's a revolution underway, and it's taking place in blenders across the nation. The age of the green smoothie is dawning, the birth of better health for everybody who jumps on board. It all begins with a base of banana and a handful of spinach. From there, the options are endless. Here you'll find some basic green smoothies, but feel free to tweak depending on your personal tastes and totally rawesome lifestyle.

# Sweet Protein

*This smoothie is a neutral backdrop that would highlight just about any flavored addition, such as cacao, carob, mesquite, or soaked goji berries. Mix and match this smoothie's delicate sweetness and subtle vanilla flavors with whatever suits your fancy.*

SERVES 1

1 frozen banana
1–2 handfuls spinach
1 cup almond milk
1 scoop vanilla-flavored protein powder or 1 scoop plain protein powder plus 1 teaspoon vanilla extract

1. Place all ingredients in a blender.
2. Process until smooth.

### Protein Powder

Many people, such as athletes, pregnant/nursing women, and anyone else for a number of reasons, may be looking to add a little extra protein into their raw diet. Fortunately, there are a wide variety of brands that offer raw protein supplements, pulled from a number of plant sources such as hemp, pea, and rice. They differ quite a bit in both taste and texture, so sample a few before you settle on a favorite. Protein powders can add a gritty, earthy quality to smoothies and may take some getting used to.

# Strawberries and Spirulina

*This smoothie packs in a wallop of a nutritional punch, starting with the easy-burning energy from the banana. The spinach offers up iron, the strawberries are rich in antioxidants, and spirulina is a source of iodine as well as complete plant protein. The whole shebang goes down easy as strawberry pie, assisted by the natural sweetness of real, ripe fresh fruit! How ridiculously rawesome!*

SERVES 1

1 frozen banana
1–2 handfuls spinach
1 cup water
1 cup strawberries, fresh or frozen
½ teaspoon spirulina, more if desired

1. Place all ingredients in a blender.
2. Process until smooth.

*Passionate* Pairings Add ground seeds like flaxseed or hempseed to your smoothies or breakfast cereals. Dry out and grind up the nut pulp left over from making milk. This can form cookies and tart crusts. Grinding grains like quinoa and millet can achieve a nonsweet crust, like a dinner quiche or a savory torte. There's so much room for interpretation, so play around and get creative!

# Strawberry Herbal

*Strawberries merge especially well with fresh, tender herbs, as both begin to ripen at the onset of summer. Strawberries are often reserved for a sweet treat, while fresh herbs are traditionally used in a savory way, but the combination of the two in this recipe makes this smoothie an unexpectedly perfect union.*

SERVES 1

1 frozen banana
1–2 handfuls spinach
1 cup water
1 cup strawberries, fresh or frozen
1 handful fresh herbs, either parsley, dill, cilantro, or basil (do not combine)

1. Place all ingredients in a blender.
2. Process until smooth.

*Do It Yourself*
Strawberries and herbs are all easy to keep alive and lend themselves very well to small-scale container gardening. You can grow the entire gang in a single large pot. Plant a strawberry bush in the center, with various herbs around the edge. Place the pot on a patio or under a windowsill and water it every few days.

# Here Comes the Sun Smoothie

*The flavor here is very mild, with just a slight sweetness from the banana, and a rich earthiness from the sunflower seeds. It's the perfect backdrop for superfood flavor enhancers, such as carob or mesquite. You could also include super fruits, like acai powder or blueberries.*

SERVES 1

1 frozen banana
1–2 handfuls spinach
1 cup water
¼ cup raw sunflower kernels (hulled seeds)
1 handful sunflower greens (sprouts from black sunflower seeds; see Soaking and Sprouting Chart in Ch. 1)

1. Place all ingredients in a blender.
2. Process until smooth.

## Smoothies for Gentle Cleansing

Blending is just an electric shortcut for chewing. But a blender does a much better job than your mouth ever could, and smoothies pretty much pour out completely predigested. This makes the following blended beverages incredibly gentle on your stomach, and it also makes the vitamins and minerals more readily available. These smoothies are a great way to give your body a break without restricting your energy input.

# Get Up and Go! Citrus Smoothie

*The sunflower lecithin in this smoothie provides a hard-to-find nutrient, choline, which is critical for cell regeneration. It also infuses recipes with an earthy richness that makes it a rawesome addition to your healthy kitchen!*

SERVES 1

1 grapefruit, peeled
1 blood orange
1 tablespoon sunflower lecithin
1 cup ice

1. Place all ingredients in a blender.
2. Process until smooth.

# Luscious Light-on-the-Tongue Purple-ade

*This icy, hydrating drink may be dark in color, but it's ultra light on the tongue—crisp and refreshing and mellow to boot! The bright purple hue harkens back to the 7-11 Slurpies that may have peppered your summers when you were a kid. You've come along way since then, and thank goodness for that! Berries taste so much better when they don't come from a machine.*

SERVES 1

1 cup water
½ cup frozen raspberries
½ cup frozen blueberries
Juice from 1 lemon, about 2
    tablespoons
1 cup ice
Optional: 1 teaspoon to 1 tablespoon
    agave syrup

1. Place all ingredients in a blender.
2. Process until smooth.

### The Healthiness Factor

The subtle flavor of this smoothie doesn't leave a lot of room for hearty additions, but you can raise the healthiness of this beverage by adding something neutral like a tablespoon of chia seeds, which will add protein, calcium, and essential omega-3 fatty acids.

# Love Your Liver Elixir

*This somewhat bitter concoction is an efficient liver cleanser that will keep you up and running. So suck it up and drink these liver-loving plants down if you think you're due for some internal housekeeping.*

SERVES 1

2 cups carrot juice
½ cup apple juice
1 cup dandelion greens
½ cup beet greens
2 tablespoons lemon juice
1 teaspoon burdock root
1 teaspoon milk thistle
½ teaspoon cayenne pepper
½ cup ice

1. Place all ingredients in a blender.
2. Process until smooth.

### Your Liver

The liver's primary function is to clean the body's blood supply. This means the liver is dealing with a broad range of toxins on a daily basis. Alcohol, sugar, stimulants, processed foods, and environmental pollutants all put an enormous strain on this super necessary organ. The restorative herbs like dandelion, parsley, wild carrot, ginger, and cayenne can help your liver maintain its optimal efficiency.

# Oh-So-Spicy Smoothie

*Sometimes you want to taste something sweet, and sometimes you want to taste something tart. And then sometimes, just sometimes, you crave something spicy, a bevvie that won't go down without a little fight. Yeah, sometimes it's one of those kinds of mornings. Yeow!*

SERVES 1

1 cup fresh young Thai coconut water

2 frozen bananas

1 cup packed watercress

½ to 2 teaspoons chlorella, to taste

1. Place all ingredients in a blender.
2. Process until smooth.

## Smoothies for Beauty

You've heard the saying, "True beauty begins on the inside"? Well, in this case, beauty begins in the blender! You don't need fancy creams or conditioners, you just need living foods. A diet that's rich in the right nutrients is the secret to gorgeous glowing skin and lustrous, healthy hair and nails. The smoothies in this section are full of vitamins A, B, C, and E, essential fatty acids, selenium, silica, and zinc—the most important elements of a lasting beauty regimen.

# Booty-Shaking Brazilian Energy Booster

*Acai is an amazing little berry that hails from the Amazon. With its rich, deep purple hue that guarantees an assortment of powerful antioxidants, this super fruit is said to increase energy, aid in digestion, and make skin glow. Why not drink something that will leave you feeling your beautiful best!*

SERVES 1

1 cup Brazil-nut milk

1½ cups frozen banana chunks

1 tablespoon acai powder

1. Place all ingredients in a blender.
2. Process until smooth.

# Make-It-Shine Smoothie

*This elegant cream-colored blend just brims over with nutrients for beauty and health. And part of the pleasure involved in this lovely beverage is, of course, its angelic coloring—which comes from it's ever-so-pale ingredient list. The gorgeous lily-white hue that makes this smoothie so special will make you even more gorgeous, too, by shining up your hair and nails, giving you radiant skin, and ensuring a gorgeous glow from within.*

SERVES 1

1 cup Brazil-nut milk
1 cup chopped cucumber, peeled
½ cup young coconut meat
1 cup ice
Optional: 1 teaspoon to 1 tablespoon
   agave syrup

1. Place all ingredients in a blender.
2. Process until smooth.

### Don't Forget to Hydrate!

If you're making your smoothies in a food processor instead of in a blender, you want to make sure that you have plenty of liquid, and may need to include more than the original recipe calls for. It helps if you make sure to always add the liquid first, with the fruits and vegetables following.

# Shiny Happy People

*Have your smoothie—and a wheatgrass shooter, too! Why not? Including the best of the cleansing foods in one powerful concoction is sure to set your skin asparkle. Shining skin makes for happy people. But remember, wheatgrass can be an acquired taste, so you may want to cut the intensity with a drizzle of agave syrup.*

SERVES 1

1-ounce shot wheatgrass juice, made
   according to the directions in Ch. 1
1 cup water (½ cup water and ½ cup
   ice if not using frozen fruit)
1 tall cup mango
1 scant cup cucumber
½ cup pineapple
Optional: 1 teaspoon to 1 tablespoon
   agave syrup

1. Place all ingredients in a blender.
2. Process until smooth.

### Spotlight on Wheatgrass

Wheatgrass shots are made by juicing young tender blades of the common wheat plant. The resulting elixir is rich in chlorophyll and enzymes, as well as many vitamins and minerals. Wheatgrass, a powerful detoxifier, is also reported to increase energy, aid in digestion, and improve skin quality.

# Totally Crave-able Carob Cherry Smoothie

*This is such a decadent drink for a totally dazzling new you! And you know what? You deserve it! So give into desire and drink in the Brazil-nut milk, which is overflowing with vitamin E, an antioxidant that plays an important role in maintaining cell membranes and mucous membranes. Hello, flawless complexion!*

SERVES 1

1 cup Brazil-nut milk

1 frozen banana, broken into chunks

1 cup pitted cherries, fresh or frozen

1 tablespoon carob powder

1. Place all ingredients in a blender.

2. Process until smooth.

Swap It Out! Carob and mesquite are similar in flavor and can be swapped interchangeably here, depending on what's available in the pantry. Cacao would work well, too. You can also hide supplements, like maca or your favorite protein, in this delicious treat.

## Stressless Smoothies

Stress can be unbelievably devastating to your body—affecting everything from digestion to sleep to impulse control. Not so rawesome, right? But one of the easiest ways to tame the beast is to bulk up on nutrients found in fresh fruits and vegetables. With optimal nutrition you'll be primed and positioned to meet your stressors head on. Whew! Don't you feel better already?

# Unbelievably Lazy Melon Mocktail

*Nothing says "lazy days" like a refreshing watermelon cooler. So pull up a hammock, lie back, and enjoy this seasonal melon blend. Icy, slushy, with spinach for a fun color and a shot of citrus to kick it up, this is one "mocktail" to mark your summers by. Cheers!*

SERVES 1

1 cup honeydew melon chunks

1 cup watermelon chunks

1 handful baby spinach

Juice from ½ lime

1 cup ice, if not using frozen fruit

1. Place all ingredients in a blender.

2. Process until smooth.

# The Motley Crew

*Sometimes opposites attract, and this unexpected mishmash of a drink marries the likes of pineapple, mint, ginger, cayenne pepper, and chocolate into one surprisingly slurp-able smoothie. The natural, clean-burning energy it provides will keep you going strong, fighting fatigue and the adrenal stress caused by fatigue. Drink it down to rev you up before you head out on a weekend evening!*

SERVES 2

1 cup fresh pineapple juice

2 frozen bananas, broken into chunks

2 tablespoons fresh mint

2 tablespoons raw cacao powder

1 teaspoon fresh ginger juice

¼ teaspoon cayenne powder

Optional: 1 tablespoon mesquite pod meal

1. Place all ingredients in a blender.

2. Process until smooth.

*Super Sweetener*

Mesquite is a unique plant with a sweet flavor reminiscent of molasses. This desert-dwelling legume is popular in Mexico and the southwestern United States and is a low-glycemic, nutrient-dense sweetener that includes the minerals calcium, magnesium, potassium, iron, and zinc. Mesquite is an optional sweetener here, and it could be replaced with the equally enlivening carob.

# Take-a-Load-Off Tropical Smoothie

*Nothing says "relaxation" like a taste from the tropics. Anyone who's ever vacationed along the equator knows that! And nothing helps your body relax like a good dose of cortisol-regulating vitamin C. This tart and tangy concoction, high in vitamin C, is perfectly reflective of essential island flavors. So sip it slowly. There's a good chance you'll be able to hear the sound of breaking waves and feel the heat of the sun on your face almost immediately. Now where's that sunscreen . . .*

SERVES 2 DRINKS OR 1 MEAL

2 oranges, peeled

4 kiwi fruits, unpeeled

2 mangoes or about 1 cup frozen chunks

½ cup ice

1. Juice the two oranges.

2. Cut off the two ends from each kiwi and rough chop, leaving the skin in place.

3. Peel and pit the mango. Roughly chop.

4. Add the ice and all other ingredients into a blender and process until smooth.

# Sweet-as-a-Peach Smoothie

*Peaches are, perhaps, the ultimate summer experience. From a decadent breakfast parfait to a delicate amuse-bouche, and in every incarnation in between, peaches star in so much more than simply crisps and cobblers—like in this smoothie where they take center stage. The peach's inherent sweetness is offset by the pungent parsley. But a little herb goes a long way, so add it slowly and taste as you go.*

**SERVES 2 DRINKS OR 1 MEAL**

1 cup water

2 ripe peaches, pitted and rough chopped

1 cup tender greens (baby spinach, baby romaine, spring mix)

2–4 tablespoons minced parsley

2 tablespoons fresh lemon juice (about 1 lemon)

1 cup ice

1. Add all ingredients into a blender.

2. Process until smooth.

■ **PRO'S TIP** If you make a lot of smoothies, you probably run through a lot of greens—which can cost you a lot of green! Next time you see bags or boxes of baby spinach on sale, why not stock up? These can be frozen and will keep this way for months. And used in a smoothie, you'll never know the difference!

## Smoothies to Stop Tummy Aches

Digestion is the cornerstone of health and longevity, hands down. If you're not properly processing your food, then you're not getting the necessary nutrients—and you won't be able to dispose of the bad stuff, either. Hydration, fiber, and probiotics are the greatest gifts you can give yourself if you're having tummy troubles. The smoothies found in this section give each of these gifts in combination with key nutrients that can help you reverse any digestive damage done by years of a not-so-great diet.

# Ginger (No Ale Added) Shake

*As nice on the tongue as it is on the tummy, this delicious, thick smoothie is as sweet as an apple pie from the freshly pressed apple juice, but is loaded with healing probiotics from the cultured yogurt. Ginger has been used for centuries to promote digestive wellness, so make it work for you!*

SERVES 1

½ cup freshly made apple juice
½ cup Creamy Coconut Yogurt or
   Totally Tangy Nut or Seed Yogurt
   (see recipes in Ch. 6)
1 banana, frozen, broken into chunks
1 knob of ginger, ½" to 1" square, to
   taste

1. Add all ingredients into a blender.
2. Process until smooth.

---

# Pom Pom Tum Tum

*Fermented foods have been used through the ages to foster healthy intestinal flora, the foundation for good digestion. The creamy cultured yogurt in this recipe provides a rich delicious base, while the apple juice adds extra fiber to keep you meal moving throughout your system.*

SERVES 1

½ cup freshly made apple juice
½ cup Creamy Coconut Yogurt or
   Totally Tangy Nut or Seed Yogurt
   (see recipes in Ch. 6)
½ cup pomegranate seeds
1 cup ice

1. Add all ingredients into a blender.
2. Process until smooth.

■ **PRO'S TIP** Some people find pomegranate seeds to be too bitter, especially when blended, so you can use the pomegranate flesh itself instead. To remove the actual seed from the fleshy pulp that surrounds it, soak the entire cut pomegranate half in an ice water bath for 10 minutes. The seeds will extricate themselves, leaving nothing but sweet, juicy fruit flesh for you to enjoy.

# Eat-Up-Those-Enzymes Smoothie

*Enzymes are a critical component of efficient digestion and effective nutrient absorption. The papaya and pineapple loaded into this smoothie are great natural sources of two unique digestive enzymes: papain and bromelain. Papain, from papayas, and bromelain, from pineapple, both aid in the breakdown and uptake of proteins. So get drinking!*

SERVES 1

1 cup papaya
½ cup pineapple, fresh or frozen
½ medium avocado
Optional: ½ cup ice if using fresh
   fruit, water to thin as needed

1. Place all ingredients in a blender.
2. Process until smooth.

# Sweet-as-Candy Smoothie

*This super-sweet smoothie is a concoction that's a pleasure to sip—but it comes with its own agenda. The delicious dried apricots here occupy the same realm as the trusty prune, and this little smoothie will keep things moving right along, which is a good thing!*

SERVES 2 SIDES OR 1 MEAL

4 unsulphured sun-dried apricot halves
1 cup coconut water kefir
½ frozen banana
1 small green pear, ripe

1. Soak the apricot halves for at least 2 hours, but ideally brewed in the coconut water kefir for a full 24–48 hours (see Cultured Coconut Kefir recipe in Chapter 14).
2. Place all ingredients in a blender and process until smooth.

## Blended Immune Boosters

There's nothing uplifting, exciting, or rawesome about spending each day fatigued, irritable, or feeling like you're fighting off a cold. If this sounds familiar, then your immune system may not be operating at maximum efficiency. Enter the smoothies in this section, which will help infuse your life with a potent cocktail of antioxidants and vitamins that will give you the immune support your body is clearly craving. So let's raise a glass to feeling great!

# Super C

*This delicious drink lives in limbo somewhere between a smoothie and a blended salad—and there's nothing wrong with that if you're rawesomely inclined! It's sweet from the fruit but has a distinctly savory capsicum undercurrent. So is it a soup? A smoothie? Does it really matter? The taste is amazing, and when you get right down to it, that's the only thing that counts!*

**SERVES 2 DRINKS OR 1 MEAL**

1 cup fresh squeezed orange juice
  (2–3 oranges)
¾ cup papaya
¾ cup mango
½ medium red bell pepper
2–6 kale leaves, to taste

1. Add all ingredients into a blender.
2. Process until smooth.

■ **PRO'S TIP** Mango and papaya are both nutritious and delicious fruits that add diversity and interest to all sorts of dishes. However, they can be expensive! If you ever come across these beauties for a great bargain, make sure you snap them up. Buy as much as you can and then peel, chop, and freeze them for later. This way, you'll always have something special on hand when the smoothie mood strikes you!

# Benefit-Your-Bladder Smoothie

*Cranberries are immune system avengers, especially when it comes to urinary tract infections. Their superpowers derive from a particular group of compounds, called proanthocyanidins, which actually prevent harmful bacteria from sticking to the bladder. Along with these impressive antioxidants, cranberries also boast brilliant levels of vitamin C and vitamin B-complex, making them a truly unbeatable immune booster.*

**SERVES 1**

1 cup freshly made apple juice
1 frozen banana
½ cup fresh cranberries plus ½ cup
  water or ⅓ cup dried unsweetened
  cranberries, soaked at least 1 hour
  in ⅔ cup water
Optional: 1 teaspoon to 1 tablespoon
  agave syrup

1. Place all ingredients (including soak water if using dried cranberries) in a blender.
2. Process until smooth.

# Very Cherry Defender

*This beautiful and brightly colored smoothie is an excellent introductory smoothie for beginners or for children. The flavor is sweet and just a little bit tart, complex enough so it won't be boring, but certainly not overwhelming. The flaxseed acts as a thickener here, so if you omit it you may want to add a half a banana or avocado, just to keep it creamy.*

SERVES 1

1 cup fresh squeezed orange juice
  (2–3 oranges)
1 cup cherries, pitted
1 tablespoon ground flaxseed
1 cup ice

1. Add all ingredients into a blender.
2. Process until smooth.

Swap It Out! This smoothie is so sweet and forgiving that it's an exceptional vehicle for super fruits! Try replacing half of the cherries with soaked goji berries or Inca berries. You can also replace the flaxseed with, or simply add, chia seeds.

# Bodaciously Blended Salad Smoothie

*Vegetables are powerful allies in the battle against* Candida—*the species that causes yeast infections. Not only do they starve the bad bugs of the sugars and molds that they need to thrive, but vegetables also absorb fungal toxins and export them out of the body. The best veggies for fighting* Candida *include alliums (garlic, onions), brassicas (brussels sprouts, broccoli), peppers, celery, asparagus, and greens.*

SERVES 2 SIDES OR 1 LIGHT MEAL

1 cup water
2 carrots
2 celery stalks
2 kale leaves
1 handful fresh parsley
1 teaspoon nama shoyu
1 teaspoon apple cider vinegar
Optional: clove of garlic, dash of raw
  hot sauce, or sprinkle of cayenne
  pepper

1. Place all ingredients in a blender.
2. Process until smooth.

## Chapter 6

# Breaking the Fast

Breakfast is a meal that was made for raw foods! From perfectly fresh fruit to sinfully delicious hand-crafted crepes, a raw vegan breakfast can be as simple or as complex as you want it to be. And a nutritious, nourishing meal that provides you with natural energy will allow you to be the very best version of yourself. Keep your breakfast light with a shake or a seasonal fruit cocktail, and marvel at how easily you digest these magnificent meals. Or go all out for brunch with friends, serving savory interpretations of the most decadent cooked-food classics. You know that rawesome means never sacrificing satisfaction! But whether it's casual or fancy or comfortable or formal, when the breakfast menu is raw it guarantees energy and a healthy foundation to an amazing day.

# Easy-Breezy Plant Milk

*Making your own plant-based milk is probably easier than you imagine. It's economical, too, and once you've mastered the skill of milking nuts, seeds, and grains, you'll have access to all sorts of fun and familiar foods that you may be missing. And what's better than that!*

**SERVES 4**

1 cup nuts, seeds, or grains
Water for soaking
4 cups water for blending
Optional: 1 date or 1 teaspoon agave
  sweetener; 1 teaspoon vanilla
  extract

1. Cover the nuts/seeds/grains in plenty of water and allow to soak for at least 2 hours, more if you want to maximize nutrients (see discussion in Chapter 1).

2. Drain and rinse the nuts/seeds/grains and add them to a blender or food processor with 4 cups fresh water. Add the optional ingredients if you choose. Process for 1–2 minutes, until the rattling stops.

3. Place a nut milk bag or fine mesh strainer in a large bowl and pour the contents of the blender into the bowl. This will strain the milk from the pulp. Use your hands to press and squeeze all the liquid out. Set aside the pulp.

4. Pour the milk into a labeled, airtight container and store it in the refrigerator. It will keep for up to 5 days.

### Milk It for All It's Worth

The most common plant milk is made from almonds, which produce a rich, slightly sweet drink. Other popular options include cashew, hazelnut, hempseed, sesame, sunflower, and oat. You can also experiment with combining these in various proportions to cover a range of flavors and nutrients.

# Brighten Your Morning Melon Mix

*Your body digests the melon in this recipe almost instantly, making it a fantastic choice for the most important meal of the day! When your body isn't working hard on digestion it can divert that energy to more important things—like renewal and repair. All melon digests just as easily, so if you want to mix things up a bit try swapping in some different melons, such as Crenshaw, Persian, or heirloom varieties and make your breakfast work for you!*

SERVES 2

2 cups honeydew melon

1 cup cantaloupe melon

1 cup watermelon

¼ cup lemon juice

¼ cup fresh mint leaves

1. Use a melon baller to carve up the honeydew, cataloupe, and watermelon.

2. Place all melons in a large bowl and toss with the lemon juice.

3. Garnish with the mint leaves and serve.

# Refreshing Three-Citrus Salad

*Just when our bodies seem to need it the most—in the very heart of winter—the exceptionally sweet citrus fruit arrives bearing its juicy flesh that hints at sun and summertime. A coincidence? Probably not! Nature gives us what we need when we need it. Pretty rawesome, right?*

SERVES 2

½ cup grapefruit, peeled and sliced

½ cup oranges, peeled and sliced

½ cup tangerines, peeled and sliced

½ cup strawberries, sliced

½ cup blackberries

½ cup kiwi, peeled and sliced

Optional: 2–4 tablespoons agave syrup, to taste

1. Toss all the fruit together in a large bowl.

2. If you wish, drizzle the agave syrup on top to sweeten.

Swap It Out! You can balance the citrus here with any fruit that has a little bit of bite. Pomegranate, cactus fruit, and tart cherry would all stand in well for the kiwi and blackberries. This tangy combination can be served with or without sweetener.

# Pick-Me-Up Papaya Salad

*The surprising flavor combinations in this beautiful fruit salad give you a fun and fantasic way to break your fast. Papayas offer unique and powerful digestive enzymes, which will settle your stomach for the long day ahead, the cilantro keeps things interesting with its unexpected flavor, and the black salt brings it all together. Equatorial fruit + exotic herb + esoteric salt = exceptional breakfast!*

SERVES 4

2 tablespoons lemon juice

1 tablespoon minced cilantro

½ teaspoon agave syrup

½ teaspoon black salt

½ cup papaya, chopped

½ cup mango, chopped

½ cup kiwi, chopped

¼ cup strawberries, sliced

1. In a large bowl, whisk together the lemon juice, cilantro, agave syrup, and black salt.

2. Add the papaya, mango, kiwi, and strawberries, and gently toss to combine. Chill for 30 minutes before serving.

# SuperFruit Superstar Fruit Cocktail

*Sometimes it takes an army to get your body ready to face the day. Fortunately, an arsenal of antioxidant power is poised to spring into action with every forkful of this fruit cocktail. Let the mighty battle begin!*

SERVES 2

¼ cup goji berries

2 tablespoons water

1 tablespoon acai powder

1 tablespoon lucuma powder

1 teaspoon agave syrup

1 apple, chopped

1 banana, sliced

½ cup blueberries

½ cup red grapes

1. Cover the goji berries in warm water and allow to soak for at least 30 minutes.

2. In a large bowl, whisk together the water, acai, lucuma, and agave syrup.

3. Add the apple, banana, blueberries, grapes, and goji berries, and gently toss to combine. Serve immediately or chill, if preferred.

Swap It Out! Here the apple and banana act as a base to anchor the dish; you can use any mild sweet fruits to stand in as background. Alternate superfruit stars include pomegranates, mangosteen, cranberries, or currants. Feel free to use any to personalize this dish.

# Sinful Sunday Fruit Fondue for Two

*This fruit fondue is so amazing that it must be naughty! In fact, "sinful" is the only way to describe the sublime pairing of fruit with chocolate. Chocolate with breakfast? Yup, how rawesome is that! Share this with your sweetheart as a perfect treat for the weekend—or any other day that delights you!*

**SERVES 2**

1 cup cashews
1 cup Easy-Breezy Plant Milk, divided
   (see this chapter for recipe)
¼ cup dates, pitted and chopped
1 tablespoon cacao powder
Fresh fruit, for dipping

**1.** Soak the cashews for at least ½ hour.

**2.** Blend the cashews with ½ cup Easy-Breezy Plant Milk. Add the dates and cacao powder, blending until smooth. Gradually add more of the Easy-Breezy Plant Milk until the proper consistency is reached—a thick sauce that will stick to the fruit.

**3.** Cut all the fruit into dipping-sized pieces, then spread them on a plate. Serve the sauce in a dipping bowl accompanied by toothpicks or fondue forks.

Swap It Out! Many fruits would work well here, so use your favorites. Strawberries, cherries, bananas, persimmons, even oranges. Watermelon? Why not? Get wild. You can also replace the cacao with carob if you prefer.

# "Mom's Apple Pie" Apple Smash

*Sometimes you just need something warm, and the warming aroma of apples and cinnamon oozing out of this recipe calls to mind comfort and wholesome charm. Try this Apple Smash fresh from the dehydrator. Heated, it's ooey and gooey and oh-so-good, just like a slice of hot apple pie. Well, like a slice of nourishing, nutrient-rich, living apple pie. Maybe not quite like Mom used to make it . . .*

## SERVES 2

**2 cups apples, chopped**

**1 cup water**

**¼ cup dates, raisins, or currants**

**2 tablespoons agave syrup**

**2 teaspoons lemon juice**

**1–1½ teaspoons cinnamon**

**½ teaspoon ground cloves**

**½ teaspoon nutmeg**

**¼ teaspoon sea salt**

1. Spread the chopped apples on a dehydrator tray. Dehydrate at 145°F for 2 hours.

2. While the apples are still dehydrating, put the rest of the ingredients into a blender and process until smooth.

3. Pour this mixture into a food processor bowl. Add the apples and pulse to combine until a chunky sauce forms.

4. Place the entire mixture into the dehydrator for an additional hour. Serve warm.

***Passionate* Pairings** Eat this alone as a porridge or mash, or spread it on bread for a saucy topping, or top it off with crunchy granola for a real apple-pie-like flavor. You could also try stirring in walnuts, flaxseed, or raisins.

# Energizer Bunny Breakfast Shake

*Need to wake up? This thick, glucose-infused breakfast-in-a-tall-glass shake may be just what you need to add a little skip to your hippity-hop step. So shake your cotton bobby tail and wiggle those big ears, 'cause you're in for a power blast, bunny rabbit. This shake is perfect for a pre-gym breakfast or before any intense activity. Just don't drink it if you're planning to sleep! This energizer will have you banging your drum for hours and hours and hours.*

### SERVES 1

1 cup Easy-Breezy Plant Milk (see recipe in this chapter)
½ cup freshly pressed carrot juice, 3–5 carrots
2 large frozen bananas, in chunks
Pinch of cinnamon

1. Add the almond milk, carrot juice, and bananas to a blender. Process until completely smooth.

2. Pour into a tall glass and garnish with cinnamon. Drink immediately.

■ **PRO'S TIP** Don't waste that "waste"! Leftover juice pulp is a fibrous, flavorful ingredient that can be integrated into any number of dishes. You can collect your juice pulp by storing it in the freezer, saving it up until you have enough to feature it in a recipe. Keep your savory pulp (greens, veggies) separate from your sweet pulp (fruits, carrots). Savory pulp is great in soups and breads, while sweet pulps can act as the base for delicious cookies and crackers (see recipes in Chapters 13 and 14).

# Totally Tangy Nut or Seed Yogurt

*Yogurt is truly a healing food. The probiotics (the good bacteria) help colonize your digestive tract, which in turn displaces the harmful bacteria. A thriving probiotic community aids in digestion, nutrient absorption, immune system functioning, and so much more. Nondairy yogurt is made in much the same way as the traditional cows'-milk counterpart—with bacterial fermentation. This produces the thick, rich texture and the telltale tang that characterizes traditional dairy yogurts.*

**SERVES 4**

**2 cups nuts or seeds**
**2 cups young coconut Thai water, or substitute plain water plus 1 teaspoon to 1 tablespoon agave syrup**
**1 teaspoon probiotic powder or 1 tablespoon Rawesome Rejuvelac (see recipe in Ch. 14)**

1. Soak nuts and/or seeds for 6–24 hours, as needed. Drain the water and replace it with fresh water every 6 hours.

2. Drain and rinse the nuts/seeds. Place them in a blender and add the young Thai coconut water or plain water with agave syrup. Process until very smooth.

3. Transfer to a large glass container. Stir in the probiotic powder or Rawesome Rejuvelac.

4. Cover the jar with a towel or cheesecloth, and secure with a rubber band. Allow it to sit for 6–8 hours at room temperature.

5. Check for tanginess before serving. Store the mixture in a glass container with a tight lid, in the refrigerator, for up to a week.

Swap It Out! You can use any raw nuts or seeds here, keeping in mind that different types will result in different tastes. You may want to experiment with blending different types in various proportions, to produce a flavor that you're crazy about!

# Creamy Coconut Yogurt

*Yogurt can be made from any number of mediums. In this case, coconuts are cultured to produce an incredibly creamy backdrop for your favorite fruit or garnish. Coconuts are high in healthy fats, which gives this tangy treat an absolutely luxurious mouthfeel. Exceptionally healthy and super tasty? Now that's a winning combination!*

**SERVES 4**

**2 cups young Thai coconut meat, from 3–5 coconuts**

**1 cup coconut water**

**1 teaspoon probiotic powder or 1 tablespoon Rawesome Rejuvelac (see recipe in Ch. 14)**

1. Open the young Thai coconuts with a large knife. Pour off water and set aside. Scoop out meat, being careful to discard any bits of shell.

2. Place coconut meat and coconut water in a blender and process until very creamy.

3. Transfer to a glass container. Stir in the probiotic powder or Rawesome Rejuvelac.

4. Cover the container with a towel or a piece of cheesecloth, secured with a rubber band. Allow to sit for 4–8 hours at room temperature.

5. Check for tanginess before serving. Store the mixture in a glass container with a tight lid, in the refrigerator, for up to 1 week.

# Orchid's Kiss Vanilla Clotted Cream

*This is a delicious, simple twist on the standard cultured coconut recipe. Real, raw vanilla beans bring an exotic and multidimensional essence to the dish that's nothing like the synthetic "vanilla" flavoring that's found in storebought yogurt. Vanilla beans come from orchids—and they're only edible orchid in existence. Yum!*

SERVES 2

2 cups Creamy Coconut Yogurt (see recipe in this chapter)
1 whole vanilla bean pod

1. Place yogurt and vanilla bean in a high-speed blender and process until smooth. If you do not have a high-speed blender, you may use a knife to split the vanilla bean and carefully scrape the seeds into the yogurt, stirring them in by hand.

2. Dress as you wish and serve. Will keep for 1 week in the refrigerator.

# Crunchy Peach Parfait

*In the Deep South, "Peach" is a term of endearment reserved for the sweetest of sweethearts. And why not? There's nothing sweeter, nothing more perfect, than a perfectly ripe, perfectly sweet, perfect peach! If you happen to disagree, you can feel free to swap in pears or plums instead. But either way, you're still a total peach!*

SERVES 2

1 cup Orchid's Kiss Vanilla Clotted Cream (see recipe in this chapter) or 1 cup yogurt plus ½ teaspoon vanilla extract
1 tablespoon agave syrup
6 walnut halves
1 cup fresh sliced peaches
½ cup raw granola or Completely Life-Changing Grain Crunchies (see recipe in this chapter)

1. Spoon yogurt into a bowl and add vanilla (if using plain yogurt) and agave syrup. Mix well to combine.

2. Crumble walnuts into large pieces and set aside.

3. In a parfait glass or champagne flute, begin layering yogurt, then sliced peaches, then granola. Repeat layering to top of glass.

4. Sprinkle walnuts on top and serve chilled.

# Spice-Berry Yogurt Cup

*Berries are such a diverse bunch, from tart juicy blackberries to mild sweet blueberries to strawberries that sing of summer and shortcake. Spices are just as varied, and a surprising number marry well with berries, offsetting their sweetness for a perfectly balanced breakfast bowl. So pick your favorite berry! Choose your favorite spice! Get ready for deliciousness!*

### SERVES 2

1 cup Creamy Coconut Yogurt or Totally Tangy Nut or Seed Yogurt (see recipes in this chapter)

1 cup berries of choice, more for garnish

1 tablespoon water

2 teaspoons agave syrup

½ teaspoon spice of choice (see sidebar, "Passionate Pairings," for suggestions)

1. In a blender or food processor, mix together yogurt and berries until smooth and completely combined.

2. In a small bowl, whisk together water, agave syrup, and spice.

3. Spoon berry-yogurt blend into two bowls and drizzle the spice sauce over the top. Garnish with fresh berries to serve.

*Passionate* Pairings If you're not sure which fruits and spices to pair, consider some of these masterful matchings: blackberries with cardamom, raspberries with ginger, blueberries with cinnamon, or strawberries with chili and salt.

# Quick and Comforting Cinnamon Toast

*Cinnamon toast is such an easy way to brighten your morning mood. Maybe you need a little lift on a dreary gray winter day. Maybe you just woke up on the wrong side of the bed! Whatever it may be, the warm, nostalgic flavors of cinnamon and brown sugar are sure to turn your day around. So treat yourself to something nice. You deserve it!*

SERVES 1

2 slices Simple Tasty Toast (see recipe in Ch. 13), or other unflavored raw bread

1 tablespoon coconut oil

1 teaspoon coconut crystals

¼ teaspoon cinnamon

1. Spread the coconut oil over the slices of bread, like butter. Place these in the dehydrator to warm, at 115°F, for an hour or so.

2. Meanwhile, in a small bowl combine the coconut crystals and cinnamon.

3. Sprinkle the sugar-spice mix over the melted coconut oil. Serve warm.

*Passionate* Pairings This recipe works with any neutral bread or cracker, though it's best with Simple Tasty Toast (recipe in Chapter 13).

# Cinnamon Toast Crunch Cold Cereal

*The Quick and Comforting Cinnamon Toast recipe can be easily adapted to produce this Cinnamon Toast Crunch Cold Cereal, which mimics the sugary, unhealthy, overprocessed version you may have loved as a kid. This delicious cereal is a blast from the past—but without the high fructose corn syrup or artificial flavorings! Real food is so much tastier, anyway.*

SERVES 4

Quadruple batch of Quick and Comforting Cinnamon Toast (see recipe on this page)

1. After adding the sugar-spice blend over the melted coconut oil, return all the slices of toast to the dehydrator. Allow to crisp up for about 2 hours.

2. Remove from the dehydrator. Break the toast into small, bite-sized cereal pieces. Serve in a bowl with Easy-Breezy Plant Milk (see recipe in this chapter).

# Completely Life-Changing Grain Crunchies

*Grain Crunchies are an endlessly diverse, rawesome ingredient, and keeping them around will allow for all sorts of incredible, on-the-fly creations. They're the base of every granola, they're perfect in a parfait, they add substance to soups and crunch to salads, and they can be ground into flour for countless raw cookies, crackers, and breads.* Note: *Soaking and sprouting times will depend on the type of grain—please refer to the Soaking and Sprouting Chart in Chapter 1.*

### YIELDS 2–6 CUPS OF CRUNCHIES

**2–6 cups grains like quinoa, buck-wheat, hulless oats, rye, wheat**

1. Soak, rinse, and sprout grains according to the Soaking and Sprouting Chart in Chapter 1.

2. Once the tails have reached sufficient length, spread the sprouts evenly over dehydrator trays. Use unlined mesh tray covers for larger grains, like buckwheat, and nonstick sheets on the trays for smaller grains, like quinoa.

3. Dehydrate at 110°F for 8–15 hours (will depend on grain) until completely dry. Remove from dehydrator and store in an airtight container in the pantry. Will keep for months.

# Simply Spiced Multi-Grain-ola

*Whole grains make for a hearty head start, with slow-burning complex carbs for fuel and plenty of heart-healthy fiber. Each of these grains just so happens to contain a complete protein (all nine essential amino acids!) as well, making this a perfectly rounded power breakfast. Shape this granola into energy bars for a quick post-workout protein boost! Delicious!*

**MAKES 2 TRAYS AND SERVES 6**

1 cup sprouted buckwheat, fresh or prepared as Completely Life-Changing Grain Crunchies (see recipe in this chapter)

1 cup sprouted hulless oats, fresh or prepared as Completely Life-Changing Grain Crunchies (see recipe in this chapter)

1 cup sprouted quinoa, fresh or prepared as Completely Life-Changing Grain Crunchies (see recipe in this chapter)

½ cup chopped dates

½ cup dried coconut

¼–½ cup agave syrup, to your taste

1 teaspoon vanilla extract

1 teaspoon cinnamon

½ teaspoon nutmeg

¼ teaspoon cloves

¼ teaspoon ginger

Pinch sea salt

**1.** Combine all ingredients in a very large bowl and toss to completely distribute agave syrup and spices. This works best if you use your hands.

**2.** Spread onto dehydrator trays lined with non-stick sheets. Dehydrate at 145°F for 2 hours, then at 110°F for 8 hours or until completely dry. Granola will store for weeks in an airtight container in the pantry.

Swap It Out! Feel free to replace the grains with any substitutions you prefer. Both millet or wheat would be healthy choices, and amaranth, another complete protein, would also be amazing!

# Rawesome Apricot-Ginger Granola with Vanilla-Scented Cashews

*Apricot, ginger, and vanilla. You know that these flavors are completely complementary, and each one sings on a different part of the tongue. The apricot hits just a little bit tart, the ginger reads with a hint of spice, and the vanilla whispers a sweet background melody that ties it all together. With multiple textures and just the right amount of crunch, this granola has it all. A symphony for the mouth!*

**MAKES 2 TRAYS AND SERVES 6**

4 cups sprouted buckwheat, fresh or prepared as Completely Life-Changing Grain Crunchies (see recipe in this chapter)

1 vanilla bean

1 cup cashew pieces

1 tablespoon coconut nectar

½ cup chopped dried apricots

¼ cup coconut oil, melted

⅓ cup agave

1" knob of ginger, peeled and finely grated

1. Carefully slice open the vanilla bean and use a knife to scrape the seeds into a mixing bowl. Add the cashews and the coconut nectar and toss to coat. Set aside.

2. In a very large bowl, combine the rest of the ingredients and mix well. Gently stir in the cashews, being mindful not to blend the flavors too much.

3. Spread onto dehydrator trays lined with non-stick sheets. Dehydrate at 145°F for 2 hours, then at 110°F for 8 hours or until completely dry. Granola will store for weeks in an airtight container in the pantry.

# Chocolate-Lover's Dream Granola

*It's pretty clear that this is a chocolate lover's dream dish. After all, nothing starts a day off right quite like chocolate! The good news here is that the raw cacao in this recipe is full of minerals and naturally energizing. It contains theobromine, a compound that's closely related to caffeine, which will help wake you up—without giving you the jitters. But more importantly, a good dose of chocolate is food for the soul.*

**MAKES 2 TRAYS AND SERVES 6**

10 dates, pitted and soaked

¼ cup coconut oil, melted

1 teaspoon vanilla extract

¼ teaspoon almond extract

2 cups sprouted rye berries, fresh or prepared as Completely Life-Changing Grain Crunchies (see recipe in this chapter)

2 cups sprouted buckwheat, fresh or prepared as Completely Life-Changing Grain Crunchies (see recipe in this chapter)

½ cup raisins

½ cup pecans halves, halved

½ cup shredded coconut

¼ cup cacao powder

**1.** In a blender, combine the soaked dates, melted coconut oil, vanilla extract, and almond extract. Process to make a thick, smooth paste.

**2.** In a very large bowl, combine the rest of the ingredients. Stir in the paste and mix very well. This works best if you use your hands.

**3.** Spread onto a dehydrator tray lined with non-stick sheets. Dehydrate at 145°F for 2 hours, then at 110°F for 8 hours or until completely dry. Granola will store for weeks in an airtight container in the pantry.

# On-the-Go Overnight Oatmeal

*Sometimes you just don't have time to linger at the kitchen table. Sometimes, you're dressed and out the door before your eyes are even completely open. If this sounds like a typical weekday for you, then this recipe is perfect! The oats in the oatmeal soften all night so you just have to blend them in and you're good to go.*

SERVES 1

½ cup hulless oats
1 teaspoon to 1 tablespoon agave
  syrup, to taste
1 teaspoon cinnamon
1 ripe banana

1. The night before, soak the oats in water for 30 minutes. Drain and rinse and transfer to the bowl of a food processor. Drizzle with agave syrup and sprinkle with cinnamon, then leave overnight to sprout.

2. In the morning, peel a banana and add it to the oatmeal mixture already in the food processor. Pulse to mix well, crumbling the oats, and making a chunky oatmeal.

3. Transfer to a bowl or a large mug for easy to-go eating.

# Completely Killer Kasha Porridge

*Most often made from buckwheat and eaten as either a sweet or savory meal, kasha—a traditional dish eaten in many Eastern European countries—has been enjoyed in various iterations for over 1,000 years. And with this recipe you'll be able to rock the kasha in its raw food form.*

SERVES 2

2 cups soaked and sprouted buckwheat groats (see Soaking and
  Sprouting Chart in Ch. 1)
1 cup apple, chopped
1 tablespoon cinnamon
2 teaspoons orange zest
½ teaspoon sea salt

1. Place all ingredients in a food processor and blend into a chunky porridge.

2. Spoon into two bowls and serve.

# Cha-Cha-Cha Chia Pearls Breakfast Pudding

*When mixed with water, chia seeds plump up to make a beaded gel that's reminiscent of tapioca pudding, which is how you get the pearls in this recipe. These seeds are high in calcium, complete protein, and essential omega-3 fatty acids, which makes them a rawesome addition to any breakfast!*

**SERVES 2**

½ cup chia seeds
1½ cups Easy-Breezy Plant Milk (see recipe in this chapter) or plain water, or combination of the two
1 teaspoon agave syrup
Spices and toppings to taste

1. Place the chia seeds in a bowl with the Easy-Breezy Plant Milk or water and the agave syrup, keeping in mind that the seeds will expand. Stir well to combine and break up any clumps.

2. Allow to sit for 15 minutes, stirring every few minutes.

3. Spoon into two bowls. Add whatever spices or toppings you prefer prior to serving.

*Passionate* Pairings Chia seeds themselves have very little flavor, so add in anything that you'd like to star in this super breakfast story. Some suggestions: cinnamon, nutmeg, carob, cacao, shredded coconut, dried fruit (raisins, gojis), fresh fruit (berries, bananas), nut butter, coconut butter, or anything else you can dream up.

# Super-Infused Super Green Chia Pudding

*As if chia seeds weren't super enough on their own, this breakfast bowl kicks it up another notch with the addition of a few fantastic superfoods. The chlorella used here is a green powder that acts as a powerful detoxifier, but it's also pretty potent. Luckily, its flavor is masked by the caramel-y, light molasses-like flavor of the sweet mesquite. Sounds delicious!*

**SERVES 2**

½ cup chia seeds
1½ cup Easy-Breezy Plant Milk (see recipe in this chapter) or plain water, plus more to pour on top
1 tablespoon mesquite powder
½–1 teaspoon chlorella, to your taste
1 cup strawberries, sliced

**1.** Place the chia seeds in a large bowl with the Easy-Breezy Plant Milk or water, the mesquite, and the chlorella. Stir to combine and break up any clumps.

**2.** Allow to sit for 15 minutes, stirring every few minutes.

**3.** Spoon into two bowls. Top with strawberries and a splash of Easy-Breezy Plant Milk.

Swap It Out! Strawberries are a nice pairing for recipe, but if you're not a fan, you can use any fresh fruit that you favor.

# Autumn Harvest Porridge

*Behold this silky smooth porridge, which is almost like a sweet breakfast soup. Rich with macadamia cream and full-bodied with all the flavors of fall, this hearty starter is just the thing for a brisk autumn morning. This purée presents a cereal-free option for those who still want that old porridge feeling, minus the gluten or grains.*

## SERVES 2

1 cup butternut squash, peeled and chopped
½ cup macadamia nuts
½ apple
½ cup young Thai coconut water
1 teaspoon cinnamon
½ teaspoon vanilla
½ teaspoon ginger juice (from a small, peeled knob of gingerroot)
½ cup dried unsweetened cranberries

1. Place all the ingredients except for the cranberries into a blender or food processor. Blend until very smooth.

2. Spoon into two bowls and garnish with dried cranberries.

Swap It Out! You can replace the butternut with sweet potatoes, which are often available year-round, if you're yearning for that seasonal taste come summer. You can also swap out the macadamias for any nut you choose—try pecans, almonds, or cashews. If you don't have any young Thai coconuts on hand, you can just use Easy-Breezy Plant Milk (see recipe in this chapter) or plain filtered water instead.

# Silver Dollar Strawberry Pancakes

*Just a bit of forethought can go such a long way, and a Friday night kitchen session will leave you sleeping soundly as you anticipate Saturday morning pancakes. These fabulous flapjacks are truly a triumph—soft and chewy on the inside, but with a nicely crisped-up crust. Smothered in fresh sliced strawberries and swimming in Unreal Maple Syrup (recipe in Chapter 9), they're definitely worth waking up for!*

**SERVES 2–4**

¼ cup Easy-Breezy Plant Milk (see recipe in this chapter)

¼ cup agave syrup

2 tablespoons coconut oil

½ teaspoon vanilla extract

½ ripe banana, mashed

2 cups almond flour, or pulp from making almond milk, finely ground

1 tablespoon lucuma powder

Pinch of sea salt

1 cup strawberries, sliced

1. Cream together the Easy-Breezy Plant Milk, agave syrup, coconut oil, vanilla extract, and banana, making sure the banana is mashed very smooth. Set aside.

2. Sift together the almond flour, lucuma powder, and sea salt. Combine the wet and dry ingredients (except strawberries) in a large bowl and mix thoroughly.

3. Spoon small dollops of batter onto a dehydrator tray lined with a nonstick sheet, flattening them and shaping them into silver-dollar-sized pancakes.

4. Dehydrate overnight, 6–8 hours, at 115°F.

5. If you'd like, in the morning you can flip them and dehydrate for another 2 hours. This is not necessary but will create a more uniform crust on both the top and bottom. Pancakes should still be pliable.

6. Serve warm from the dehydrator, topped with strawberries and Unreal Maple Syrup (see recipe in Chapter 9).

# Positively Perfect Pear Crêpes

*Crêpes, very flat pancakes stuffed with either sweet or savory fillings, are traditional French fare. Elegant and a little bit laborious, crêpes are generally reserved as a special occasion food, but you're living a special occasion life! So bon appétit!*

SERVES 4

2 cups young Thai coconut meat

4 cups pears, chopped

2 cups sliced bananas

Optional: sprinkle of coconut crystals

½ cup Unreal Maple Syrup or Unbelievable Raspberry Coulis (see recipes in Ch. 9)

1. Place the coconut meat and chopped pears in a blender or food processor and purée until completely smooth.

2. Spread the mixture in a thin layer onto dehydrator trays fitted with nonstick sheets. Dehydrate at 115°F for 4 hours.

3. Score the resulting fruit leather into circles, about 8" in diameter, to make the crêpes.

4. Mash the bananas with a fork. Place a crêpe on a plate and spread a layer of mashed banana on it. If you wish, sprinkle the coconut crystals over the banana. Roll the crêpe.

5. Place the crêpe rolls on a platter and drizzle with Unreal Maple Syrup or Unbelievable Raspberry Coulis to serve.

# Fantastique Fig Crêpes

*The wrappers for this delicate crêpe are cashew-based and extra-chewy, with a fruity compote filling that charmingly befits any French cottage. So set your shabby chic table with chipped china and mismatched flatware and pull up that white wicker chair, 'cause it's time for a taste that's straight from a countryside villa.*

SERVES 4

For the crêpe wrapper:
2 cups cashews, soaked 2–4 hours
3 tablespoons agave syrup
2 tablespoons lemon juice
¼ teaspoon salt

For the fruit filling:
1 cup dried figs, soaked 8–12 hours
1–2 tablespoons agave syrup
½ teaspoon vanilla
½ teaspoon cinnamon
¼ teaspoon sea salt
2 tablespoons water

1. To make the crêpe wrappers, place all ingredients in a blender and process until completely smooth. Spread a thin layer of mixture onto dehydrator trays fitted with nonstick sheets. Dehydrate at 110°F for 12–18 hours.

2. When drying is complete (wrappers should still be pliable), cut into circles about 8" in diameter.

3. To make the crêpe filling, remove the soaked figs from the water, cut and discard the stems, and then finely chop and place them in a mixing bowl with the agave syrup, vanilla, cinnamon, and sea salt. Toss to completely coat.

4. In a food processor or blender, blend ¼ cup of the fig mixture until it becomes a paste. Add the water, 1 teaspoon at a time as needed, to create a thick sauce. Pour this sauce back into the chopped figs and stir to create a compote.

5. Place a crêpe wrapper on a plate and spread a layer of fig compote over it. Roll up the crêpe. Place the crêpe rolls on a platter and top each crêpe roll with another dollop of compote. Serve.

# Crunch-Tastic Breakfast Tacos with Tangy Ruby Raspberry Filling

*As far as greens go, romaine is not at the top of the nutritional tower, but it more than makes up for this small indiscretion by bringing something amazing to the table: the crunch factor. And when it comes to making raw tacos, nothing else on earth could be more crunch-tastic.*

**SERVES 2**

1 ruby red grapefruit

1 cup raspberries

½ cup peaches, diced

½ cup nectarines, diced

Optional: 1 teaspoon to 1 tablespoon
   agave syrup

4–8 romaine leaves, choose large
   and sturdy ones

1. Use a sharp knife to remove the peel and pith from the grapefruit. Remove the seeds and slice the membrane from each segment. Slice each segment in half. Discard the peel, pith, seeds, and membrane.

2. Combine all the fruit in a large mixing bowl and toss with the agave. Spoon into romaine leaves and serve.

Swap It Out! The fruit used in the filling is a lovely colorful blend of sweet and tart flavors. However, you can feel free to make substitutions: citrus for citrus, berries for berries, etc. You could even replace the peaches with apples, or the nectarines with kiwi. Whatever you wish!

# Bite-Sized Breakfast Sushi Roll

*Sushi goes sweet—and raw vegan! Adapted for the palate of a raw vegan, this contemporary, interpretive take on the traditional Japanese "fast food" resembles the original in form alone. The flavors are entirely new for sushi, but they're classic in their own delicious way.*

**MAKES 8 SUSHI WRAPPERS**

**4 cups sliced strawberries**

**1 cup pears, peeled, cored and chopped**

**8 tablespoons almond butter (1 per sushi roll)**

**8 bananas (1 per sushi roll)**

1. Place strawberries and pears into a food processor or blender and purée until smooth. Spread mixture in a thin layer onto dehydrator trays lined with nonstick sheets. Dehydrate at 115°F for 6–8 hours.

2. Once the wrappers are cooled, score them into fourths and peel them off the trays. To store them, roll them up and wrap them in plastic, and keep them in the fridge for up to two weeks.

3. To make a sushi roll, lay out a wrapper on a plate. Spread 1 tablespoon of almond butter down the center. Place a banana on top of the almond butter. Roll it up and slice into 8 sushi pieces. You can also leave it unsliced for a more portable meal.

# California Benedict with Herbivore's Hollandaise

*Traditional Eggs Benedict is made with poached eggs, Canadian bacon, and hollandaise sauce. In other words: cholesterol, carcinogens, and other objectionable crud. However, this raw version riffs on the original with a reminiscent presentation and a flavor that's remarkably spot-on. Ultrarich and over-the-top decadent, save this recipe for your most special occasion.*

## SERVES 2

1 very large or 2 medium red round slicing tomatoes

12 slices Sweet and Spicy Zucchini Jerky (see recipe in Ch. 13)

1 whole avocado, peeled, pitted, and sliced

½ cup Herbivore's Hollandaise Sauce (see recipe in Ch. 9)

2 green onions, diced

1. Slice tomatoes into 4 large slabs, about ½" thick.

2. Place 2 tomato slices on each plate. Top each tomato slice with 3 pieces of Sweet and Spicy Zucchini Jerky (spread overlapping, not stacked), followed by ¼ of the sliced avocado.

3. Drizzle Herbivore's Hollandaise Sauce over each stack. Sprinkle with green onions to garnish.

## Chapter 7

# Step Into Salads

As an experienced raw foodist, you're probably used to hearing, "So what do you eat, like, salads?" And of course, the answer is yes! Raw foodists eat salads—among many, many other things—but the salads you consume are more than the standard, sad pile of pitiful veggies. No, your salads are celebrations! They sing to the bounty of each season, and they're carefully crafted to highlight each delicate flavor and soft tender texture that nature gifts through her myriad produce. These are some of the most artisan, inspired meals that you eat!

And, you know that your salads don't mess around. Hearty, satiating, nutrient-rich, and bountiful, these salads can just as easily steal the show as a complete meal. So serve them on their own or serve them as a side, but either way you serve them, serve them up with pride!

# Lettuce Lover's Little Slice of Heaven

*Variety is the spice of life, so they say, and so it goes with greens especially. Each species bears a unique nutrient profile, so rotate through the spectrum in order to reap the full rewards. Kale, collards, red oak, frisée, endive, butter leaf, romaine, chard, bok choy, pak choi, cabbage, and more. With so many options, you'll never get bored!*

SERVES 4

2 cups romaine lettuce, chopped
1 cup Bibb lettuce, chopped
1 cup endive, torn
½ cup arugula, torn
½ cup red-leaf lettuce, torn
⅓ cup celery, sliced
¼ cup carrots, sliced
2 tablespoons olive oil
4 teaspoons coconut vinegar
¼ teaspoon agave syrup
¼ teaspoon sea salt
⅛ teaspoon hot paprika
⅛ teaspoon garlic powder
⅛ teaspoon onion powder
¼ cup grape tomatoes, sliced

1. Combine romaine, Bibb, endive, arugula, red-leaf, celery, and carrots in a large bowl. Toss to mix.

2. Whisk together the olive oil, vinegar, agave syrup, and spices to make dressing.

3. Drizzle dressing over salad and toss thoroughly to coat. Garnish with sliced grape tomatoes and serve.

### Tomato Typing

Cherry, plum, pear, grape—there are a lot of little tomatoes around! Each has its own unique flavor, and each originates from a slightly different region. Grape tomatoes hail from Southeast Asia, and have the distinctly sweet taste of their cousins, the cherry tomatoes.

# Warmed-and-Wilted Spinach Salad with Raspberry-and-Red-Onion Vinaigrette

*Elegant. Charming. Ever-so-refined. Gently wilted spinach is truly a treasure, tender and delicate on the tongue. This simple salad allows that unique feature to take center stage. The focus is on the texture and the amazing dressing, which marries the sweetness of fresh raspberries with the slight pungency of raw onion. A match made in heaven—or at least in your totally rawesome kitchen!*

**SERVES 4**

1½ cups fresh raspberries, divided
¼ cup red onion, chopped
¼ cup coconut vinegar
1 teaspoon basil, minced
½ teaspoon sea salt
¼ teaspoon fine black pepper
¼ teaspoon dried thyme
¼ teaspoon dried parsley
⅛ teaspoon cumin
½ cup extra-virgin olive oil
4 cups baby spinach
½ cup walnut halves

1. In a blender or food processor, combine 1 cup raspberries with the onion, vinegar, basil, salt, pepper, thyme, parsley, and cumin. Process until smooth.

2. With the machine running, slowly add the oil until fully emulsified.

3. Toss with the spinach and walnuts until thoroughly coated. Place bowl in dehydrator and allow to warm at 115°F for at least an hour.

4. Serve warm from the dehydrator, garnished with additional raspberries.

# Rawkin' Secret Caesar

*This is a raucous take on a classic recipe. Traditional Caesar employs eggs for creaminess and anchovies for a salty undertone—both of which you just want to avoid. This raw vegan, no-compromise version doesn't make any flavor concessions, but it does include plenty of heart-healthy plant fats to ensure an awesome flavor. Et tu, Brute? Nope, no traitors here. This recipe rawks!*

SERVES 2

½ medium avocado

½ cup hempseed

2 tablespoons olive oil

2 tablespoons lemon juice

1 tablespoon apple-cider vinegar

1 clove garlic

1 teaspoon agave syrup

1 teaspoon sea salt

½ teaspoon black pepper

½ teaspoon kelp granules

¼ cup water

½ cup pine nuts

4 cups romaine lettuce, chopped and plated

1 cup Garlic Lover's Greatest Crackers (see recipe in Ch. 13), crumbled

1. In a blender or food processor, combine the avocado, hempseed, olive oil, lemon juice, vinegar, garlic, agave syrup, salt, pepper, kelp granules, and water. Process until completely smooth to make dressing.

2. In a coffee grinder or food processor, process pine nuts until crumbly.

3. Pour dressing over plated romaine. Sprinkle with pine nuts and crackers. Serve.

# Escarole's Eclipse

*Escarole is a broader-leafed, slightly less bitter cousin of endive. It's a lovely pairing with mild, nutty lamb's lettuce and assertive, dulcet citrus. Between the oranges and the currants, this salad presents an explosion of colors and flavors atop a perfect, neutral palate. It's gorgeous to look at, but it's even more amazing to bite into!*

SERVES 4

1 head escarole

2 cups lamb's lettuce

2 large seedless oranges

2 tablespoons mineral water

2 tablespoons lemon juice

2 teaspoons olive oil

⅛ teaspoon sea salt

2 tablespoons fresh red or pink currant

1. Wash, drain, and shred the escarole and lamb's lettuce. Set aside in large bowl.

2. Peel the oranges. Remove pith and membranes and separate into segments. Set aside.

3. Whisk together the mineral water, lemon juice, olive oil, and sea salt to make dressing.

4. Toss dressing with escarole and lamb's lettuce. Top with oranges and currants. Refrigerate or serve immediately.

# Tantalizing Tangerine, Licorice, and Mint

*This is another dish that plays with a diverse array of elements and includes seemingly at-odds ingredients, which combine synergistically to form a cohesive taste. The various threads—citrus, fennel, and mint—create a tightly woven tapestry of unified flavor that will leave you and your guests begging for seconds!*

SERVES 2

1 whole head green lettuce, chopped

2 tangerines, peeled, pith removed, and sectioned

1 bulb fennel, sliced thin

⅓ cup chopped walnuts

2 tablespoons chopped fresh mint

2 tablespoons olive oil

Sea salt and pepper to taste

1. Gently toss together the lettuce, tangerines, fennel, walnuts, and mint.

2. Drizzle with oil, then add salt and pepper before serving.

Swap It Out! For a fun twist, try replacing the olive oil with cold-pressed walnut oil instead, and taste this bouquet as it blooms on a whole other level.

# Feeling Feisty, Spicy, and Nice

*This powerful starter packs a flavor punch all on its own, so you want to serve it as your first course. But it's a show-stopper, so follow it up with something that isn't going to compete, like a sweeter or creamier entrée. You want this salad to shine like the feisty, fiery little star that it is!*

SERVES 4

¼ cup olive oil

2 tablespoons apple-cider vinegar

1 teaspoon fresh ginger, peeled and minced

½ teaspoon garlic, minced

½ teaspoon dried mustard powder

½ teaspoon nama shoyu

1 cup Pink Lady apple, diced

½ cup cucumber, thinly sliced

¼ cup leeks, diced

3 cups watercress, chopped

2 cups spinach leaves, torn

1 tablespoon almond slivers

1. Shake oil, vinegar, ginger, garlic, mustard powder, and nama shoyu together in a lidded glass jar, until well-blended. This dressing is best if the flavor is allowed to mature in the refrigerator for 24 hours.

2. Toss the apple, cucumber, and leeks together in a large bowl. Mix in the dressing until thoroughly coated.

3. Fold in the watercress and spinach, gently tossing to coat. Serve garnished with the slivered almonds.

---

### Spotlight on Watercress

Watercress is a brassica, like cabbages and cauliflower. It's most closely related to mustard and shares its distinctive fiery flavor. Watercress is high in iron, calcium, folic acid, and iodine, as well as vitamins A, C, and K. It's believed to strengthen thyroid functioning, and recent research suggests that it may suppress the growth of certain cancer cells.

# Fishing for Compliments Salad

*This unique little number features disparate textures and divergent flavors that end up singing together in perfect harmony. The peppery arugula is offset nicely by the slightly sweet dressing, and the crispy pears partner up and play nice with the creamy avocado. Light/Dark. Push/Pull. Eat/Yum!*

SERVES 4

3 cups arugula leaves

1 cup Asian or Bosc pear, thinly sliced

½ cup avocado, cubed

¼ cup grape tomatoes, diced

¼ cup sunflower seeds

2 tablespoons olive oil

1 teaspoon apple-cider vinegar

1 teaspoon agave syrup

¼ teaspoon lemon zest

¼ teaspoon dried mustard powder

¼ teaspoon fine black pepper

1. Toss the arugula, pear, avocado, grape tomatoes, and sunflower seeds together in a large bowl.

2. Whisk the olive oil, vinegar, agave syrup, lemon zest, mustard powder, and pepper together to make the dressing.

3. Drizzle the dressing over the salad and toss to coat. Serve immediately.

# Good, Clean Green Eats

*This unreal salad is a triumph that combines the crunch of cruciferous broccoli and cauliflower with equally crispy celery and cucumbers. All that texture is balanced out by the tender baby greens that provide the bedding. This is simple fare, just good, clean, eating. Rawesome, right?*

SERVES 2

1 cup broccoli florets
1 cup cauliflower florets
½ cup English cucumber, sliced
½ cup celery, chopped
¼ cup Supremely Silica-Rich Dressing (Ch. 9)
1 tablespoon pesto of choice (see recipes in Ch. 9)
2 cups baby mixed greens, torn

1. Place the broccoli and cauliflower in a large bowl. Break up any large florets. Add the cucumber and celery. Toss.

2. Whisk together the salad dressing and pesto. Drizzle over the vegetables and toss to thoroughly coat.

3. Fold in the baby greens and gently mix. Serve immediately.

# Totally Tasty Mediterranean Tomatoes

*This salad is the epitome of Mediterranean simplicity: the freshest fresh produce highlighted in an uncluttered sauce. No muss, no fuss, no pomp and circumstance. Just pure flavors and purifying foods. Perfecto!*

SERVES 4

2 cups juicy tomatoes (like Beefsteak or Heirloom), sliced
1 cup cucumber, chopped
⅓ cup yellow bell pepper, chopped
¼ cup radish, sliced
¼ cup flat-leaf parsley, chopped
1 clove garlic, minced
2 tablespoons olive oil
1 tablespoon lemon juice
2 cups baby spinach leaves
Salt and pepper to taste

1. Combine tomatoes, cucumber, bell pepper, radish, and parsley together in a large bowl with the garlic, olive oil, and lemon juice. Toss thoroughly to coat.

2. Divide spinach onto four plates and top with dressed mixture. Season with salt and pepper to taste, then serve.

**Passionate** Pairings Serve this as a starter to pizza margherita, pasta marinara, or alongside your favorite Italian-inspired soup.

# Ginger-Spiked Raw-ldorf

*The traditional Waldorf salad revolves around apples, walnuts, and an abundance of eggy, artery-clogging mayonnaise, which will not do. This recipe keeps the healthy fruit and nuts, but then kicks the old-school Waldorf up a notch with a shot of fresh ginger juice for fantastic flavor and a bit of unexpected flair. Now you're talking— and rawkin'—with that Waldorf!*

**SERVES 4**

2 apples, your preference

Juice of ½ lemon

2 large carrots, grated

¼ cup dried unsweetened
  cranberries

12 walnut halves

¼ cup olive oil

2 tablespoons apple-cider vinegar

1 teaspoon fresh ginger juice

1 teaspoon agave syrup

½ teaspoon sea salt

Optional: mixed greens

1. Core and chop the apples. Place them in a mixing bowl and toss with the lemon juice.

2. Add the carrots, cranberries, and walnut halves to the apples. Toss and set aside.

3. In a small bowl, whisk together the olive oil, vinegar, ginger juice, agave syrup, and sea salt to make the dressing.

4. Pour the dressing over the apple mixture and toss to mix well. Serve in small bowls, or over mixed greens.

# Relaxed and Groovy Collard Greens

*Collards are kale's scruffy streetwise cousins, and they can be quite the little ruffians. Collards can be thick and tough, anything but tender. If you don't know how to handle them, they're liable to give you lip, so approach this salad with a firm yet loving approach, a little coaxing if you will. Remember, it's all in the wrist . . .*

SERVES 2

3 cups young collard greens
1 teaspoon salt
3 tablespoons lemon juice, divided
½ cup pine nuts
2 tablespoons olive oil
½ teaspoon garlic powder
½ tablespoon fresh basil
½ tablespoon fresh oregano
2 cups tomatoes, diced
1 cup red bell peppers, diced
¼ cup green onions, diced

1. Remove the stems from the collard greens and discard. Roll the greens up and chop them into small pieces. Sprinkle with salt. Massage them by hand to work the salt into the greens so they begin to wilt.

2. Pour 2 tablespoons lemon juice onto the greens and mix well. Let them sit for 1–2 minutes to further wilt.

3. In a blender or food processor, blend the pine nuts, olive oil, garlic powder, and 1 tablespoon lemon juice until smooth. Add the basil and oregano and briefly pulse until the herbs are mixed in but still chunky.

4. Add tomatoes, bell peppers, and onion to the collard greens. Toss everything together with the pine nut dressing and serve.

# Keep-It-Simple Stir-No-Fry Salad

*This recipe shows you how to make an awesome Asian standby in a totally rawe-some new way! This easy-to-grab salad offers all the standard stir-fry veggies, in a fry-sauce-inspired salad dressing instead. All of the stir with none of the fry! So put away the wok full of smoking oil and dive into this crisp, refreshing bowl full of crunchy saucy goodness.*

### SERVES 4

1½ cups sugar snap peas, trimmed
 and halved

1 cup bok choy, diced

½ cup red bell pepper, julienned

½ cup red onion, sliced

¼ cup carrot, diced

3 tablespoons sesame oil

2 tablespoons nama shoyu

2 tablespoons coconut vinegar

½ teaspoon lemon zest

¼ teaspoon gingerroot, ground

2 tablespoons cashews, chopped

1. Place prepared sugar snap peas, bok choy, bell pepper, onion, and carrot in a large bowl. Set aside.

2. In a small bowl, whisk together sesame oil, nama shoyu, vinegar, lemon zest, and ground gingerroot to make dressing.

3. Drizzle dressing over vegetables and toss thoroughly to combine.

4. Cover bowl and place in refrigerator. Allow to marinate for 30 minutes. Mix well, garnish with cashews, and serve.

Swap It Out! Like a traditional stir-fry, the veg-etables in this dish are totally transferable. Don't like red onion? Replace it with Walla Walla Sweets! Not into cashews? Try almonds instead! Any of these ingredi-ents can be exchanged for youtr favorite equivalent— just one of the many reasons why salads totally rawk!

# Sweetie-Pie Scarlet Salad

*Red may be the color of love, but it's also an indicator of mighty antioxidant power. Romantic, huh? This salad derives its amorous complexion from plant-based angels like betalains and terpenoids. So move over Cupid—and eat this salad for a healthy heart!*

SERVES 4

3 cups baby mixed greens

3–4 small beets, peeled and grated

1 cup sliced strawberries

½ cup chopped pecans

¼ cup olive oil

2 tablespoons coconut or apple-cider vinegar

2 tablespoons agave syrup

2 tablespoons fresh orange juice

Salt and pepper to taste

1. In a large bowl, combine mixed greens, beets, strawberries, and pecans.

2. In a small bowl, whisk together the olive oil, vinegar, agave syrup, and orange juice to make the dressing.

3. Pour the dressing over the vegetables and gently toss to coat.

4. Season generously with salt and pepper before serving.

# Sweet Green and Grain

*Quinoa is a South American seed that hails from a plant called the goosefoot, which is closely related to beets and spinach. But goosefoot is not a grass, and therefore quinoa is not actually a grain. In fact, it's called an ancient grain, or a pseudograin. But no matter what you call it, quinoa offers up all nine essential amino acids, making it a great source of complete protein.*

SERVES 4

1 bunch mesclun greens

1 cup walnuts, chopped

½ cup sprouted quinoa (see Soaking and Sprouting chart in Ch. 1)

2 apples, cored and chopped

1 red bell pepper, seeded and chopped

¼ cup olive oil

2 tablespoons apple-cider vinegar

2 cloves garlic

1 tablespoon agave syrup

2 pitted dates

⅛ teaspoon cinnamon

2 tablespoons water

1. In a large bowl combine the mesclun, walnuts, quinoa, apples, and bell pepper. Set aside.

2. In a blender or food processor, combine the oil, vinegar, garlic, agave syrup, dates, and cinnamon. Purée until smooth, adding the water a tablespoon at a time as needed to thin.

3. Pour the dressing over the greens and grain, and toss well to thoroughly coat. Serve immediately.

# An Intricate Apricot Duet

*Complexity in an appetizer is best appreciated when the dish is served on its own, and this complex salad shines when it's paired with nothing else at all. Serve it before or after your entrée, lest it attempt to overshadow the other dish. Or, add some lemony sprouted lentils and call it a complete meal. But whatever you do, don't you dare call it boring!*

SERVES 4

3 tablespoons sesame oil

3 tablespoons lemon juice

4 teaspoons orange juice

½ teaspoon sea salt

⅛ teaspoon cayenne pepper

⅛ teaspoon finely ground black pepper

2 cups fresh apricots, diced

¼ cup dried apricots, diced

⅓ cup fennel bulb, sliced

½ cup celery, sliced

2 cups romaine, chopped

1 cup oak-leaf lettuce, torn

1 cup alfalfa sprouts

¼ teaspoon orange zest

1. Whisk the sesame oil, lemon juice, orange juice, sea salt, cayenne pepper, and black pepper together in the bottom of a mixing bowl until salt dissolves.

2. Add both kinds of apricots, fennel, and celery to the dressing bowl. Toss thoroughly to coat. Cover bowl and place in refrigerator to marinate for at least 15 minutes.

3. Place the romaine, oak-leaf, and alfalfa sprouts in a large salad bowl. Gently fold in the marinated mixture and all the dressing, carefully tossing to combine completely.

4. Garnish with a sprinkle of orange zest and serve.

# Scrumptious Herbal Surplus

*All three of the herbs in this recipe are potent antibacterial agents. Mint is a good source of vitamins A and C and the mineral manganese. It also contains special phytochemicals that help protect against cancer. Basil is high in calcium, iron, and magnesium, and has anti-inflammatory properties. And fresh oregano contains unique antioxidents as well as omega-3 fatty acids. Now that's a powerful pile of greens!*

**SERVES 4**

5 cups romaine leaves, finely torn

⅓ cup fresh mint leaves

¼ cup fresh basil leaves

¼ cup green onions, finely chopped

1 tablespoon fresh oregano, chopped

¼ cup olive oil

2 tablespoons water

2 teaspoons apple-cider vinegar

1 teaspoon dried mustard powder

½ teaspoon sea salt

½ cup Tomato, Basil, and Flax Crackers (see recipe in Ch. 13) or other crackers, crumbled

1. In a large bowl, combine the romaine with the mint, basil, green onions, and oregano. Toss to mix well. Set aside.

2. In a jar with a lid, mix the olive oil, water, vinegar, mustard powder, and sea salt to make the vinaigrette. Shake well until completely blended. Drizzle half the vinaigrette over the salad and gently toss to mix well. Add more vinaigrette if needed. Store any extra dressing in the fridge—it makes a great veggie dip!

3. Top with crumbled crackers before serving.

# Cactus in the Raw

*Believe it or not, cactus pads are commonly eaten in the southwest United States and all through Mexico. Cooked to make a dish called* nopalitos, *the pad is a pain to prepare, but this fun and funky ingredient is truly a pleasure to eat. Just be careful cleaning it—you don't want to prick your precious fingertips!*

SERVES 4

2 cups cactus pads, prepared and cut into strips (see sidebar, "Working with Cactus Pads")

1½ cups red tomatoes, chopped

⅓ cup raw black olives, pitted and halved

⅓ cup radishes

2 tablespoons fresh cilantro

¼ cup olive oil

¼ cup apple cider vinegar

1 clove garlic, crushed

½ teaspoon sea salt

1 teaspoon ground white pepper

½ teaspoon cayenne pepper

Optional: mixed greens

1. Mix the cactus, tomatoes, olives, and radishes with the cilantro in a large mixing bowl.

2. In a small lidded glass jar, combine the oil, vinegar, garlic, salt, and both types of pepper. Shake well to mix.

3. Pour the dressing over the vegetables and toss to thoroughly combine. Cover and allow to sit for at least 30 minutes in the refrigerator. Serve as is or over a bed of mixed greens.

### Working with Cactus Pads

To clean and prepare a cactus pad, begin by using a potato peeler or paring knife to dig out the thorns and "eyes." Wash the pads thoroughly in cold water, and then trim away any discolored skin using a potato peeler. Finally, use a sharp knife to slice the pad into thin strips. It's as easy as that!

# Sweet and Hot Sunset Salad

*This pretty pile of piquant perfection is an absolute joy to behold, with bright, beautiful colors that foretell the tastes to come. A little bit spicy, a little bit sweet, this salad has a whole lot of* oomph! *Serve it chilled as a midday treat on a hot summer day, with a heaping side of guacamole. There's nothing like slightly spicy vegetables to refuel your afternoon.* ¡Caliente!

SERVES 4

2 cups cubed pineapple
2 cups romaine lettuce, chopped
1 cup red-leaf lettuce
½ large red bell pepper, julienned
1 small jalapeño, seeded and minced
½ cup fresh pineapple juice
2 tablespoons apple-cider vinegar
¼ teaspoon sweet paprika
⅛ teaspoon sea salt
⅛ teaspoon finely ground black
  pepper
1 tablespoon fresh chives, diced

**1.** In a large bowl, combine pineapple cubes, lettuces, and bell pepper. Toss to mix.

**2.** Combine the jalapeño and pineapple juice in a small bowl. Add the vinegar, paprika, sea salt, and black pepper to make a dressing.

**3.** Toss the dressing with the salad and chill prior to serving. Garnish with fresh chives.

# East African Kachumbari

*This classic African appetizer lies somewhere between a salsa and a slaw. Either way, the spicy side can be eaten all on its own, served over greens, tossed into a wrap, or piled up on veggies with guacamole, like a salsa. After all, variety is the spice of life!*

SERVES 4

1 medium jalapeño, seeded and minced

2 cups green cabbage, shredded

1½ cups tomatoes, thinly sliced

¾ cup red onion, thinly sliced

3 tablespoons lemon juice

3 tablespoons fresh cilantro, chopped

½ teaspoon sea salt

1. Combine the jalapeño with the cabbage, tomatoes, and red onion.

2. Sprinkle the vegetables with lemon juice, cilantro, and sea salt. Toss gently to mix and coat. Serve immediately or cover and chill for up to 4 hours.

Swap It Out! This appetizer is as variable as you are, so don't be afraid to alter the ingredients list. Any shredded veggies will mix in well, though a base of cabbage, tomato, and pepper will keep it tasting traditional.

# Garden Shredder

*This multicolored slaw combines a cornucopia of produce into one nutrient-rich and flavor-packed rawesome celebration. Use your food processor's shredding disc attachment to speed up all the prep work. Or, just put on some good tunes and rock out as you get down with your hand grater. Either way, enjoy the bounty that this recipe brings with its bunches of vitamins, minerals, and phytonutrients!*

**SERVES 4**

1½ cups red cabbage, shredded
1 cup carrot, shredded
¾ cup yellow squash, shredded
¾ cup zucchini, shredded
½ cup green bell pepper, julienned
⅓ cup white onion, slivered
¼ cup fresh pineapple juice
3 tablespoons apple-cider vinegar
2 tablespoons water
1 tablespoon agave syrup
¼ teaspoon paprika
¼ teaspoon celery seeds
⅛ teaspoon garlic powder
⅛ teaspoon red pepper, ground

1. In a large bowl mix the cabbage, carrot, squash, zucchini, bell pepper, and onion.

2. In a small mixing bowl, combine pineapple juice, vinegar, water, agave syrup, and spices. Whisk to blend.

3. Pour the dressing over the vegetables and toss well to thoroughly coat.

4. Refrigerate for at least 4 hours. Toss again prior to serving.

### What Color Is That Cabbage?

Some people call it red cabbage, and others call it purple cabbage, and some are just confused! So who's correct? The truth is, these leaves actually change their color depending on their environment. They'll even turn blue under certain conditions! The variable hue is mostly due to pH balance. For some fun kitchen chemistry, juice a head of cabbage into a glass bowl, add a little lemon juice, and watch what happens. Then drink it down. Yum!

# "Sunfish" Salad

*Tuna fish salad is practically a staple food for children, and many of us share fond memories of those charming, simple sandwiches—crusts cut off! Of course, these days you know better. Thank goodness for this perfect mimic, which hits every note you may remember, minus the mercury and environmental destruction. Truly, this salad is a blessing to behold. Get ready to lick your fingers like a kiddo—because you won't want to miss a bit!*

**SERVES 4**

2 cups sunflower seeds, soaked at least 2 hours

½ cup Good Gracious Garlic Aioli (see recipe in Ch. 9)

4 celery stalks, sliced

2 tablespoons minced red onion

2 tablespoons dulse flakes or 1 teaspoon dulse powder

2 teaspoons apple-cider vinegar

½ teaspoon sea salt

½ teaspoon black pepper

Optional: 2–4 diced Crunchy Cultured Dill Pickles (see recipe in Ch. 10) or storebought pickles (Bubbies is a raw brand), plus a splash of pickle juice

1. Rinse and drain soaked sunflower seeds and transfer to a food processor. Pulse to make a chunky mixture; do not overprocess.

2. Transfer to a large mixing bowl and add the rest of the ingredients. Use a large spoon to mix thoroughly.

3. This tastes best if allowed to marinate for a few hours in the fridge. Serve in a sandwich or atop mixed baby greens.

# Spicy Southwestern Three-Sprout Salad

*Red rocks, purple sunsets, giant cacti looming lonesome in an endless sky. These are the sights of the southwest desert, and this is the imagery your meal will surely call to mind. Hot wind, scaly critters, and crunching-crumbling under foot. Thank goodness you've got your own little oasis. So hang a hammock between two palm trees. Put your feet up by the wellspring. And beat the heat with this tasty Tex-Mex treat.*

**SERVES 6**

1 cup lentil sprouts (see Soaking and Sprouting Chart in Ch. 1)

1 cup green pea sprouts (see Soaking and Sprouting Chart in Ch. 1)

1 cup yellow pea sprouts (see Soaking and Sprouting Chart in Ch. 1)

1 red or yellow bell pepper, chopped

1 large tomato, diced

⅔ cup corn kernels

1 small red onion, diced

⅓ cup olive oil

¼ cup lime juice

½ teaspoon chili powder

½ teaspoon garlic powder

½ teaspoon sea salt

¼ teaspoon cayenne pepper

¼ cup chopped fresh cilantro

1 avocado, cubed

**1.** In a large bowl combine all the sprouts with the bell pepper, tomato, corn kernels, and onion. Gently toss and set aside.

**2.** In a small separate bowl, whisk together the oil, lime juice, chili powder, garlic powder, sea salt, and cayenne pepper.

**3.** Pour the dressing over the vegetables and toss to coat. Stir in the cilantro.

**4.** Chill for at least 1 hour to allow flavors to mingle. Garnish with cubed avocado.

Swap It Out! Feel free to substitute whatever types of sprouts you wish. Chickpeas, mung beans, or quinoa would all stand in well here as sprouted alternatives.

# Nontraditional Tabbouleh, Starring Quinoa

*Tabbouleh is a classic Middle Eastern dish that can lean more towards a salad or more towards a pilaf, depending on how much parsley you prefer. Here it's presented in salad style, with bunches of the fresh, grassy herb. Serve this healthy, healing dish as an appetizer to share, or keep it all for yourself as a perfectly balanced, rawesomely delicious meal.*

SERVES 4

1 clove garlic, pressed or finely minced

¼ cup olive oil

Juice of 1 lemon

Sea salt to taste

1½ cups sprouted quinoa (see Soaking and Sprouting Chart in Ch. 1)

2 cups fresh parsley, minced

3 green onions, minced

1 cup plum tomatoes, halved lengthwise

1. Whisk together the garlic, olive oil, lemon juice, and sea salt in a large bowl.

2. Toss with all the rest of the ingredients, mixing well to completely distribute the dressing. Adjust seasoning before serving.

# A Conversation Between Crispy and Creamy

*This is a salad that speaks up for its raw vegan beliefs and walks to the beat of its own drum. This quirky salad matches crunchy red radishes and crisp purple plums with smooth, silky avocados. The result is a chorus of flavor, a circus of color, a delight for all the senses. Sensational!*

SERVES 4

2 tablespoons lemon juice

2 tablespoons olive oil

1 tablespoon agave syrup

1 teaspoon coconut vinegar

Pinch of sea salt

2 cups red radishes, quartered

2 cups baby plums, pitted and halved

½ cup walnuts, chopped

2 avocados, cubed

1. In a medium bowl, whisk together the lemon juice, olive oil, agave syrup, vinegar, and sea salt.

2. Add the radishes, baby plums, and walnuts to the bowl. Toss well to completely coat with dressing.

3. Add the avocado and gently stir. Do not over-mix or the avocado pieces will break down and lose their shape.

4. Chill for at least 10 minutes before serving.

# Spiked Citrus Curried Quinoa Salad

*Sprouted quinoa is a power player in the raw kitchen because it provides an excellent source of protein. Quinoa protein is complete, meaning it contains all nine of the amino acids that are necessary to secure dietarily. Combined with the spinach that's packed with iron, and the vitamin C–rich orange juice that makes the iron more absorbable, this salad is practically a superfood in and of itself. Or, perhaps, a super*meal!

**SERVES 4**

3 cups sprouted quinoa (see Soaking and Sprouting Chart in Ch. 1)

¾ cup golden raisins

¾ cup slivered almonds or pine nuts

¼ cup red onion, diced

½ cup orange juice

2 tablespoons olive oil

1 teaspoon Curry Seasoning Spice Blend (see recipe in Ch. 12) or storebought curry powder

½ teaspoon coriander powder

4 cups baby spinach

2 scallions, chopped

1. In a large bowl combine the quinoa, raisins, almonds or pine nuts, and onion. Toss to mix. Set aside.

2. In a smaller separate bowl, whisk together the orange juice, olive oil, Curry Seasoning Spice Blend, and coriander powder to make dressing.

3. Drizzle the dressing over the quinoa mixture. Toss thoroughly to coat. This tastes better if allowed to marinate for at least 1 hour.

4. Serve over baby spinach, garnished with scallions.

Swap It Out! This delicious dish lends itself well to interpretation, so feel free to play with substitutions or throw in any additions. Try currants or other dried fruit in place of the raisins, or replace the nuts with any seed that suits your fancy. Sliced jalapeños for a bit of a kick? Why not! A few chunks of tangerine for a tart taste sensation? Have at it! From freshly shelled green peas to sprouted lentils to shredded coconut, this exceptional salad can handle whatever you decide to throw its way.

# Cleansing Cucumber and Cilantro Salad

*The cucumbers, green beans, sprouted lentils, and sunflower seeds packed into this delicious recipe all contain molybdenum, a chemical element that's essential for proper metabolic functioning. Molybdenum plays a critical role in many of our important biochemical reactions, and is actually a component of some of the enzymes themselves! So keep that metabolism purring—and enjoy!*

**SERVES 4**

4 cucumbers, sliced

2 tomatoes, chopped

½ red onion, minced

1 cup Totally Tangy Nut or Seed Yogurt or Creamy Coconut Yogurt (see recipes in Ch. 6)

1 tablespoon lemon juice

2 tablespoons fresh cilantro, chopped

¼ teaspoon cayenne pepper

Salt and pepper to taste

1. Toss all ingredients in a large bowl, stirring well to combine.

2. Chill for at least 2 hours before serving. This allows all the flavors to mingle and marinate. Toss again prior to plating.

# Spicy Sweet Sunomono

*Japanese sunomono, or vinegared vegetables, is a light and refreshing traditional cleanser. The cool, crisp cucumbers and the bit of spice in this recipe make for an interesting combination that doesn't overwhelm or interfere with the taste of other dishes, so serve this version to aid in digestion at the start of a meal, or to clear the palate in between courses.*

SERVES 2

1 cup cucumbers, very thinly sliced
¾ teaspoon sea salt
¼ cup coconut vinegar
1 teaspoon agave syrup
1 teaspoon sesame oil
¼ teaspoon red pepper flakes
½ cup white onion, thinly sliced

1. In a large, shallow container, spread the cucumbers in a single layer and sprinkle with sea salt. Allow to sit at least 10 minutes.

2. Drain any excess water from the cucumbers and place them in a large bowl. Set aside.

3. In a small separate bowl, whisk together the vinegar, agave syrup, oil, and red pepper flakes to make a dressing.

4. Pour dressing over the cucumbers, add the onion slices, and toss gently.

5. Allow to sit at least 10 minutes before serving to allow flavors to mingle. Best served cold.

# Mountain of Minerals: Kale and Seaweed Salad

*The straight shot of concentrated nutrition in this recipe is just the thing to pick you right back up and get you go-go-going if you're having a tough day. Kale is a super vegetable if ever there were one, with an amazing nutrient profile that includes off-the-charts levels of vitamins A, C, and K; the minerals calcium, iron, and manganese; amino acids; and antioxidants galore! And that's really just the tip of the iceberg. Wakame is a sea-veggie supreme, with high levels of calcium and iron, as well as the hard-to-find and ever-important iodine. So get off the couch—and into your kitchen!*

SERVES 4

4 cups curly kale
1 teaspoon sea salt
2 tablespoons lemon juice
½ avocado
1 tablespoon sesame oil
¼ cup dried wakame, rehydrated for 20 minutes in warm water, then drained
1 tablespoon sunflower seeds
1 tablespoon sesame seeds
3 tablespoons sliced green onions

1. Remove the stems from the kale and discard. Tear the leaves into small pieces. Sprinkle the salt over them, and massage them by hand so they begin to wilt.

2. Pour 2 tablespoons of lemon juice onto the kale and mix well. Allow to sit for 1–2 minutes to further wilt.

3. In a small bowl, mash the avocado with the sesame oil. Mix well to make a thick but smooth sauce.

4. Pour the sauce over the kale and use your hands to massage it in. Make sure it's evenly spread and completely coating the kale.

5. Fold in the wakame, sunflower seeds, and sesame seeds. Gently toss. Garnish with the sliced green onions before serving.

*Chapter 8*

# Soups for All Seasons

Soups are the afternoon equivalent of smoothies in that they are fantastically effortless to whip up, delightfully quick to prepare, endlessly adaptable, and easily customized to fit the individual contents of your pantry. Like smoothies, raw soups can get a micronutrient boost via fresh greens, or you can add satiety and bulk by putting in protein powders or superfoods. And of course, raw soups are as delicious as they are nutritious!

From the simple blended veggie bisques to the more texturally complex preparations such as hearty chowders or chunky gazpachos, raw soups provide a blank canvas for culinary artistry. Once you've explored the following recipes, try venturing out on your own raw soup exploration. You just may strike recipe gold!

# Sweet Honey Melon with Heat

*Don't you dare call this soup a dessert! This recipe may revolve around honeydew melon, but the flavors here are surprisingly complex—and anything but saccharine. The interplay of sweet and spicy, silky and acidic is perfect for a hot summer's night. Listen to the serenading cicadas, look out for the flickering fireflies, and linger over every last delicious bite.*

SERVES 4

1 small ripe honeydew melon, seeded
  and cubed
½ cup lime juice
½ cup Totally Tangy Nut or Seed
  Yogurt or Creamy Coconut Yogurt
  (see recipes in Ch. 6)
Sea salt and pepper to taste
½ jalapeño, seeded and minced
½ cup slivered almonds
¼ cup chopped fresh mint

1. In a food processor, purée the melon, lime juice, yogurt, salt, pepper, and jalapeño. Refrigerate until completely chilled.

2. Serve garnished with slivered almonds and mint.

■ **PRO'S TIP** Plan ahead! As soon as you bring home a melon, carve it up into bite-sized chunks. Spread the pieces on a baking tray and stick it in the freezer. Once they're frozen you can transfer them to a lidded container—this method will keep the pieces from freezing together. In the future, you'll always have amazing melon on hand for a special summer-inspired treat.

# Summer's Sunrise

*Imagine rainbow sherbet in a soup tureen. Perfectly pastel like the dawning sky, delicate sweet and a touch of tart, a harmonic blend of real fruity flavors and citrus to accent it all. This soup does duty on many levels: from a breakfast to a starter to a simple dessert. However you decide to eat it, rest assured that you'll enjoy its pure, unparalleled freshness.*

SERVES 4

1 ripe cantaloupe, seeded and cubed

1 cup fresh raspberries, plus 4 extra raspberries for garnish

½ cup orange juice

Juice of ½ lemon

Juice of ½ lime

4 large fresh mint leaves

1. Put the cantaloupe in a blender or food processor and blend to make a smooth purée. Pour into a large bowl.

2. In the blender or food processor, process the 1 cup fresh raspberries into a smooth purée. If not using a high-speed blender, pour the purée through a fine mesh strainer into a small bowl in order to remove the seeds. This should yield about ½ cup (repeat with more raspberries if it comes up short).

3. Stir the purées together, then add the juices and stir to blend.

4. Garnish each bowl with a raspberry and a mint leaf.

# Chunky Cherry Walnut Gazpacho

*This yogurt-based soup makes for a fun and fabulous first course. Why? Because probiotics are a beneficial way to begin a meal; they prime your stomach up to handle anything that follows them down the hatch. So start your dining experience right with this light, refreshing soup. Your tummy will thank you for it.*

SERVES 2

1 cup diced cucumber

2 tablespoons walnut oil

1 clove garlic, minced

¼ teaspoon pepper

¾ cup cherry tomatoes

1 cup Totally Tangy Nut or Seed
   Yogurt or Creamy Coconut Yogurt
   (see recipes in Ch. 6)

Optional: 2 tablespoons fresh
   chopped dill

Optional: 2 tablespoons chopped
   walnuts

1. Toss the diced cucumber with the walnut oil, minced garlic, and pepper. Allow this mixture to marinate in the refrigerator for at least 2 hours.

2. When the mixture is done marinating, drain the cucumbers. Add the cherry tomatoes and the yogurt, stirring well.

3. Pour the soup into serving bowls. Garnish with dill and walnuts, if desired.

■ **PRO'S TIP** Cucumber flesh is very mild in flavor and made of mostly water, but it also contains ascorbic and caffeic acids, which sooth skin and reduce swelling. The thicker, dark green skin is a rich source of silica, essential for skin elasticity and healthy connective tissue. To minimize any bitterness, peel your cucumbers. To maximize the beauty benefits, leave the peels intact. Keep this in mind as you use cukes in all your other uncooking recipes.

# Farmer's Harvest Hearty Gazpacho

*Looking for a farmer's market in your bowl? Well, this soup has it all, from small popping-sweet corn kernels to crunchy-textured broccoli florets to tender, carved zucchini cubes. Truly, this is a cornucopia of flavor and nutrition. Bless the bounty!*

SERVES 4

2 large tomatoes
2 ears corn
½ cup green beans
2 zucchinis
1 summer squash
1 cup broccoli florets
½ cup shelled fresh peas
4 cups tomato juice
Sea salt and cracked black pepper
   to taste

1. Chop and seed the 2 tomatoes, husk the corn and cut the kernels from the cob, and trim the green beans. Cut the zucchini and the summer squash into bite-size chunks. Combine together with the fresh peas.

2. In individual soup bowls, pour the tomato juice. Divide the raw vegetables equally among the bowls. Top each bowl with cracked black pepper and a sprinkle of sea salt.

# Quick and Creamy Cucumber Bisque

*This dream of a cucumber bisque comes together in minutes, and it's the perfect choice when you want something light and need something now. It's elegant enough that you still feel like you're getting a real meal, but with no fuss, no muss, and most of all, no worries!*

SERVES 2

1 cucumber, halved and seeded
¼ cup chopped scallions
¼ cup chopped fresh mint
2 cups Easy-Breezy Plant Milk (see
   recipe in Ch. 6)
1 cup Totally Tangy Nut or Seed
   Yogurt or Creamy Coconut Yogurt
   (see recipes in Ch. 6)
Sea salt and pepper to taste

1. Purée the cucumber, scallions, and mint in a food processor or blender.

2. Add the Easy-Breezy Plant Milk and yogurt and process until smooth.

3. Transfer to a large bowl and stir in the salt and pepper.

Swap It Out! If you don't have any yogurt on hand, try adding ½ cup more Easy-Breezy Plant Milk along with a large handful of cashews. The taste will be out of this world!

# Little Miss Green Goddess Gazpacho

*This is a down-to-earth soup, perfect for a relaxing afternoon filled with meandering conversation and loving, lighthearted laughter. Mother Nature is serene in spring, as the wild world awakens and life blooms lively all around so serve this creamy cucumber blend on a warm spring day spent with friends. Drink it down and savor the season!*

**SERVES 6**

5 medium cucumbers

1 medium sweet onion

2 large red peppers

1 medium jalapeño pepper, seeded and chopped

4 medium cloves garlic, smashed and peeled

¾ cup fresh mint leaves, chopped

½ cup parsley, chopped, plus 2 tablespoons, minced, for garnish

2 cups Totally Tangy Nut or Seed Yogurt or Creamy Coconut Yogurt (see recipes in Ch. 6)

1 teaspoon sea salt

3 tablespoons coconut vinegar

¾ cup olive oil

2 cups water

½ cup pine nuts

1. Seed and chop the cucumbers. Hold back 1 cup for garnish.

2. In a food processor, process the remaining cucumber in batches. Remove cucumbers to a bowl and set aside.

3. Core, seed, and chop the onion, red pepper, and jalapeño; pulse them to chop in the food processor. Add this mix to the cucumbers.

4. In the processor, purée the garlic, mint, parsley, yogurt, sea salt, and vinegar. While machine is running, add oil slowly through feed slot.

5. Fold the purée into the cucumber mixture. Add the water, stirring to combine.

6. Adjust the seasonings and refrigerate until chilled. Serve topped with pine nuts, the reserved chopped cucumber, and minced parsley.

# Nourishing Noodle Soup

*This recipe calls for miso paste, although technically miso is not raw. Instead, it's made from a base of fermented cooked legumes or grains (often soy, but also barley, chickpeas, or others). However, miso is cultured and therefore it's a living food. For that reason many raw foodists include it in moderation. If you aren't comfortable consuming miso, you can still enjoy this delicious soup: simply replace the miso with 1 tablespoon of nama shoyu.*

**SERVES 4**

4 cups water

1 tablespoon nama shoyu

4 teaspoons mellow white miso paste

2 teaspoons lemon juice

1 clove garlic

½" knob ginger, peeled

2 tablespoons dried wakame, rehydrated in warm water

1 12-ounce package kelp noodles

½ onion, very thinly sliced

2 medium carrots, julienned

2 green onions, sliced on the diagonal

1 zucchini, peeled, seeded, and cubed

4 tablespoons pumpkin seeds

1. To make the stock, blend water, nama shoyu, miso, lemon juice, garlic, and ginger in a blender until garlic and ginger are completely incorporated.

2. Pour stock into a large bowl. Add the rehydrated wakame. Open the package of kelp noodles and rinse them under warm running water, untangling them gently as you rinse. Place the noodles in the stock and allow them to sit for 15 minutes—they will plump and soften a bit.

3. Next, add the onion, carrots, green onions, and zucchini to a large bowl and mix them together.

4. Spoon the noodles and broth into 4 serving bowls. Top with the vegetable mixture and garnish with pumpkin seeds.

# Energizing Sea and Sprouts Soup

*You're bound to enjoy this grounding, mineral-rich green masterpiece that's sure to leave you full, but without the listlessness that often come hand-in-hand with a big meal. The dulse found in this soup offers many of the same trace minerals that are found in human blood, such as chromium and copper, and it's a powerful anti-inflammatory, anticancer, anticoagulant, antithrombotic, and antiviral. That's a lot of bang for just a little bowl of soup!*

**SERVES 2**

¼ cup whole dulse or 1 tablespoon powdered dulse
1 cup apple, chopped
2 cups sunflower seed green sprouts (see Soaking and Sprouting Chart in Ch. 1)
½ cup pine nuts
1 cup water
½ cup avocado, chopped

1. Soak the whole dulse for 5 minutes in water and drain. The powder does not need to be soaked.

2. Place all the ingredients, except the avocado, in a food processor or blender and process until smooth. Briefly blend in the avocado last.

3. Serve immediately at room temperature.

---

### Spotlight on Sunflower Seed Greens

Sunflower seed sprouts are some of the most common sprouts, because they're highly nutritious and quick to grow. Sunny sprouts are available in small trays at most health food stores. Or, you can grow them yourself by buying small black sunflower seeds and sprouting them according to the Soaking and Sprouting Chart in Chapter 1.

---

Open-Faced Avo-Smash
(Chapter 11)

"Spicy Sour" Green Juice
(Chapter 4)

Fearsome Fiery Red Hot Sauce
(Chapter 9)

Asian Noodles with Spicy Almond Sauce
(Chapter 12)

Spring Brings Asparagus Soup
(Chapter 8)

California Benedict with
Herbivore's Hollandaise
(Chapter 6)

Easy Entertainer's Onion Dip
(Chapter 10)

Not-Roasted
Red Pepper Wrap
(Chapter 11)

Silver Dollar Strawberry Pancakes
with Unreal Maple Syrup
(Chapters 6 and 9)

Can't Get Enough
Chocolate Pots
(Chapter 14)

Mountain of Minerals Kale and
Seaweed Salad
(Chapter 7)

Secret Success Zucchini Hummus
with Good Earth Crackers
(Chapters 10 and 13)

Chewy Chocolate Nib Cookies
(Chapter 14)

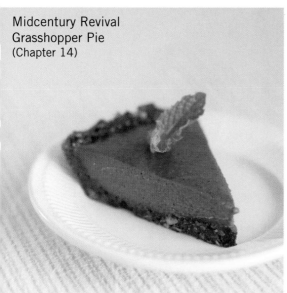

Midcentury Revival
Grasshopper Pie
(Chapter 14)

Sherbet Herb Spring Rolls
(Chapter 11)

Fruit Sushi Rainbow Roll
(Chapter 12)

Marvelous Coconut Cashew Mayonnaise,
Kreative Ketchup, and Must-Have Mustard
(Chapter 9)

Orange and Almond Macaroons dipped in
Chocolate "Magic Shell" Sauce
(Chapter 14)

Horn of Plenty Ratatouille
(Chapter 12)

Mega Maca Burger Patties on Onion Bread
or Buns with Sweet Tater French Drys
(Chapters 11 and 13)

Chia-mole
(Chapter 10)

Incredible Italian Minestrone
(Chapter 8)

Protein Pesto Sprout Stacks
(Chapter 12)

# Dreamy Creamy Corn Chowder

*Chowders are, by nature and by design, rich and filling and full of flavor, and this particular chowder is a perfect accompaniment for a cool autumn night. Pair it with a vibrant, simple mixed green salad for a satisfying meal. Thick and chunky and hearty and good, this chowder easily stands alone as a main course. Bonus: it's even better the next day!*

SERVES 4

4 cups corn kernels, divided

1½ cups Easy-Breezy Plant Milk (see recipe in Ch. 6), more if needed to thin

½ cup cashews, soaked at least 2 hours

¼ cup sweet onion

1 clove garlic

½ teaspoon salt

¼ teaspoon cayenne pepper

½ cup finely diced red bell pepper

2 teaspoons fresh thyme

1. In a blender or food processor, combine 3 cups of corn kernels with the Easy-Breezy Plant Milk, cashews, onion, garlic, salt, and cayenne pepper. Blend until smooth. Transfer to a large bowl.

2. Fold in the 1 cup of corn kernels, the red bell pepper, and the thyme. Stir to mix well, adjust seasoning, and serve.

# Simple Sugar Pea Soup

*Some of the earliest harbingers of spring are the sugar snap and snow peas that fight their way through the final frost. These friendly little legumes can be found around the first farmers' market of the year, and their crisp, tender, deliciously sweet flesh is a lovely reminder of the future bounty the season will bring. This simple soup is an homage to these, the prettiest little peas.*

**SERVES 2–4**

1 pound fresh sugar snap or snow peas, trimmed

1 cup Easy-Breezy Plant Milk (see recipe in Ch. 6) or almond milk

Meat from 1 young coconut, roughly ½ cup

1 medium avocado, peeled, seeded, and cubed

2 tablespoons lemon juice

1 medium cucumber, chopped

¼ teaspoon sea salt

¼ teaspoon pepper

1 tablespoon lemon zest

1. Combine all ingredients except for the lemon zest in a high-speed blender. Process until completely smooth.

2. Pour into serving bowls and garnish with lemon zest.

# Buttery Smooth Butternut Curry Soup

*Buttery scrumptious, this exotic blender soup is built around basic winter squash. Butternuts are widely available in the fall through early spring, but most people don't realize that they can be eaten raw! Hearty starches like these make for heavy, comforting fare, just the kind of food to sustain you through the colder seasons. Warming spices add a special winter flare to this dish.*

**SERVES 2**

1 cup cucumber, chopped
2 cups cubed butternut squash
½ cup red bell pepper, chopped
1 cup pine nuts
¼ cup leeks, diced
2 teaspoons fresh minced or grated ginger
1 tablespoon Curry Seasoning Spice Blend (see recipe in Ch. 12) or storebought curry powder
Water for blending
Optional: ¼ cup fenugreek sprouts

1. In a food processor or blender, blend the cucumber until it's liquefied, and then add the squash. Continue blending.

2. Gradually add the bell pepper, pine nuts, leeks, ginger, and Curry Seasoning Spice Blend, and blend until smooth. Add small amounts of water gradually, if needed.

3. Let the soup sit for 15 minutes before eating, to enhance the flavor. Garnish with fenugreek sprouts and serve.

# Spring Brings Asparagus Soup

*Asparagus season is short and sweet, so finding this veggie at its peak is an absolute treasure. Seek out an organic source and look for thin, pliable stalks with small, compact heads. Asparagus is such a unique little treat of a vegetable! It's low in calories, high in protein and fiber, incredibly rich in vitamins (A, C, and K especially), and is a good source of folate and iron. That's one green wonder-veggie worth taking advantage of!*

**SERVES 4**

1 bunch of asparagus

1 cup Easy-Breezy Plant Milk (see recipe in Ch. 6)

1 medium avocado

2 tablespoons sweet onion, minced

1 tablespoon lime juice

½ tablespoon oregano

¼ teaspoon chipotle powder

**1.** Chop the asparagus, setting aside the tips for garnish.

**2.** Place the chopped asparagus and all other ingredients into a blender or food processor and blend until smooth and creamy.

**3.** Pour into 4 soup bowls and top with asparagus tips.

---

### Don't Miss Out!

Don't let the short season deprive you of asparagus year-round! It's easy to freeze and freezing doesn't degrade any of the nutrients, making it an ideal preservation technique. Simply wash and trim the spears as normal, then lay them out in single layers on baking sheets, stacked in the freezer. Once they're frozen you can remove them and package them in airtight containers for long-term storage. This method will prevent them from freezing together in unruly clumps.

---

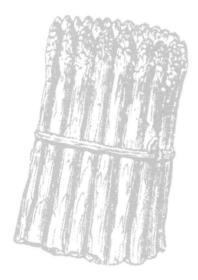

# Creamy Fennel and Tomato Bisque

*Sometimes the simplest things in life are actually the most profound. Like this rich, full-bodied, absolutely flavorful fennel bisque. Like five simple ingredients, combining to create something oh-so-much greater than the simple sum of its simple parts. Simply splendid!*

SERVES 4

1 cup fennel bulb, chopped (reserve fennel fronds for garnish)

4 cups chopped tomatoes

1 cup cashews, soaked for at least 2 hours

Juice of 2 lemons (about 4 tablespoons)

½ teaspoon sea salt

1. Combine all ingredients in a food processor or high-speed blender and process until completely smooth.

2. Pour into 4 bowls and garnish with fennel fronds.

# Incredible Italian Minestrone

*Healthy and hearty, with a thick, tangy tomato base that's a live ringer for the minestrone you remember. The soup carries all of the comfort with none of the cons of canned soup. In this version, sprouted lentils stand in for noodles, offering texture, heft, and an extra kick of essential protein.*

SERVES 2

1 cup sprouted lentils, divided

8 sun-dried tomato halves, soaked for at least 2 hours, 1 cup soak water reserved

2 tablespoons apple-cider vinegar

¼ cup onion, diced

1 clove garlic

1 tablespoon nama shoyu

1 teaspoon dried basil

1 teaspoon dried oregano

¼ teaspoon black pepper

¼ teaspoon sea salt

1. In a blender or food processor, combine ½ cup of the lentils with the rest of the ingredients (including 1 cup tomato soak water). Pulse until well-mixed but not completely smooth.

2. Transfer to serving bowls and top with the remaining sprouted lentils.

Swap It Out! Add your favorite veggies for a complete and well-rounded meal, or serve this Italian soup alongside a fresh and garlicky green salad. Your Nonna would be so proud!

# A Soft-Serve Salad

*Is it a green smoothie, a blended salad, or a creamy soup? And when it tastes this good, does it really matter what you call it? It boasts all the classic dinner salad vegetables piled on top of avocado for silky richness and garlicky fresh herbs for a formidable flavor. A little bit of heat takes your taste buds over the edge, into the realm of purely rawesome. Fabulous!*

**SERVES 4**

2 cucumbers, diced

2 large slicing tomatoes, diced

2 avocados, diced

¾ cup ice-cold water

½ red onion, diced

½ cup fresh chopped cilantro

2 tablespoons lime juice

1 tablespoon coconut vinegar

4 cloves garlic

1 fresh chili pepper (jalapeño, serrano, or cayenne)

Sea salt and pepper to taste

1. Combine all of the ingredients in a food processor or blender. Process until completely smooth.

2. Transfer to bowls and serve very cold.

---

### Avocado Soup?

Say what? It may sound strange, but avocados make an amazing base for blended dishes. They're full of healthy fats, which means they're absolutely ultra creamy, but their flavor disappears completely behind whatever it is they're paired with. Give it a try—and prepare to be delighted!

## Chapter 9

# Dressings, Sauces, and Condiments

A meal without condiments is a mundane meal indeed. Lucky for you, you never need let your veggies sit alone on a plate, your sandwich take the stage undressed, your crackers lead a lonely existence. . . . No, with the recipes that follow, you'll be able to spiff up every entrée imaginable and add some creativity to your crudités or a little bit of bling to an otherwise boring spread.

Condiments like ketchup, mustard, mayo, and barbecue sauce can all add a comforting sense of familiarity to your raw dinner table. The right dressing can make or break a salad, and a delicious dipping sauce is priceless to have around for those unexpected snack attacks. As a general rule, dips and dressing will last for up to a week in the fridge, so it's easy to keep them on hand. Let the following recipes inspire you as you let your mind wander to all the amazing meals that they could complement. That is, after all, what condiments are for!

# Tangy Raw Ranch

*Ranch dressing is something of a modern marvel, the perfect cooling condiment for crunchy crackers or simple crudités. Drizzle it over your pizza, serve it with your kale chips, and of course, toss it with your favorite greens for an easy and amazing salad. However you use it—and the possibilities really are endless—you can't go wrong with ranch!*

YIELDS ABOUT 3 CUPS

1 cup water, more to thin to desired consistency

1 cup Totally Tangy Nut or Seed Yogurt or Creamy Coconut Yogurt (see recipes in Ch. 6; Creamy Coconut Yogurt works best here)

½ cup cashews, soaked at least 2 hours

2 tablespoons apple-cider vinegar

1 tablespoon agave syrup

1 teaspoon nama shoyu

2 medium cloves garlic

1 tablespoon fresh chives, plus more for garnish

1 tablespoon fresh curly parsley

½ teaspoon dried dill

¼–½ teaspoon sea salt, to taste

¼–½ teaspoon cracked black pepper, to taste

1. Place the water, yogurt, cashews, vinegar, agave syrup, nama shoyu, and garlic in a high-speed blender or food processor. Blend until completely smooth.

2. Pour into a mixing bowl and stir in the chives, parsley, dill, salt, and pepper. If serving as a dip, garnish with extra chives.

# Supremely Silica-Rich Dressing

*There's no two ways about it: cucumber is a woefully underappreciated vegetable. But this gorgeous green underdog provides so much more than just wonderful crunch! Cucumbers are rich in the minerals responsible for building connective tissues like bones, skin, hair, and nails. They're also incredibly hydrating and naturally cooling. Here, they add a delicate flavor and a full body that allows for the reduction of oil, making this a delicious and lower-calorie dressing option.*

**YIELDS ABOUT 1 CUP**

1¼ cups chopped cucumber, peeled and seeded (leave peel if using a high-speed blender)

2 tablespoons apple-cider vinegar

1 tablespoon flat-leaf parsley, chopped

2 teaspoons cilantro, chopped

1 small garlic clove

¼ teaspoon salt

¼ teaspoon ground black pepper

¼ teaspoon ground red pepper

¼ teaspoon dried dill

¼ cup extra-virgin olive oil

1. Add the cucumber, vinegar, parsley, cilantro, garlic clove, salt, black pepper, red pepper, and dill to a food processor or small blender. Process the mixture until totally smooth.

2. As the machine is running, slowly add the olive oil. Continue to process for 15 seconds, or until oil is thoroughly incorporated.

3. Pour the dressing into a glass bottle with a tight lid. Store in the fridge and shake well before each use.

■ **PRO'S TIP** Here's a nifty trick for quickly removing the cucumber seeds: Slice the cuke in half lengthwise, then use a melon baller to scoop out the seeds down the center of each half. Once the seeds are out of the way, you're free to slice and dice the veggie as needed. In lieu of a melon baller, you can use a small spoon.

# Ruby Dragon Garlic Dressing

*With a bit of bite from the garlic and a hearty texture that stands up to any vegetable you can toss its way, this lively, tantalizing dressing will add a lovely fiery flair to all your favorite dippers and hors d'oeuvres. The ground flax also acts as thickener while adding healthy fiber and essential omega-3 fatty acids. Just watch out for that dragon breath!*

**YIELDS ABOUT ¾ CUP**

¼ cup water

1 small tomato, chopped

2 garlic cloves, minced

2 tablespoons apple-cider vinegar

1 tablespoon lemon juice

1 tablespoon ground flaxseed

¼ teaspoon celery seed

⅛ teaspoon finely ground black pepper

**1.** Place all ingredients in a blender or food processor and blend until smooth.

**2.** Pour the dressing into a glass bottle with a tight lid. Store in the fridge.

### All about Fiber

Fiber is, simply put, indigestible plant matter. As the bulk moves through your bowel, it picks up lingering debris along the way—essentially sweeping up. The American College of Gastroenterology reports that increasing dietary fiber has been shown to improve a number of digestive disorders. Some of these ailments include chronic constipation, hemorrhoids, diverticular disease, elevated cholesterol, irritable bowel syndrome, and colorectal cancer.

# Topaz Dragon Ginger Dressing

*Lemon and ginger. Agave and onion. Tart and spicy. Sweet and piquant. This is a dressing for all the senses, a sauce that hits with impact in* aroma *in addition to* flavor. *And it's sure to have you adding* sound *to your sensory list, as you sigh, moan, or groan with glee. Just one* touch *on the tongue and you'll swoon, just you wait and* see. . . .

**YIELDS ABOUT 1 CUP**

2 tablespoons water

2 teaspoons agave syrup

1 teaspoon lemon zest

1 teaspoon gingerroot, peeled and finely minced

¼ teaspoon sea salt

¼ teaspoon onion powder

¼ teaspoon ground ginger

¼ teaspoon finely ground black pepper

¼ teaspoon sweet Hungarian paprika

¼ cup lemon juice

⅓ cup flax oil

1. Combine the water, agave syrup, lemon zest, gingerroot, sea salt, onion powder, ground ginger, black pepper, and paprika in a glass bottle. Twist the lid on the bottle and shake to mix well.

2. Add lemon juice and oil to the bottle. Secure the lid and shake until thoroughly mixed. Store in the fridge and shake well before each use.

# You Are a Goddess Dressing

*A staple in vegan restaurants and hippie potlucks across the nation, Goddess Dressing is as functional, fabulous, and ubiquitous in health circles as ranch dressing is out in the real world. This version—all raw of course!—is an uncomplicated and stripped-down template that will make you feel as pampered as a goddess yourself!*

**YIELDS ABOUT 1½ CUPS**

⅔ cup tahini
¼ cup apple-cider vinegar
¼ cup nama shoyu
2 teaspoons lemon juice
1 garlic clove
½ teaspoon agave syrup
⅓ cup olive oil

**1.** Process all the ingredients, except olive oil, together in a blender or food processor until smooth.

**2.** With the machine still running, slowly add in the olive oil, blending for another full minute, allowing the oil to emulsify.

**3.** Pour dressing into a bottle and chill in the refrigerator for at least 10 minutes before serving; dressing will thicken as it chills. Shake dressing before each use.

Swap It Out! Feel free to play with it however you see fit, from add-ins like minced onion or pickles, to fresh herbs, to any spices you can dream up. The greatest thing about Goddess Dressing is never making it the same way twice!

# Red Russian Dressing

*Traditional Russian dressing is a amazing modern concoction combining ketchup, mayonnaise, and spices. This delicious blend is based around the amazing Good Gracious Garlic Aioli (see recipe in this chapter), and combines sweet sun-dried tomatoes, creamy almond milk, and tangy pickles that tickle the tongue. Yum!*

**YIELDS ABOUT 2 CUPS**

¼ cup Good Gracious Garlic Aioli (recipe in this chapter)

20 sun-dried tomato halves, about 1 cup, soaked

1 cup Easy-Breezy Plant Milk (see recipe in Ch. 6)

2 tablespoons apple-cider vinegar

1 teaspoon paprika

¼ teaspoon sea salt

1 Crunchy Cultured Dill Pickle (see recipe in Ch. 10) or storebought pickle (Bubbies is a raw brand), minced

1. Combine all ingredients except the pickle in a blender or food processor. Blend until completely smooth.

2. Transfer to a mixing bowl and stir in the pickle. Adjust seasonings and serve. Store in a lidded glass jar in the refrigerator.

***Passionate* Pairings** This delicious dressing is infinitely healthier than the gloppy, processed American classic, and tastes amazing on the Marvelously Modern Mushroom Reuben (see recipe in Chapter 11).

# Sassy Sprout Sauce

*Radish sprouts are spicy—like the root itself—and infuse this dressing with a subtle kick . . . some may even call it* sass. *Add more avocado if you want a thicker veggie dip, or thin it out with water for a fun, feisty salad dressing*

YIELDS ABOUT 1 CUP

½ cup red bell pepper
½ cup tomato
¼ cup radish sprouts
¼ cup alfalfa sprouts
¼ cup avocado
1 tablespoon lemon juice
2–4 tablespoons water

1. Place all the ingredients into a blender and blend together until smooth, adding the water gradually to reach desired consistency.

2. Pour over your favorite salad or store in a lidded glass jar in the fridge.

### So Much More Than Salad

Each of these recipes does its duty with so much more than simply salad! You can use any of these diverse dressings as dips for crudités or crackers, as a spread for sandwiches or wraps, as a marinade for mushrooms or veggies, and even as a sauce to top your pizza pie. Don't limit yourself when it comes to these dynamic dressings: think outside the bowl!

# Cashew Creamsicle

*A serious salad dressing or a sweet little dipping sauce? A practical cracker spread or a pretty party dip? If you're not sure, you could just stand over the blender and lick it off the spoon before it's even had a chance. No one will ever know. And with just three ingredients, it's always easy to whip up another batch. In case the first one, you know, mysteriously disappears. . . .*

YIELDS ABOUT 1 CUP

½ cup cashews, soaked at least 2 hours
¼ cup extra-virgin sesame oil
1 cup orange juice

1. Place all the ingredients into a blender and blend until smooth. Continue to blend until the cashews are fully emulsified.

2. Pour the dressing into a glass bottle with a tight lid. Store in the refrigerator.

# Totally Out-of-This-World Tahini

*Tahini is an important element that lends both credibility and a certain* je ne sais quoi *to anything and everything related to hummus. It's also the secret weapon hiding in every authentic Goddess Dressing, as well as countless other raw vegan creamy sauces. Premade tahini can cost a pretty penny, but it's just made of ground sesame seeds—which are cheap! Make sure that you get the unhulled ones, as they're raw and retain important minerals like calcium.*

### YIELDS ABOUT 2 CUPS

2 cups sesame seeds
¼–½ cup olive oil, to preference
Optional: ½ teaspoon paprika

1. Place sesame seeds and olive oil in a high-speed blender and process until smooth and creamy.

2. Transfer to a lidded glass jar to store in the fridge. Or, if serving as a dip, garnish with paprika.

# Addictive Almond Dipping Sauce

*This dipping sauce is an amazing creation, surprisingly diverse as a veggie dunker, a spring roll sauce, a sandwich spread, or a noodle dressing. The assertive Asian flavors balance perfectly here, making certain that this will be one addictive dip! It's a good thing the recipe results in a rather large batch, because once you've tasted it, you'll be thinking up new and creative ways to put it into action. Happy imagining!*

### YIELDS ABOUT 2 CUPS

1 cup almond butter
⅔ cup water
½ cup cilantro, loosely packed
1 jalapeño, seeded
2 tablespoons nama shoyu
1 tablespoon agave syrup
1 tablespoon sesame oil
1 tablespoon apple-cider vinegar
¼ teaspoon sea salt
4–6 garlic cloves, to taste

1. Place all ingredients in a blender or food processor and blend until completely smooth.

2. If not serving immediately, transfer to a lidded glass jar and store in the refrigerator, up to a week.

Swap It Out! Almonds make for a creamy, flavorful base, but the truth is that any nut or seed will do. Try sunflower seeds, which are easy on the wallet, or hazelnuts, which are rich and delicious. Or, try a blend of nuts and seeds to encourage a wide variety of nutrients and an incredible depth of flavor.

# Magical Multidimensional Mole Sauce

*Mole is a Mexican masterpiece, an intricate web of subtle flavor threads that traditionally can take days to develop. This rawesome riff is a bit simpler, though like the original the unique combination of spices is an unexpected delight. Conventional mole includes such ingredients as chocolate, peppers, nuts, and plantains—all of which have a perfect raw counterpart that you'll find here. So don't be afraid to indulge a little!*

**YIELDS ABOUT 2 CUPS**

1 cup chopped tomato
¾ cup banana, sliced
2 tablespoons onion, diced
2 tablespoons raw cacao or carob
1 tablespoon jalapeño pepper,
    seeded and minced
1 tablespoon olive oil
1 tablespoon agave syrup
½ teaspoon sea salt
½ teaspoon cinnamon
¼ teaspoon cloves
½ teaspoon oregano
½ cup avocado

1. In a blender, combine all ingredients except the avocado. Process until smooth.

2. Add the avocado last and blend until the sauce becomes creamy.

# Triple Seedy Sauce

*With the powerful combination formed by this trio of mighty seeds, nothing will stand in the way of a delicious meal. Three times the seeds means triple the nutrients—like zinc from the pumpkin, calcium from the sesame, and omega-3 fatty acids from the hemp. With these forces combined, you can rule the world . . . or at least your kitchen.*

**YIELDS ABOUT 2 CUPS**

½ cup water, more to thin if needed
½ cup tahini
¼ cup pumpkin seeds
¼ cup sesame seeds
¼ cup hempseed
2 tablespoons apple-cider vinegar
1 tablespoon nama shoyu
1 tablespoon lemon juice
1 clove garlic
¼–½ teaspoon sea salt, to taste

1. Place all ingredients in a blender or food processor and blend until completely smooth. Add additional water to reach desired consistency.

2. If not serving immediately, transfer to a lidded glass jar and store in the refrigerator for up to a week.

# Cilantro Pumpkin Seed Pesto Perfection

*This looks like such a simple recipe. Unassuming, perhaps even mundane. But somehow this combination of average ingredients, in just the right proportion, creates a cohesion that's simply unparalleled. Why is this pesto so good? The world may never know.*

**YIELDS ABOUT 2 CUPS**

½ cup pumpkin seeds

⅓ cup olive oil

1 large bunch cilantro (leaves and stems), 4–5 cups loosely packed

2 cloves garlic

Juice of 2 limes, about 4 tablespoons

1 scant teaspoon finely ground black pepper

½ teaspoon sea salt

1. Place all ingredients in a food processor and pulse to create a chunky sauce. Do not overprocess.

2. If not serving immediately, transfer to a lidded glass jar and store in the refrigerator for up to a week.

■ **PRO'S TIP** Pesto is easy to make and freezes exceptionally well. When fresh herbs like cilantro, basil, and parsley are in season, you can take advantage and make big batches of pesto. Portion the sauce into an ice cube tray and place it in the freezer. Once it's frozen, transfer your pesto cubes to an airtight container, which will last for months in the freezer. And voila! Thaw them one or two at a time for "fresh" pesto whenever the mood strikes.

# Sweet Creamy Cashew Basil Pesto

*Traditionally, pesto is made from basil blended into a chunky paste with pine nuts and Parmesan. But recent revisionist cooking has seen a wide selection of herbs combined with any and every nut imaginable. And why not? This particular recipe lies somewhere between classic and modern. The inclusion of basil is left intact, but this recipe incorporates cashews for an ultimately creamy, absolutely decadent twist. Use it like a regular pesto on kelp noodles or spiraled squash pasta, or let it act as a spread for sandwiches, crackers, or crudités.*

**YIELDS ABOUT 1½ CUPS**

1 cup cashews, soaked
¼ cup sweet onion
¼ cup packed basil leaves
Juice from ½ lemon (a little over 1 tablespoon)
½ teaspoon sea salt
½ teaspoon black pepper

1. Place all ingredients in a blender or food processor and process until completely smooth.

2. If not serving immediately, transfer to a lidded glass jar and store in the refrigerator for up to a week.

# Kreative Ketchup

*Ketchup is such an old standby, a penultimate classic condiment that accompanies so many controversial comfort foods like french fries, tater tots, burgers, and more. Until now. This rawesome ketchup goes renegade, turning its back on grease and guilt and gluttony. Now this sauce allows you to get creative and reinterpret all the old classics. The sky's the limit!*

**YIELDS ABOUT 1 CUP**

½ cup chopped fresh tomato
¼ cup sun-dried tomatoes, soaked at least 2 hours, then drained
¼ cup chopped red bell pepper
1 clove garlic, chopped
1 tablespoon chopped dates
1 tablespoon apple-cider vinegar
½ teaspoon sea salt

1. Place all of the ingredients in a blender or food processor and blend until smooth.

2. Store in a lidded glass jar in the refrigerator for up to a week.

# Must-Have Mustard

*Mustard is another important condiment for mimicking basic cooked-food favorites, like burgers, brats, or pretzel bread. The spicy sauce comes in many varieties, like yellow, brown, or Dijon. This recipe is similar to a basic brown mustard, sweet and spicy and universally delicious.*

### YIELDS ABOUT 1 CUP

½ cup mustard seeds

½ cup cashews, soaked at least 2 hours

¼ cup lemon juice

3 tablespoons agave syrup

1 tablespoon nama shoyu

1 tablespoon apple-cider vinegar

¼ teaspoon turmeric powder

1. Soak the mustard seeds for 8–12 hours. Drain and rinse. Use as is or sprout for 3 days, then use sprouts.

2. In a blender, blend all ingredients until smooth.

3. Store in a lidded glass jar in the refrigerator. Keeps for 2–4 weeks.

*Passionate* **Pairings** Try this mustard on the Slammin Sliders (Chapter 11) or with the New York Rye bread (see recipe Chapter 13). Or, come up with your own creative culinary applications!

# Sweet and Savory Rawbecue Sauce

*Okay, so you may not be heading out to the deck to fire up the grill, but that doesn't mean you can't enjoy "barbecue" on a hot summer day! Studies have shown that the char created while barbecuing meat is actually carcinogenic, so let's keep our veggie kebabs nice and cool now, shall we? This sauce is delightfully tangy and works well as a dressing, dip, or marinade. Have fun with it, but leave the fire pit alone!*

**YIELDS ABOUT 2 CUPS**

1 cup sun-dried tomatoes, soaked, with ½ cup soaking water reserved

1 cup fresh tomato, chopped

1 dried pepper, soaked

2 tablespoons apple-cider vinegar

2 tablespoons yacon syrup

2 teaspoons chili powder

1 teaspoon nama shoyu

½ teaspoon salt

1 clove garlic

1. Blend all the ingredients with the tomato soak water in a blender until smooth.

2. Store in a lidded glass jar in the refrigerator for up to 2 weeks.

# Fearsome Fiery Green Hot Sauce

*Caution: Not for amateurs! This super-spicy sauce is just the thing to kick up your raw tacos, to take your stir-dry to the next level, or to add a little va-va-voom to your vegetable sandwich. But no messing around here! This baby is packing heat— and you'll be howling for some almond milk relief if you're not careful. So play nice!*

**YIELDS ABOUT 2 CUPS**

1 pound jalapeño peppers
2–6 fresh Serrano chilies, depending on heat preference
6 cloves garlic
1 tablespoon sea salt
1 tablespoon nama shoyu
1 tablespoon agave syrup
½ cup apple-cider vinegar

1. Clean and seed the jalapeños and chilies. Remove the stems but leave the little crown. Chop them all up.

2. Add all of the ingredients to a food processor or blender. Blend until smooth.

3. Over a large bowl, pour the mixture through a nut milk bag or metal mesh to strain it. If you use your hands to squeeze or press the pulp, wear gloves or wash well with soap immediately after.

4. Store your hot sauce in a lidded glass jar in fridge. Will keep for months.

# Fearsome Fiery Red Hot Sauce

*Sriracha, or "rooster sauce," is a type of hot sauce that hails from Thailand. It's usually cooked to develop the flavors, but here the process of fermentation accomplishes that work. And work it does! This is a full-bodied, fruity, and dynamic spicy condiment that's perfect for spring rolls, Asian noodles, sushi, or burgers. You can't go wrong with a spot of sriracha. But be careful—this puppy packs some real heat!*

**YIELDS ABOUT 2 CUPS**

1 pound red jalapeños
3–6 fresh Serrano chilies
½ cup coconut vinegar, plus a splash (divided)
1 tablespoon sea salt
1 tablespoon nama shoyu
1 tablespoon agave syrup
4 cloves garlic

1. Clean, seed, and chop the jalapeños and Serranos. Remove the stems but leave the crown, which will add to the depth of flavor.

2. Add both types of chilies, the ½ cup vinegar, salt, nama shoyu, agave syrup, and garlic to a food processor or blender. Pulse to purée but keep it chunky.

3. Transfer the mixture to a Mason jar and top it off with another splash of vinegar. Cover the jar with a loose lid or a rag secured with a rubber band.

4. Leave the jar on the counter at room temperature for 3 days, out of direct sunlight.

5. Transfer everything to a blender and process until completely smooth. Add water if needed.

6. Store sriracha in a lidded glass jar in fridge. Will keep for months.

# Marvelous Coconut Cashew Mayonnaise

*Mayonnaise is a thick and creamy emulsion that's traditionally made from oil and egg. But this rawesome recipe results in a mayonnaise that even the fanciest French chef would approve of: silky smooth but stand-up thick, with just the right amount of acid, and no cholesterol to clog you up! With a distinctive tang and subtle notes of lemon juice, mayo makes a rich, decadent spread for countless classics like burgers and sandwiches. So spread it on thick and enjoy that gooey white goodness, guilt free!*

**YIELDS ABOUT 2 CUPS**

½–1 cup water

½ cup cashews, soaked at least 2 hours

Meat from 1 young coconut, about ½ cup

2 teaspoons lemon juice

¼ teaspoon sea salt

1. In a food processor or blender, blend all ingredients with ½ cup of the water, until completely smooth and slightly whipped, adding more water if needed. This may take up to 10 minutes. Stop to scrape down sides as needed.

2. Store in a lidded glass jar in the fridge. Keeps for up to 2 weeks.

### Young Coconut Water

The liquid inside of young coconuts is an incredible elixir. Naturally sweet but low in fat and sugar, it's been hailed as "nature's sports drink" for its hydrating prowess and electrolyte balance. Make sure that when you come across recipes like this one—which calls for coconut meat but not water—that you put that precious liquid to good use. Use it in another recipe, as a base for a soup or smoothie, or just drink it straight up. It's delicious!

# Soured Coconut Cream

*Sour cream is a staple in American and European cuisine. A similar version, called crema, is also featured prominently in Latin American cooking. And Tex-Mex, which combines the flavors of these regions, leans heavily on the deliciously creamy condiment, but you don't need to compromise your values just for some extra taste. Just a dollop of this tangy sauce will take your raw tacos over the top. ¡Que auténtico!*

**YIELDS ABOUT 1 CUP**

1 cup **Creamy Coconut Yogurt (see recipe in Ch. 6)** or ¾ cup fresh young coconut meat plus ½ cup water
2 teaspoons lemon juice
½ teaspoon garlic powder
½ teaspoon onion powder
Water to thin as needed

1. In a food processor or blender, blend all ingredients until completely smooth and slightly whipped.

2. Store in a lidded glass jar in the fridge. Keeps for up to 2 weeks.

# Good Gracious Garlic Aioli

*Light and fluffy, pale and perfect, this aioli is essentially whipped olive oil . . . and it is spectacular. This mayonnaise alternative uses familiar ingredients found in almost any raw kitchen, and comes together super quickly. You could almost say that there's no excuse* not *to make it!*

**YIELDS ABOUT 2 CUPS**

½ cup **Easy-Breezy Plant Milk (see recipe in Ch. 6;** almond milk works best here)
2 cloves garlic
1 tablespoon lemon juice
¼ teaspoon salt
1½ cups olive oil

1. Combine all ingredients except oil in a food processor or blender. Process until completely smooth.

2. With the machine still running, slowly drizzle in the oil. Allow it to run on highest speed for as long as necessary until the oil seizes up and the entire mixture becomes firm and creamy.

3. Store in a lidded glass jar in the refrigerator for up to 2 weeks. Separation may occur; stir or reblend if needed.

# Herbivore's Hollandaise Sauce

*Is there anything richer, anything more sinful, anything more symbolic of unabashed epicurean glee than traditional French hollandaise sauce? Incorporating a mountain of butter and egg yolk into every bit, hollandaise sells itself on its fantastic flavor alone. And now, for the health-minded and plant-based among us, there's an equally indulgent alternative. Enjoy this lemony cream sauce on the California Benedict (see recipe in Chapter 6), over dinner vegetables, or over . . . pretty much everything!*

**YIELDS ABOUT 1 CUP**

¾ cup macadamia nut butter

½ cup Goodness Gracious Garlic Aioli (see recipe in this chapter)

2 tablespoons lemon juice

1 teaspoon nama shoyu

¼ teaspoon paprika

¼ teaspoon ground mustard

Pinch of salt

Water to thin, if needed (up to ¼ cup)

1. Place all ingredients into a blender and purée on high for up to 5 minutes, until completely creamy and lightly whipped.

2. Serve warm from the blender or store in a lidded glass jar in the refrigerator for up to 2 weeks.

# Unreal Maple Syrup

*Maple syrup is a natural, healthier sweetener that's a great stand-in for sugar or corn syrup. For this reason, it has been embraced by the health community and is featured in many raw recipes. However, maple syrup is boiled as part of the distillation process, which means that, although it's better than high-fructose corn syrup by a mile, it's not actually a raw food. This syrupy sauce, made mostly from dates, is a really great, really rawesome alternative.*

**YIELDS ABOUT 1½ CUPS**

**1 cup dates, halved and pitted**
**1 cup filtered water for soaking**
**2 tablespoons yacon syrup**
**1 tablespoon agave syrup**

1. Place the dates in a large bowl. Cover with the water. Allow to soak for at least 4 hours, and as many as 8. You want them to get good and waterlogged so that the skins loosen up.

2. Drain the dates, reserving the soak water. Peel the skins off each date half and discard.

3. Place the date meat in a blender along with the soak water, yacon syrup, and agave syrup. Process until completely smooth. This will take a while. Mixture will thicken a bit when chilled.

4. Store in a glass jar in the fridge. This syrup will keep for up to 2 weeks.

---

### Super Sweetener: Dates!

Most raw sweeteners are pressed, evaporated, or otherwise extracted. But dates are unique, because they offer sweetness via the whole food, which means they're consumed just exactly as nature intended. There's no questioning that dates are healthy treats, with their high levels of iron, calcium, copper, potassium, and manganese. Dates are also fiber-full, and offer a source of instant energy.

---

# Unbelievable Raspberry Coulis

*It truly is unbelievable that something so simple, containing only two ingredients, could taste so spectacularly divine. Or maybe it's not so unbelievable, considering the magic and the mystery that reveals itself when you're eating real, raw, whole plant foods. Regardless, the bottom line remains: this is a seriously rawkin' sauce.*

YIELDS ABOUT ½ CUP

½ cup raspberries
1 tablespoon agave syrup

1. Combine ingredients in a food processor or blender and process until smooth. If you want to, you may strain it through a nut milk bag or metal mesh to remove the seeds.

2. Store in a lidded glass jar in the fridge for 3 days.

*Passionate* Pairings Enjoy Unbelievable Raspberry Coulis with your favorite dessert, on vanilla ice cream or berry pie, or use it to sweeten up your morning fare, over pancakes or a parfait.

*Chapter 10*

# Dips, Spreads, and Sides

To some people, a dip is just something they serve at parties, an infrequent, unimportant player—the minor leagues of culinary play. But raw vegans know better.

You know that the right dip can become a meal unto itself. The right spread can take a flatbread and transform it into a fancy affair. Guacamole puts a crown on anything it graces, and takes it to the next level of amazing. Raw hummus is a key component of countless incredible 5-minute-meals, and there's at least three fantastic spreads in your fridge at any given time. Exciting side dishes, like exotic slaws or fermented veggies, can take a simple dinner and quickly elevate it to the status of "spectacular." And entertaining is always easy when you keep a few fun side dishes tucked away for a special occasion. So what are you waiting for? Dig in!

# Party-Ready Pico de Gallo

*Pico de Gallo, sometimes called salsa fresca, is a Mexican dip as ubiquitous as America's beloved ketchup. It's naturally raw, too, so no modifications need be made. Just ordinary, fresh food combined into a slightly spicy, refreshing topper for tacos, salads, or your favorite crackers. Pico is also the perfect party food, so get all your friends together—whether they're raw vegan or not!—and enjoy!*

## PLEASE ENTER RECIPE YIELD

4 cups slicing tomatoes, diced
½ cup white onion, diced
1–2 fresh jalapeño peppers, seeded
  and minced
Juice of 1 small lime
1 clove garlic, crushed
1 teaspoon sea salt

1. Combine all ingredients in a large bowl, stirring well.

2. Marinate for 1 hour in the fridge prior to serving.

# Chunky Sweet Corn Salsa

*This is a salsa that's all about contrast. With pops of sweet from tomatoes and corn, and spikes of heat from garlic and jalapeño, it all comes together for a dynamic flavor. The contrasting texture between the soft tomatoes, crunchy onions, and chewy corn kernels keeps things interesting for your tongue—and there's nothing wrong with interesting!*

## YIELDS ABOUT 3 CUPS

3 cups cherry tomatoes, halved
½ cup fresh sweet corn kernels
¼ cup chopped fresh cilantro
1 tablespoon jalapeño pepper, minced
1 tablespoon fresh ginger, minced
1 tablespoon lime juice
1 tablespoon olive oil
½ teaspoon salt
1 clove garlic, minced

1. Combine all ingredients in a large bowl, stirring well.

2. This salsa tastes best if allowed to marinate for up to 1 hour prior to serving.

*Passionate* **Pairings** Serve this dip with a creamy guacamole for a major taste sensation!

# Mucho Mango Tropical Salsa

*Have you ever put fruit in your salsa? It really is a treat, that delicious dichotomy that dances on the tongue. Spicy? Sweet? From pineapples to peaches to apricots to pears, consider this a heartfelt urging to give this unlikely combo a spin. And why not start here, with mild mango and chunky tomatoes, all lazing about together in a zesty citrus swimming pool? Does that sound like a good time? Good, because you're officially invited to join the fun!*

**YIELDS ABOUT 3 CUPS**

1 mango, chopped
2 tangerines, chopped
½ red bell pepper, chopped
½ red onion, minced
3 cloves garlic, minced
½ jalapeño pepper, minced
3 tablespoons chopped cilantro
2 tablespoons lime juice
½ teaspoon sea salt
¼ teaspoon black pepper

1. Gently toss together all the ingredients in a large mixing bowl.

2. Allow to rest at room temperature for 15 minutes prior to serving, so that flavors can mingle. Or, cover and refrigerate until ready to serve.

---

### Low-Calorie Raw Options

Most raw foodists don't pay much mind to calorie counts, but if you happen to be looking for an easy way to add a whole lot of flavor without much caloric density, salsa is your one-stop shop. It's easy to customize to fit your mood, it's full of fresh healthy vegetables, it adds tons of flavor to any dish, and of course, it's incredibly calorie-light.

# Chia-mole

*Guacamole makes everything taste better, and that's a fact. But what could possibly make guacamole taste better? How about the amazing, miniature beads of the super-nutritious chia seed? These tiny plump pearls add protein, calcium, and essential fatty acids to everyone's favorite dip. But above their nutritional accolades, they impart a subtly nutty flavor and an incredible, chewy texture. If you've ever wanted to eat guacamole as a complete meal (and really, who hasn't?), then this is just the way to add that extra* oomph!

**YIELDS ABOUT 3 CUPS**

¼ cup chia seeds

¾ cup water

3 tablespoons lime juice, divided

1 medium tomato, diced

¼ cup diced red onion

2 cloves garlic

Salt and pepper to taste

2 avocados, pitted and peeled and cubed

1. In a small mixing bowl, stir together the chia seeds, water, and 2 tablespoons of the lime juice. Make sure to break up any clumps. Allow to sit for 10–20 minutes, stirring every few minutes, until the chia seeds have absorbed all the liquid.

2. In a larger mixing bowl, combine the chia mixture with the rest of the ingredients, except for the avocados. Mix well. Gently fold in the avocado, but do not overmix or the avocado will break down and lose its shape.

# Cumin-Spiced Avocado Spread

*This delicious dish acts as either a dip or a spread. Serve it as part of a party platter, or smear it over flatbreads for a quick and satisfying bite. The cumin is subtle and hard to pin down, leaving your diners pleasantly surprised and wondering aloud "This tastes amazing—what is it?" Keep it as your little chef's secret, or share the cumin love. Just keep the spread coming!*

## YIELDS ABOUT 2 CUPS

2 medium ripe avocados, peeled and seeded

2 tablespoons fresh lemon juice

2 tablespoons olive oil

1 tablespoon fresh chives

1 teaspoon ground cumin

1 teaspoon sea salt

¼ teaspoon garlic powder

Optional: dash of raw hot sauce

1. In a medium-size bowl, mash the avocado until smooth. Add the remaining ingredients, mixing to combine completely.

2. Letting this dip sit for 15 minutes helps to blend the flavors. Refrigerate, covered, until ready to serve.

---

### Oxidizing Avocados

Avocados are super sensitive to enzymatic browning, which leads to discoloration. In other words, your dip will turn dull if you leave it for too long. So if you plan to prep in advance, there are a few of tricks you can use to keep your dip looking fresh. First, save your avocado pits. Float them in the finished dip until you're ready to use it. Second, a liberal dousing of lemon or lime juice over the surface will create a protective barrier between the dip and the air. And finally, keep your dip tightly covered and refrigerated, then give it a good stir just before you serve—the browning only occurs on the very surface!

---

# Not-Roasted Red Pepper Lentil Dip

*Pâtés, especially of the nut and seed variety, are a great way to add some extra protein to your diet. However, nuts and seeds are high in fat and often very filling. If you're looking for something that's a little less heavy but equally high in important protein, this is the dip for you! Refreshing and light, it's a simple spin on conventional roasted red pepper hummus. Use redried sprouted lentils to achieve maximum rich and creamy results.*

### YIELDS ABOUT 2½ CUPS

2 cups sprouted brown lentils
1 medium red bell pepper
⅓ cup tahini
3 tablespoons lemon juice
2 cloves garlic
½ teaspoon sea salt
¼ teaspoon cayenne pepper
Liquid to thin, if needed (water, oil, Easy-Breezy Plant Milk, or lemon juice, as preferred)

1. Place all ingredients in a food processor or blender and process until completely smooth, stopping to scrape down the sides as needed.

2. Serve in a large bowl or store in a lidded glass jar in the refrigerator for up to a week.

### Redried Lentils?

Redrying is a simple technique that allows you to prepare large batches of sprouted legumes. Simply sprout the legume—lentils in the recipe above—as normal, then spread the sprouts on a dehydrator tray lined with a nonstick sheet. Dehydrate at 110°F for 10–15 hours (drying time will depend on the size of the legume; they are done when they are completely dry), then store in a lidded container in the pantry. Redried legumes will keep for months, ready to go whenever you need them.

# Sprouted Chickpea Hummus

*Hummus is a Mediterranean staple food that has become a major player in American vegan cuisine. Authentic hummus is made with chickpeas, tahini, and lemon juice, with variable herbs and spices. This version brings authenticity to the raw masses, using softened sprouted chickpeas in the place of the classic cooked ones. All the other ingredients are the same, making this a truly* rawthentic *dish.*

**YIELDS ABOUT 3 CUPS**

1 cup garbanzo beans

5 cups water

¼ cup tahini

¼ cup lemon juice

1 clove garlic, minced

½ teaspoon cumin

½ teaspoon salt

¼ cup olive oil, as needed for consistency

Optional: 1 tablespoon jalapeño pepper, minced

1. Soak the chickpeas in water for 12 hours. Drain and rinse.

2. Sprout the chickpeas for at least 12 hours. Rinse them a couple times during the sprouting process. They are ready when their tails are at least as long as the bean.

3. In a food processor or blender, process all the ingredients except the olive oil. Gradually add the olive oil until the mixture becomes creamy.

# Secret Success Zucchini Hummus

*Let's be honest, there are a lot of zucchini hummus recipes already out there in the world. But here's the thing: fresh zucchini holds a lot of water, and most zucchini hummus recipes end up tasting watered down. Either they lack flavor and depth, or else extra oils or heavy nuts are added to make up the difference. But here, you can achieve rich and creamy hummus without any added fat. Just a simple extra step, a quick secret trick, and you've got a delicious, low-fat dip. You're welcome!*

**YIELDS ABOUT 3 CUPS**

2 large zucchinis shredded (should equal between 4–6 cups, not packed)

½ cup tahini

Juice from 1 lemon, about 2 tablespoons

2–4 cloves garlic, to taste

½ teaspoon cumin

½ teaspoon paprika

½ teaspoon sea salt

1. Pour shredded zucchini into a nut milk bag or wrap it in cheesecloth. Use your hands to squeeze, extracting as much juice as possible. You may also place the wrapped zucchini in a colander with something heavy on top, and leave it for a few hours.

2. Place the zucchini and all the other ingredients into a food processor or blender. Process until completely smooth.

3. Serve immediately or store in a lidded glass container in the fridge for up to a week.

# Bountiful Baba Ganoush

*Baba ganoush is a lovely Lebanese classic that combines cooked eggplant with olive oil and spices to create a uniquely flavored and viscous dish. Baba ganoush is a great addition to a mezza party platter, alongside hummus, tabbouleh, and falafel. Eggplant can be difficult to deal with in the raw, but here the bitterness and texture are managed with a long soak in a sea salt bath. Sounds pretty nice, right? Don't you just wish you were an eggplant, too?*

**YIELDS ABOUT 1½ CUPS**

2 cups eggplant, sliced thin

2 cups cold water

2 teaspoons salt

3 tablespoons lemon juice

2 tablespoons tahini

1 clove garlic, minced

1 teaspoon cumin

½ teaspoon black pepper

Sea salt to taste

1 teaspoon paprika, for garnish

1 teaspoon olive oil, for garnish

2 tablespoons fresh chopped parsley, for garnish

1. Place the eggplant strips in a bowl or casserole dish. Mix together the water and the 2 teaspoons salt and cover the eggplant strips with the salt-water solution. Soften the eggplant by letting it soak 6–12 hours in the refrigerator. This works well overnight.

2. Drain the eggplant.

3. Place the eggplant, lemon juice, tahini, garlic, cumin, black pepper, and sea salt in a food processor or blender and purée until smooth.

4. Pour the mixture into a serving bowl. Sprinkle it with paprika and drizzle a little olive oil on top. Garnish with fresh parsley.

# Totally Traditional Tzatziki

*Tzatziki is a cool and refreshing cucumber yogurt dip that hails from the heart of ancient Greece. It's excellent served as part of a mezza platter, alongside hummus and the like, but it's equally fantastic when eaten on its own. Try it as a dip for flatbread or crackers. Try it as a spread in wraps. You can even eat it as a sort of soup! It's super versatile, healthy, hydrating, and it's easy to whip up, too. Why not declare this as your go-to summer snack?*

YIELDS ABOUT 3 CUPS

1½ cups Soured Coconut Cream (see recipe in Ch. 9), Totally Tangy Nut or Seed Yogurt, or Creamy Coconut Yogurt (see recipes in Ch. 6)

1 tablespoon olive oil

1 tablespoon lemon juice

4 cloves garlic, minced

2 cucumbers, grated

1 tablespoon chopped fresh mint or fresh dill

1. Whisk the yogurt with the olive oil and lemon juice until well-combined.

2. Add all the remaining ingredients, stirring well to completely mix.

3. Chill for at least 1 hour before serving. Garnish with additional mint or dill.

# Briny Black and Green Olive Tapenade

*Tapenade is a classic Provençal spread that dates back over a thousand years, which means it's gotta be good! It's most commonly used to top hors d'oeuvres or to stuff into entrées, but it also amazing as a simple dip for crackers and crudités. Delicious!*

YIELDS ABOUT 1 CUP

¾ cup raw black olives, pitted

½ cup raw green olives, pitted

2 cloves garlic

2 tablespoons lemon juice

2 tablespoons olive oil

¼ teaspoon oregano

¼ teaspoon black pepper

1. Place all ingredients in a food processor or blender and process until finely ground and well-incorporated. You do not want it to be completely smooth.

2. Serve at room temperature.

***Passionate* Pairings** As a party dip or a dinner starter, pair it with something neutral so that it won't have competition in the flavor spotlight.

# Easy Entertainer's Onion Dip

*Onion dip is the quintessential centerpiece of any American party platter. And with good reason! It's flavorful and satisfying, and pairs perfectly with almost every vegetable. Best of all, it's a breeze to whip up. With just a few ingredients, a bowl, and a spoon, you can have this recipe on the table and ready to serve in no time flat. Impromptu parties, commence!*

**YIELDS ABOUT 1½ CUPS**

1 cup Marvelous Coconut Cashew Mayonnaise or Soured Coconut Cream (see recipes in Ch. 9) or Creamy Coconut Yogurt (see recipe in Ch. 6)

4 green onions, diced (both green and white portions), some reserved for garnish

1 tablespoon lime juice

1 teaspoon onion powder

½ teaspoon agave syrup

Sea salt and cracked black pepper, to taste

1. Combine all ingredients in a mixing bowl and stir to combine.

2. Garnish with extra green onions and serve in a large bowl, or store in a lidded glass jar in the refrigerator for up to a week.

# Zesty Italian Walnut Pâté

*Pâtés play an important part of many people's raw food diets. They offer versatility, portability, satiety, and ease. They're fun to play with, too: You can use them as veggie dips, plop them on tomato or zucchini rounds, spread them over crackers, layer them in wraps, and so much more. This particular pâté is especially adaptable, as the flavors lend themselves very well to many types of meals. Keep a batch of this blend in your fridge, and you're food choices will always be inspired!*

## YIELDS ABOUT 2 CUPS

2 cups walnuts
¼ cup sun-dried tomatoes
2 tablespoons tahini
½ cup red bell pepper, chopped
¼ cup raw olives, pits removed
2 cloves garlic
4 tablespoons cilantro
1 tablespoon In-Your-Face Italian Seasoning Spice Blend (see recipe in Ch. 12) or storebought Italian seasoning
1 teaspoon olive oil
¼ teaspoon sea salt

1. Soak the walnuts for 6–10 hours. Soak the sun-dried tomatoes for at least 4 hours, reserving the soak water.

2. In a food processor or blender, process the walnuts and tahini until smooth.

3. Add all remaining ingredients and blend until smooth again. Pour in ¼ cup of the soak water from the sun-dried tomatoes for a more intense tomato flavor.

4. Serve in a large bowl or store in a lidded glass container in the refrigerator for up to a week.

# Magical Mushroom Pâté

*No, not that kind of magical mushroom, silly. Though some would say that all mushrooms possess "magical" powers—like the potential to assist in healing our bodies in ways we have yet to understand. Throughout the ages mushrooms have been used in tinctures and tonics, broths and brews, in order to fight disease and prevent harm. So enjoy this dip and re-energize your essential life force with these mystical, marvelous little mushrooms.*

**YIELDS ABOUT 3 CUPS**

**1 cup almonds**
**¼ cup black sesame seeds**
**1 cup portobello mushrooms**
**½ cup crimini mushrooms**
**2 tablespoons nama shoyu**
**1 tablespoon grated ginger**
**1 teaspoon sage**
**1 teaspoon thyme**
**¼ teaspoon sea salt**
**Scant ¼ teaspoon cayenne pepper**

1. Soak the almonds in water for at least 12 hours, rinsing every 6 hours or so. Soak the black sesame seeds in water for 1 hour. Drain and rinse both.

2. Process the almonds and sesame seeds in a food processor or blender until well-broken-down. Add the remaining ingredients and purée until smooth.

3. Serve in a large bowl or store in a lidded glass container in the refrigerator for up to a week.

# Homemade Basic Nut/Seed Butter

*Buying preground nut and seed butters from the grocery store is costly on many levels. It takes a toll on your wallet—those little jars are expensive, especially if you're getting organic. It impacts the environment, with all that extra shipping and packaging. And finally, you can never be certain of what you're getting, from the quality of the ingredients to the potential contamination from shared equipment. With all this in mind, grinding your own rawesome butters really makes sense. And it's easier—and more fun—than you may think. So get ready to play!*

**YIELDS ABOUT 1–3 CUPS**

**2–4 cups nuts, seeds, or any combination of these**

1. Place all nuts/seeds in the bowl of a food processor fitted with an S-blade. If you have a high-speed blender, you may use that instead.

2. Run the machine for up to 10 minutes, stopping every so often to scrape down the sides as needed. This may take longer than expected, and the mixture will go through a number of stages—meal, powder, flour, sticky, a big ball clumped together, etc. At some point the mixture will relax and release its oils. That indicates when it's done. You may need to take long breaks to keep the nut butter from overheating.

3. Store your butter in a lidded glass jar in the refrigerator. It will keep for months.

■ **PRO'S TIP** We all know the importance of soaking/sprouting our nuts and seeds, as discussed in Chapter 1. But there are certain recipes, like this butter for example, where freshly soaked and waterlogged ingredients just won't work. So as a preemptive practice, try soaking/sprouting *all* your nuts/seeds as soon as you get them home from the grocery store. You can then dehydrate them, and store them dried as usual. That way you'll always have nuts and seeds ready to spring into recipe action.

# Very Vanilla Almond Butter

*Give this Very Vanilla Almond Butter a try atop any of your favorite savories, such as celery sticks or salty crackers, or use it to top off your favorite desserts. You'll be surprised by how well this simple topping goes with pretty much anything! It's like the little black dress of toppings!*

YIELDS ABOUT 2 CUPS

2 cups almonds, soaked

2 tablespoons olive, sesame, or flax oil

1 teaspoon vanilla extract

½ teaspoon sea salt

1. Blend the almonds in a food processor, stopping to scrape down the sides as needed, and continuing until the almonds stick to the walls.

2. Gradually add in the olive oil, vanilla, and salt, and continue to process until creamy. Serve immediately or keep in the fridge for up to a month.

***Passionate* Pairings** This recipe is especially lovely when paired with carob or apricots. And a small spoonful, stuffed into a pitted date, makes for a decadent and nutrient-dense snack!

# "Silk Chocolate" Hazelnut Spread

*Nutella is a popular, nonraw, nonvegan novelty spread made from hazelnuts and milk chocolate. It's delicious stuff, but it's just not rawesome enough for you! So what's a Nutella lover to do? Raw to the rescue! This smooth spread is made from whole hazelnuts, is infused with raw cacao, and is rich with the inclusion of healthful fats from the coconut. Once again, raw does it right!*

**YIELDS ABOUT 2 CUPS**

2 cups hazelnuts
2 tablespoons liquid coconut oil or
  cacao butter
½ cup raw cacao powder
2 tablespoons agave nectar
1 teaspoon vanilla extract
½ teaspoon salt

1. Process the hazelnuts in a food processor or blender until they become a powder. Gradually add the coconut oil or cacao butter and continue processing until smooth. (These oils are usually in solid form, so they add stability to the spread.)

2. Add the remaining ingredients and process until smooth.

3. Serve at room temperature. Store in a lidded glass container in the refrigerator for up to a month.

# Buttery Garam Masala Spread

*Garam masala is a basic spice blend popular in Indian and Southern Asian cuisine. This savory nut pâté features the special seasoning and offers a hearty, filling accompaniment for crackers or crudités. So take your taste buds on a tour of the exotic today, and give this unique nut butter a try!*

**YIELDS ABOUT 1 CUP**

1 cup macadamia nuts
½ cup young coconut meat
Optional: 4 tablespoons ground
  sesame seeds
1 teaspoon garam masala spice
½ teaspoon sea salt
½ teaspoon paprika or ¼ cup cilantro, diced

1. Place the macadamia nuts, young coconut meat, and sesame seeds (if using) in a food processor or blender. Process until the nut butter is well-mixed and chunky.

2. Add the garam masala spice, sea salt, and either paprika or diced cilantro. Blend again and serve.

# Gooey Garlicky Coconut Butter

*Is a vampire—literally the walking dead—the absolute antithesis of a raw foodist? Raw foodies are the walking living, vibrating bright and full of fresh plant life. And if that doesn't frighten a vampire away, well then, this butter surely will. Its garlic-heavy goodness is a sure fit for the greatest of garlic aficionados, and this delicate, flavorful spread stands in anywhere that traditional garlic butter would. Vampires beware!*

**YIELDS ABOUT 2 CUPS**

½ cup coconut oil
Warm water
2 cups young coconut meat
1–2 teaspoons minced garlic
¼ teaspoon salt

1. Place the jar of coconut oil in warm water until it becomes liquid.

2. Add all the ingredients to a food processor or blender and process until whipped and completely smooth.

3. Place the mixture in a lidded glass container and put it in the refrigerator for 1 hour until it becomes solid. Serve or store in the fridge for up to a week.

# Simple Starter for Seed Cheese

*This recipe is very pared down and is meant to be a jumping-off point for your own cheese mongering experiments. Raw cultured cheese-making is an artisan craft that can become quite complex. Begin with the basic recipe once or twice, and then branch out by adding herbs, spices, dried fruits, or olives to your cheeses. Feel free to get creative!*

**YIELDS ABOUT 1 CUP**

**1 cup sunflower seeds**
**3 cups water, divided**
**1 teaspoon probiotic powder**

1. Soak the sunflower seeds in 2 cups of water for 6–8 hours. Drain and rinse.

2. Blend the sunflower seeds with 1 cup of fresh water and the probiotic powder.

3. Transfer the mixture to a glass jar and allow it to sit at room temperature for 8–12 hours. Bubbles will form.

4. The cheese will separate from the liquid whey. Pour out the whey. If you stop here, you have a usable cultured seed cheese that resembles conventional cheese, with a sour and tangy taste. Here is where you will mix in any additions, if you wish.

5. If you want a product that resembles a cream cheese, you'll want to add this last step. Put the cheese in a nut milk bag or cheesecloth and squeeze out the remaining liquid. Hang the bag over the sink for 4 hours or longer to culture it. Either way, store the cheese in lidded glass container in the refrigerator. It will last for up to 2 weeks.

Swap It Out! Try changing up the base by using cashews, hempseed, or macadamias instead of sunflower seeds. Play around with fermentation time and temperature as well. Who knows, maybe there's a raw cheesemonger hiding inside of you!

# Pine Nut Parmesan

*Parmesan cheese is the topping supreme for salads, pastas, and pretty much every-
thing in between. But when it comes right down to it, what Parmesan really offers is
that salty, fatty quality that we all love so much. Luckily, that amazing taste is easy
to mimic, and this recipe is completely capable of holding its own in the rich-and-
savory-topping department.*

**YIELDS ABOUT 2 CUPS**

**2 cups pine nuts**
**½ cup cashews**
**½ teaspoon lemon juice**
**½ teaspoon sea salt**

1. Place all ingredients in a food processor and pulse until crumbly. Do not overmix.

2. Store in a lidded glass jar in the fridge for up to a month.

### Using Yeast

If you keep and use nutritional yeast (a nonraw health food that's embraced by many high-raw foodists), then feel free to toss a teaspoon in to really take this over the top into cheeseland. If you're a raw purist, then no worries, this recipe as-is will still be delicious!

# BBQ's Best Friend (Classic Coleslaw)

*As a raw vegan, do you sometimes feel left out of all the summer fun? Good news! You never again have to endure a friendly cookout with nary a bite to eat! Say goodbye to family picnics that leave you starving and surly. This Classic Coleslaw will give you something amazing to share, and you don't even need to tell anybody that it's raw! They'll love it and you'll finally get to go home happy—and well-fed. This year summer is going to* rawk!

**SERVES 6**

1 medium head of cabbage

¼ cup plus 2 tablespoons Good Gracious Garlic Aioli (see recipe in Ch. 9)

2 tablespoons apple-cider vinegar

1 tablespoon agave syrup

½ teaspoon sea salt

½ teaspoon black pepper

1. Shred the cabbage using either a sharp knife or a food processor fitted with a shredding disc.

2. Combine all ingredients in a very large mixing bowl and toss well to completely coat the cabbage.

3. Allow to marinate in the fridge for at least 1 hour, overnight if possible. Toss again before serving.

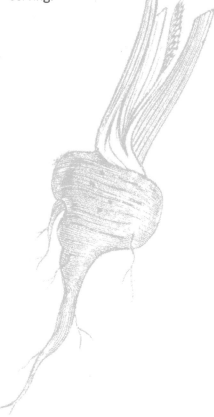

# Coleslaw, "Well-Cooked"

*This tart and tangy slaw is simply saturated in flavors, sublime after a night spent stewing in the fridge. There's an unexpected interplay here, too, between the sweet apple juice and the spicy mustard and paprika. Take this tasty slaw to your next summer potluck, or simply spoon it into a giant bowl for your supper.*

**SERVES 6**

4 cups green cabbage, shredded

2 cups carrots, shredded

¾ cup green onions, thinly sliced

¾ cup fresh apple juice

⅔ cup apple-cider vinegar

1½ teaspoons paprika

1 teaspoon mustard seeds

½ teaspoon mustard powder

½ teaspoon garlic powder

½ teaspoon celery seeds

½ teaspoon black pepper, ground

½ teaspoon sea salt

1. In a large bowl, combine the cabbage, carrots, and green onions. Set aside.

2. In a jar with a secure lid, combine the remaining ingredients. Tightly screw on the lid and shake vigorously.

3. Pour the dressing over vegetables. Toss lightly to coat.

4. Cover and refrigerate overnight. Toss well before serving.

# Fiesta-Ready Multicolored Tex-Mex Slaw

*This vibrant, rainbow-painted dish is inspired by the colors and flavors of Mexico and the southwestern United States and the onions, peppers, and salty olives are ready to dance the night away under the desert moon. So grab your sombrero and slip on your castanets. Mock margaritas are optional, but raw slaw is a must.*

**SERVES 6**

4 cups green cabbage, shredded

½ cup green bell pepper, diced

½ cup raw black olives, pitted and sliced

⅓ cup yellow onion, diced

¼ cup sweet red peppers, diced

½ cup apple cider vinegar

3 tablespoons olive oil

1 tablespoon agave syrup

1½ teaspoons sea salt

1 teaspoon sweet Hungarian paprika

½ teaspoon dry mustard

1 teaspoon celery seeds

1. In a large serving bowl, combine the cabbage, bell pepper, olives, onion, and sweet red peppers; toss gently until well-mixed. Set aside.

2. In a small glass jar with a lid, combine the remaining ingredients. Cover and shake until well-mixed.

3. Pour the dressing over the veggies and toss gently until thoroughly incorporated. Cover and refrigerate for at least 1 hour before serving.

■ **PRO'S TIP** For coleslaw that's especially extra-crispy, submerge your head of cabbage in ice water immediately before slicing it up. Then, once you've shredded it, stick it right into the refrigerator. This will guarantee the crispiest coleslaw you've ever served!

# Picnic-Ready "Potato" Salad

*Jicama is a root crop indigenous to Mexico. The crispy tuber has white flesh, like a potato, but unlike its underground-growing brother, jicama can be eaten raw. This salad looks and tastes a lot like classic American potato salad and is a rawesome addition to any summer raw potluck party.*

**SERVES 6**

1 cup Marvelous Coconut Cashew Mayonnaise (see recipe in Ch. 9)

½ teaspoon celery seed

½ teaspoon dry mustard

½ teaspoon white pepper

2 pounds jicama, peeled and chopped

⅔ cup yellow onion, thinly sliced

2 tablespoons fresh parsley, chopped, for garnish

⅛ teaspoon paprika, for garnish

1. Whisk the mayonnaise, celery seed, dry mustard, and white pepper together in a large mixing bowl.

2. Add the jicama and onion and toss to completely coat.

3. Sprinkle with parsley and paprika. Serve immediately or store covered in the refrigerator for up to a week.

# Minted Lemongrass "Potato" Salad

*Once again featuring jicama as a stand-in for cooked potatoes, this sumptuous salad steals its flavor profile from far-away locales, borrowing the beauty of Southeast Asian cuisine. The exotic ingredients used in this recipe make for amazing edibles, and the combination of lemongrass and mint is undeniably mouth-watering. It's a totally living twist on an old American classic—and it's sure to be an instant raw favorite*

### SERVES 6

2 pounds jicama, peeled and diced

¼ cup green onion, diced

2 tablespoons coconut vinegar

2 tablespoons sesame oil

1½ teaspoons fresh lemongrass, minced

½ teaspoon garlic, minced

¼ teaspoon sea salt

¼ teaspoon red pepper flakes

1 tablespoon fresh mint, finely minced

½ teaspoon sesame seeds

1. Place the jicama and onions in a large mixing bowl. Set aside.

2. In a smaller bowl, whisk together the vinegar, oil, lemongrass, garlic, sea salt, and red pepper flakes to make a dressing. Pour the dressing over the jicama-and-onion mixture and toss to completely coat.

3. Add the mint to the mix and gently fold it in. Garnish the salad with sesame seeds.

4. Serve the salad immediately or cover the bowl and chill up to 24 hours before serving.

# You Won't Believe How Simple Sauerkraut

*Fermenting vegetables may seem intimidating at first, but it's easier than you think. It's just a matter of timing and technique, which comes quickly with a little practice. The key to a successful sauerkraut is to keep everything submerged beneath the brine. As long as you're careful about that, everything should go off without a hitch!*

**YIELDS 1 LARGE JAR**

**1 pound green or purple cabbage**
**1 tablespoon sea salt**

1. Set aside 5–6 whole large leaves of cabbage, then shred the rest thin, using either a sharp knife or a food processor fitted with the shredding disc.

2. In a giant mixing bowl, use your hands to work the salt into the cabbage. Put some muscle into it! After a while the cabbage will wilt and release its liquid.

3. Place the softened cabbage in a ceramic crock, a large glass jar, or a stainless steel container. Press it down to pack it in as much as you can—you want it very tight and you want the liquid released in Step 2 to completely cover the cabbage. Fill the container to just ¾ full. (This leaves room for the fermentation to cause expansion.)

4. Place the reserved whole leaves over the top of the shredded cabbage to completely cover the surface.

5. Gently press down on cabbage leaves to compress and submerge them. Use something to weigh them down, like a plate with a few canned goods on top, or a jar filled with water (this will depend on the fermenting vessel you use and how large the opening is).

6. Keep the fermenting vessel in a room with a temperature of 59°F–71°F for 1 week. Check each day to make sure the leaves remain submerged. Press down if needed.

7. At the end of the week, remove the weights and the cabbage leaves, and skim off any mold that may have grown. As long as the vegetables under the brine smell okay, then it's safe to eat. If the vegetables smell rotten, you'll have to discard the batch.

8. Transfer sauerkraut to smaller lidded glass jars and store in the refrigerator. Fermented foods will keep indefinitely in the refrigerator.

# Crunchy Cultured Dill Pickles

*Pickles are just plain fabulous. Salty and crisp, they add flavor and texture to any dish you deem fit to fill with them. Untuna? Potato salad? A sammie or wrap? The possibilities are endless and, with these pickles, so are the benefits. These carefully cultured, fermented favorites are full of those amazing probiotics that keep us all so healthy. What more reason do you need to add a little pickle to your plate?*

## YIELDS 1 LARGE JAR

¼ cup sea salt

5 cups warm water

2–4 heads fresh flowering dill

8–10 garlic cloves, peeled

2 teaspoons dill seeds

Small bunch of fresh strawberry, grape, or horseradish leaves

2 pounds pickling cucumbers

1. Stir to dissolve the salt in the 5 cups of warm water. Set aside. This is brine.

2. Place the fresh flowering dill face down in a very large jar (or split between two medium jars). Add the garlic and dill seeds, then top with the fresh strawberry, grape, or horseradish leaves.

3. Add the pickling cucumbers, leaving room for at least 2" of liquid on top. Cover with the salt water. Put the lid on the jar but leave it very loose—just set it on top. Make sure that the cucumbers remain submerged.

4. Leave your pickles in a warm spot for 3–5 days to ferment. Check the liquid levels daily and add more brine, which you can make using the same proportion of salt to water, if needed.

5. Transfer to the refrigerator and store, tightly lidded, indefinitely.

### Strawberry, Grape, or Horseradish Leaves

Why add these leaves to your pickles? These plants contain tannins, and tannins act to keep the pickles supercrisp. Nobody likes a mushy pickle, so make sure to layer in the leaves, and keep those pickles full of *crunch*!

# Spicy Snappy Ginger Pickles

*This recipe is a great way to keep away a tummy ache. Drawing on a double dose of digestive aid, it combines the ancient use of ginger to calm the belly with our more modern understanding of the power in probiotic foods. That's an effective duet, dutifully keeping guard over your most sensitive stomach. Begin each meal with a piece of pickled ginger to stoke your digestive fire. The fuel will keep you running smoothly and assist you in absorbing all the nutrients that you eat up!*

**YIELDS 1 LARGE JAR**

**4 pounds gingerroot**
**1 tablespoon sea salt**
**1 cup distilled water**
**1 teaspoon probiotic powder**

1. Peel and cut the ginger into very thin slices. A mandoline would work well here.

2. Using a wooden mallet or the flat side of a large knife, pound the ginger slices to expel the juices.

3. Transfer the pounded ginger and its juices into a glass jar; mix with salt and water.

4. Add the probiotic powder. Make sure that all the ginger is submerged. Loosely seal the jar with its lid.

5. Let it sit at room temperature for 3–5 days, then transfer to the refrigerator and store indefinitely.

# Traditional Korean Kimchi

*Every cultural region has its own form of fermented food, and kimchi hails from Korea. There are thousands of variations, but most authentic versions will contain cabbage and some sort of hot spice. Kimchi is amazing whether it's served alone as an appetizer, as part of a soup, on top of a salad, or as a component of certain entrées. Never fear, you'll find it used as an ingredient in recipes throughout this book, too!*

**YIELDS 1 LARGE JAR**

4 cloves garlic
1 cup onion, chopped
4 fresh hot red peppers
2 dried hot red peppers
2 tablespoons gingerroot
4 heads green cabbage
½ daikon radish
3 tablespoons salt

1. In a food processor or blender, combine the garlic, onion, both kinds of hot peppers, and gingerroot into a kimchi sauce.

2. Grate, shred, or chop the cabbage and daikon radish. Mix in the salt and squeeze or pound the cabbage to create a brine.

3. Mix the cabbage and daikon with the kimchi sauce.

4. Pack the kimchi into a 1 gallon glass jar or ceramic crock. Make sure there are no gaps or air pockets. Place a weight over the kimchi to keep it covered in the brine. Place a loose lid over the opening, one that that will allow the pressure to release.

5. Let the kimchi sit at room temperature. Check every day to make sure the vegetables remain submerged beneath the brine. It will be ready to eat in 4–5 days. Transfer it to smaller glass jars and store in the refrigerator. Fermented foods will keep indefinitely in the fridge.

Swap It Out! Cabbage is the quintessential kimchi base, but this fermented superfood can be made with all sorts of alternatives. Some ideas to try: bok choy, kale, radishes, Brussels sprouts, or Swiss chard.

## Chapter 11

# Sandwiches, Wraps, and Rolls

It's the centerpiece of almost every lunchbox across America, the iconic midday menu item, the one thing most associated with the word "lunch." The sandwich! The good news is that there are a million ways to make a raw vegan sandwich, wrap, or roll. From dehydrated bread encasing a collection of your favorite veggies, to open-faced Italian-style bruschetta, to wraps made with collards and rolls of nori seaweed, you'll never need feel left out around the lunch table again. There's even a classic PB&J, which is truly not to be missed.

So start salivating! It's guaranteed that you'll wish you could make a sandwich for every meal. Hey, wait a minute . . . you can!

# Completely Rawesome Coconut Wrappers

*Bread is off the table for raw vegans, but never fear. This recipe gives you a sweet, chewy, and sturdy vehicle that you can use to usher all your most favorite fillings into your mouth, from simple slaws and hearty pâtés to just plain fresh raw veggies. These coconut wrappers are a blank canvas that melds well with many types of flavors. Have fun playing with your own creative stuffings, or stick to the plan and prepare the following recipes that put this wrapper into action!*

SERVES 2

2 cups young coconut meat
1 cup mango
¼ teaspoon sea salt

1. Blend together all ingredients in a food processor or blender.

2. Spread the wrap mixture in a thin layer onto dehydrator trays fitted with nonstick sheets. Dehydrate at 115°F for 4 hours.

3. Serve immediately, or wrap in plastic and store in the cupboard for up to a week.

# Sherbet Herb Spring Rolls

*These golden creamsicle-colored wrappers can be used to brighten up your standard spring rolls. They're not actually ice cream, but these wrappers may be equally as refreshing on a hot summer evening.*

**SERVES 4**

½ of a 12-ounce package of kelp noodles, rinsed and soaked in warm water for 15 minutes

1 tablespoon nama shoyu

1 teaspoon sesame oil

½ teaspoon minced gingerroot

¼ cup shiitake mushrooms, diced

1 carrot, grated

8 Completely Rawesome Coconut Wrappers (see recipe in this chapter)

½ head green leaf lettuce, chopped

1 cucumber, sliced very thin

1 bunch fresh mint

1. In a large bowl, toss together the drained kelp noodles, nama shoyu, sesame oil, ginger, mushrooms, and carrot.

2. Place a coconut wrapper on a plate. Add a bit of lettuce to the center of the wrapper. Add a scoop of the noodle mixture, a thin layer of cucumbers, and a few leaves of mint on top.

3. Fold the bottom of the roll over the filling, then fold in each side, and then roll it up. Repeat with all wrappers. Serve.

■ **PRO'S TIP** Wrapping spring rolls can come with a learning curve: too tight and they split their sides, but too loose and everything inside slides out. Luckily, there are a few tricks that can help you along the way. First, keep a small bowl of warm water at your work station. Frequently dipping your fingertips will prevent sticking. For the filling, make sure it's not too large or lumpy; you may want to use scissors to trim noodles short. Don't overfill! Use water to seal seams as you go. This will help to keep everything held together. And finally, again: Don't overfill!

# Fiesta Slaw Salad Rolls

*There's a party going on in that salad-roll wrapper! These bold, bright flavors combine with a rainbow of color to make for an amazing presentation. Oh, and these rolls taste pretty spectacular as well! Wraps like these make such great appetizers for a fun and casual get-together with friends, so call up all your rawesome buddies and have a great time!*

SERVES 4–8

8 Completely Rawesome Coconut Wrappers (see recipe in this chapter)

2 cups Fiesta-Ready Multicolored Tex-Mex Slaw (see recipe in Ch. 10)

1 cup Cumin-Spiced Avocado Spread or Chia-mole (see recipes in Ch. 10)

**1.** Place a coconut wrapper on a plate. Add ¼ cup of Fiesta-Ready Multicolored Tex-Mex Slaw to the center of the wrapper. Top with about 2 tablespoons of Cumin-Spiced Avocado Spread or Chia-mole.

**2.** Fold the bottom of the roll over the filling, then fold in each side, and then roll it up. Repeat with all wrappers. Serve.

Swap It Out! Feel free to make alterations to this recipe based on what you're craving on any given day. You can substitute another favorite slaw, or use avocado slices in place of guacamole.

# Jamaican Jerk-Spiced Collard Wraps

*The term "jerk" actually describes a style of cooking—of cooking meat, in fact. Of course, there's nothing like that going on around here. In this case "jerk" is referring to the seasonings used—a very hot mixture made from allspice and Scotch bonnet peppers, among others. So let's borrow the best—the spice blend, the style, and the mood—and leave the rest—the meat and the grill. It's a postmodern world, after all, and we raw vegans are making our own rules!*

**SERVES 2**

¼ cup flaxseed
1 cup almonds, soaked
¼ cup celery, chopped
1 tablespoon olive oil
½ tablespoon Jamaican jerk
  seasoning
½ tablespoon jalapeño pepper,
  minced and seeds removed
¼ teaspoon salt
½ clove garlic, minced
2 collard leaves
1 cucumber, finely julienned
1 sweet red pepper, finely julienned

1. Grind the flaxseed to a powder in a coffee grinder.

2. To make the filling, process the flax, almonds, celery, olive oil, jerk seasoning, jalapeño, salt, and garlic in a food processor or blender, until smooth.

3. To make the wrap, remove the stems from 2 collard leaves and cut them in half. Spread a layer of the filling onto each collard green half. Lay a few pieces of cucumber and red pepper on top.

4. Tightly roll up each collard green. Stick a toothpick through the middle to hold them together.

# Not-Roasted Red Pepper Wrap

*This is a robust wrap, perfect for a solid square lunch or quick hearty dinner. Best of all, this recipe provides a very well-rounded meal, with protein from the sprouted lentil pâté, healthy fats from the avocados, and burnable carbohydrates in the plethora of vegetables. There's also plenty of fiber as well as micronutrients like minerals and antioxidants. Now that's complete!*

**SERVES 2**

2 large collard leaves
1 cucumber, thinly sliced
1 cup Not-Roasted Red Pepper Lentil Dip (see recipe in Ch. 10)
1 sweet red pepper, in strips
1 avocado, sliced
Optional: ½ cup alfalfa sprouts

1. To assemble the wrap, remove the stems from 2 collard leaves and cut them in half. Lay down a few cucumber slices on each collard half, and spread ¼ cup of the Not-Roasted Red Pepper Lentil Dip over them. Top with sweet red pepper strips and avocado slices. Add sprouts if using them.

2. Tightly roll up each collard green leaf. Stick a toothpick through the middle to hold them together.

*Passionate* Pairings Serve this wrap with your favorite dipping sauce for a fun and extra-flavorful experience!

# Terrific "Tuna" Roll-Ups

*The contrasting textures and complementary flavors of this recipe allow it to shine. As with all simplicity dining, try to use only the highest-quality ingredients here—you'll be glad you did when you taste the difference it can make!*

SERVES 4

4 large romaine lettuce, red leaf lettuce, or green leaf lettuce leaves

1⅓ cups "Sunfish" Salad (see recipe in Ch. 7)

1 slicing tomato, cut into 8 slices

Optional toppings: grated carrot, slivered red onion, or alfalfa sprouts to taste

1. Hold open a lettuce leaf on a plate. Spread ⅓ cup "Sunfish" Salad down the center and top with 2 slices of tomato.

2. Add any additional toppings you like. Fold one side of the lettuce over the toppings and tuck it under, continuing to roll the wrap all the way up.

3. Repeat with each lettuce leaf. Serve.

# Oh-So-Spicy Korean Hand Rolls

*This rawesome recipe is fusion dining at its finest! This recipe borrows from a number of Eastern regions, most notably with a nori roll base from Japanese-style sushi, and a filling of traditional Korean kimchi. Any rough spots in this collision of two distinctly unique cuisines are smoothed over by the creamy avocado. Oh, avocado—is there anything you can't do?*

SERVES 2

4 sheets raw nori

1⅓ cups Traditional Korean Kimchi (see recipe in Ch. 10) or store-bought kimchi

1 cucumber, thinly sliced

4 red or green lettuce leaves

1 avocado, sliced

1. Lay 1 nori sheet on a flat surface. Spread ⅓ cup of kimchi down the center. Top the kimchi with ¼ of the cucumber slices, 1 lettuce leaf, and ¼ of avocado slices.

2. Use your hands to carefully roll the nori into a cone shape, closed at one end and wide at the other. Repeat with other nori sheets and serve.

# Scrumptiously Sunny Pickle Rolls

*These radical rolls are totally unique. It's almost certain that you've never had any-thing quite like them, between the sunflower seeds and buckwheat, the pickles and the nori seaweed, and the strangely synchronous spice blend. But really, isn't that what raw food is all about? Of course it's fun to recreate and raw-ify your old favor-ites, but in the end, this recipe is on the cutting edge of rawesomeness! It's something totally new! Enjoy!*

SERVES 4

1 cup sunflower seeds, soaked

1 cup buckwheat, sprouted

½ cup cauliflower, chopped

½ cup Crunchy Cultured Dill Pickles (see recipe in Ch. 10) or store-bought pickles (Bubbies is a raw brand), chopped

¼ cup onion, chopped

3 tablespoons lemon juice

2 tablespoons agave syrup

1 tablespoon coconut vinegar

1 tablespoon fresh dill, minced

1 tablespoon In-Your-Face Italian Seasoning Spice Blend (see recipe in Ch. 12)

2 teaspoons garlic, minced

½ teaspoon salt

½ teaspoon cayenne pepper powder

4 raw nori sheets

1. Process the sunflower seeds and buck-wheat in a blender or food processor until well-broken-down.

2. Add all remaining ingredients, except the nori sheets, to the blender or food processor and pulse until they are well-broken-down but still chunky.

3. Lay a nori sheet flat on a bamboo sushi mat. Place 2 scoops of the mixture onto each nori sheet and use the bamboo mat to roll. Alterna-tively, roll by hand.

4. Chop the nori rolls into quarters and serve.

# Practically Perfect Puttanesca Bruschetta

*Bruschetta is traditionally an Italian appetizer, though here it makes for a light meal. Think of it more like an open-faced sandwich, a modern interpretation of the old classic. Bruschetta can include any number of toppings, and this one spotlights a salty southern Italian sauce called puttanesca. Usually puttanesca is served with spaghetti, but again, we're being creative here. Just taste it—you won't object to the culinary creative license.*

### SERVES 2

2 cups chopped tomatoes

¼ cup raw Kalamata olives, or other raw olives, pitted and halved

2 tablespoons diced white onion

2 tablespoons olive oil, more to garnish

2 teaspoons fresh basil, minced

1 teaspoon fresh oregano, minced

½–1 teaspoon red pepper flakes (traditionally, puttanesca should have a kick)

2 cloves garlic, crushed

Sea salt and cracked black pepper, to taste

4 slices of flatbread, such as Tomato, Basil, and Flax Crackers; Garlic Lover's Greatest Crackers; Seriously, Sauerkraut Crackers; or any others (see recipes in Ch. 13)

1. In a large mixing bowl, combine the tomatoes, olives, onion, olive oil, basil, oregano, red pepper, garlic, salt, and pepper. Mix well, cover, and refrigerate for 1 hour to allow flavors to mingle.

2. Lay flatbread out on 2 plates. Spoon the puttanesca over the flatbreads and if you'd like, drizzle with a little extra olive oil before serving.

# Open-Faced Avo-Smash

*This recipe is about as easy as it gets, but for all its simplicity, it's far from boring. Actually, this is the kind of food that many long-time raw enthusiasts find themselves eating again and again. Nothing fancy, nothing too obscure. Just a good, solid go-to recipe that lends itself to alteration depending on what's in the crisper. Sometimes simple really is best.*

**SERVES 2**

1 large avocado (or 2 small)

4 slices of flatbread, such as Good Earth Crackers; Tomato, Basil, and Flax Crackers; Simple Tasty Toast; or any others (see recipes in Ch. 13)

1 very large or 2 medium tomatoes

Sea salt and fresh cracked pepper to taste

1. Open the avocado by cutting it in half, and remove the pit. Scoop out each half. Divide the flesh into 4 equal amounts. Put equal amounts of avocado on each piece of flatbread. Use a fork to gently mash the avocado over each slice of bread, being careful not to crack the bread.

2. Slice the tomato into thick slabs. Layer the slabs over the avocado.

3. Add any additional desired topping before serving (see sidebar, "Swap It Out"), and sprinkle with salt and pepper.

Swap It Out! There's a lot of room to play around in this recipe. You can add veggies like grated carrot, thin-sliced cukes, or minced mushroom caps. It's also great with an added dressing, from homemade hot sauce to Secret Success Zucchini Hummus (see recipe in Chapter 10) to Tangy Raw Ranch (see recipe in Chapter 9). For a boost of protein, try sprinkling hempseed or sprouted lentils over the avocado layer.

# Eggplant Bread Sammie

*An "egg"cellent alternative to heavier, nut- or seed-based crackers, this recipe steps in when you want a sandwich that really feels familiar, and lettuce leaves just won't cut it. Once dehydrated, eggplant becomes remarkably breadlike. However, eggplant does grow increasingly bitter as it ages, so try to get them as fresh as possible, and use them up immediately. Sandwiches all around!*

**SERVES 2**

**1 eggplant, as fresh as possible**
**Sea salt**
**Fillings of choice (see sidebar, "Swap It Out")**

1. Peel the skin off the eggplant and cut it into toast-like slices, at least 1" thick.

2. Sprinkle each side of each slice with sea salt. Set in a pan and allow to sweat for about an hour. This will help remove some of the moisture and bitterness.

3. Rinse off the salt, pat dry, and spread the eggplant slices on a dehydrator tray. Dehydrate at 145°F for 2–3 hours.

4. Layer 1 slice with your fillings of choice, top with another slice, and serve.

Swap It Out! You can use whatever you like as a filling here, such as lettuce, tomatoes, cucumbers, or red peppers. A spread always adds a fun little flair, so why not try some Triple Seedy Sauce (see recipe in Chapter 9), Sweet and Savory Rawbecue Sauce, (see recipe in Chapter 9), Cumin-Spiced Avocado Spread (see recipe in Chapter 10), or either Zesty Italian or Magical Mushroom Pâté (see recipes in Chapter 10). You could add the Simple Starter for Seed Cheese (recipe in Chapter 10), or go for a savory, meatlike feel with some Sweet and Spicy Zucchini Jerky (recipe in Chapter 13). There are so many options to choose from, so play around and make this sandwich your own!

# Marvelously Modern Mushroom Reuben

*There is a lot of mythology and speculation surrounding the birthplace of the salty, sloppy sandwich known as the reuben. Characterized by its various parts, the reuben includes rye bread, corned beef, Swiss cheese, sauerkraut, and Russian dressing. Not very raw, nor very vegan. And yet, here you have it: a veganized, raw-rific version that plays on each important element of the original. Served warm from the dehydrator, this comforting concoction is a true pleasure!*

**SERVES 2**

2 portobello mushroom caps

1 sweet onion

¼ cup olive oil

1 tablespoon nama shoyu

½ teaspoon onion powder

½ teaspoon garlic powder

½ teaspoon black pepper

4 slices New York Rye bread (see recipe in Ch. 13)

½ cup You Won't Believe How Simple Sauerkraut (see recipe in Ch. 10)

2 tablespoons Red Russian Dressing (see recipe in Ch. 9)

Optional: ¼ cup Simple Starter for Seed Cheese (see recipe in Ch. 10)

1. Use a mandoline or sharp knife to very thinly slice the mushrooms and onions. Toss these in a glass mixing bowl with the olive oil, nama shoyu, and spices. Allow to marinate, covered, for 1–4 hours.

2. Toss again and then transfer the entire bowl to a dehydrator. Dehydrate at 115°F for 4 hours, stirring occasionally.

3. To assemble the sandwiches, place a slice of rye bread on a plate. Pile on half of the mushroom-and-onion mix. Top with sauerkraut, Russian dressing, and seed cheese, if you'd like. Place another piece of rye on top, and serve.

# Fabulous Spiced Almond Falafels

*Falafels are the fast food of the Middle East. Like hot dog vendors in New York City and taco trucks in SoCal, falafel carts can be found on street corners all throughout Arabia. The delicious, addictive little balls of goodness are made of fresh beans and then deep fried, served in warm pita with sauce. And these awesome raw renditions are . . . not! Nope, no frying, no transfats, no processed wheat bread, no suspicious sauce. Just amazing, wholesome, healthy ingredients that more than meet the criteria for "delicious, addictive little balls of goodness." So go for it—get your falafel on!*

**SERVES 2**

**2 cups almonds, soaked**
**1 garlic clove**
**2 tablespoons lemon juice**
**2 tablespoons liquid coconut oil**
**1 tablespoon sage**
**¼ teaspoon cayenne pepper powder**
**4 cabbage leaves**
**1 cup Secret Success Zucchini Hummus or Sprouted Chickpea Hummus (see recipes in Ch. 10)**

1. In a food processor or blender, process all the ingredients except the cabbage leaves and hummus.

2. Form the mixture into little balls and place on dehydrator trays. Dehydrate at 145°F for 2 hours. Turn down the temperature and continue dehydrating at 115°F for 12 hours.

3. To serve, lay the cabbage leaves on a plate. Spread the hummus onto each leaf and place falafel patties on top. Roll up into a sandwich wrap.

# Shining Sun-Sprout Burgers

*Sometimes you float along through life, feet barely touching the floor, head in a daydream, planning all the possibilities in your fantasy future. Sometimes life just sweeps you up, as you flit from place to place, and you graze on light fare, sustain yourself on simple foods, thrive with fresh, hydrating, easy on-the-go produce. And then sometimes, you need to get* grounded. *And that's when you want food that will center you, hearty fuel to bring you into your body. A burger? Yes, a burger will probably fit the bill quite nicely.*

SERVES 4–6

2 cups sunflower seeds, soaked

½ cup mixed sprouts (alfalfa, fenugreek, mung, lentil, green pea, etc.)

¼ cup celery, chopped

¼ cup red or white onion, chopped

4 tablespoons agave syrup

2 tablespoons flaxseed, ground

1 tablespoon nama shoyu

1 tablespoon In-Your-Face Italian Seasoning Spice Blend (see Ch. 12)

1 clove garlic, minced

1. In a food processor or blender, mix all ingredients together. Leave some texture and chunkiness to the mixture.

2. Form the mixture into 4–6 burger patties and dehydrate at 110°F for 4 hours. Flip over burgers and continue to dehydrate for 2–4 more hours.

3. Optional: Serve on bread or in a cabbage leaf, topped with lettuce and tomato. Dress with a sauce from Chapter 9.

# Slammin' Sliders

*Sliders are simply miniature hamburgers. They were first popularized by the fast food chain White Castle, though they've become somewhat of a hot food trend in recent years. Doctor up these ridiculously rawesome sliders however you wish and serve them as appetizers or even hors d'oeuvres. Or, pile a few on each person's plate to make a meal of it.*

**SERVES 4**

2 cups sunflower seeds (soaked), or walnuts (soaked) (see Soaking and Sprouting Chart in Ch. 1)

½ cup flaxseed, ground

2 tablespoons lemon juice

¼ cup water, as needed

1 cup diced carrot

¼ cup diced onion

4 tablespoons basil, minced

2 tablespoons dill, minced

1 tablespoon jalapeño pepper, minced

½ teaspoon salt

1 clove garlic, minced

1 recipe Onion Bread or Buns (see recipe in Ch. 13)

2 tomatoes, thinly sliced

½ red onion, thinly sliced

Optional: dressing and/or sauces of choice

**1.** In a food processor or blender, process the sunflower seeds and flaxseed with the lemon juice and a little water to create a batter the consistency of creamy peanut butter.

**2.** Add the carrot, onion, basil, dill, jalapeño, salt, and garlic to the food processor and process until well-mixed but still chunky. You may need to add a little extra water to make it easier to form the mixture into patties.

**3.** Form the veggie burger mix into small patties measuring about 3" wide and ⅜" thick.

**4.** Prepare the Onion Bread or Buns recipe according to the instructions, but form the dough into small buns measuring about 5" wide.

**5.** Dehydrate both the veggie burgers and onion bread at 110°F for 12 hours.

**6.** Create a sandwich with the veggie burger in the middle of 2 onion buns. Top the burger with sliced tomatoes and red onion. Add whatever other toppings you like.

Swap It Out! Variety is the spice of life, so feel free to dress each one of your sliders differently and enjoy the overflow of so many delicious flavors.

# Mega Maca Burger Patties

*Maca is a powerful superpowder made from an Andean root vegetable. It's also an adaptogen, which means it aids the body in regaining balance wherever imbalance arises. This ingredient can also increase energy and stamina, fight disease, regulate hormones, and decrease your stress. But best of all, maca is also a powerful aphrodisiac. So enjoy that burger, baby!*

**SERVES 4**

1½ cups walnuts, soaked
¼ cup flaxseed
2 cups chopped zucchini
½ cup chopped celery
1½ cups crimini or portobello mushrooms, minced
½ cup chopped red onion
1 clove garlic, minced
1 tablespoon nama shoyu
1 cup water
2 tablespoons maca
1 tablespoon minced sage
3 tablespoons minced basil

1. Grind 1 cup walnuts to a powder in a food processor. Grind the flaxseed into a powder with a coffee grinder. Pour them into a large mixing bowl.

2. Briefly process the remaining ½ cup walnuts in a food processor. Add the zucchini, celery, mushrooms, onion, and garlic and process until well-mixed and still chunky. Add this to the mixing bowl containing the ground flax and walnuts. Set aside.

3. Stir the nama shoyu into 1 cup water.

4. Add all ingredients to the walnut-and-flax mixture and stir well. Form the mixture into burger patties, about ½" thick.

5. Dehydrate the patties at 145°F for 2 hours. Turn down heat to 110°F. Flip the patties and continue dehydrating for an additional 8–12 hours.

# "Grilled Cheese" and Tomato

*This is a great simple supper if you're ever feeling under the weather. Well-rounded in macronutrient ratios, it provides all that you'll need without a lot of thought. Served warm, it's soothing and nostalgic, and paired with soup it's the perfect answer to aches, pains, and minor ailments. Funny how some foods are just magic like that.*

SERVES 1

**2 slices bread of choice (see side-bar, "Passionate Pairings")**
**¼ cup Simple Starter for Seed Cheese (see recipe in Ch. 10)**
**1 ripe tomato, sliced**

1. Spread the cheese over 1 slice of bread and layer on the tomatoes. Top with the other slice of bread.

2. Heat in the dehydrator at 115°F for 1 hour, or until warmed through.

***Passionate* Pairings** This recipe works well on a number of breads. Some suggestions: Traditional Sprouted Essene Bread, Onion Bread or Buns, New York Rye, and Simple Tasty Toast (see recipes in Chapter 13). Serve it alongside your favorite soup, such as Creamy Fennel and Tomato Bisque, Incredible Italian Minestrone, or Dreamy Creamy Corn Chowder (see recipes in Chapter 8).

# Perfect PB&J

*Sometime that semisweet almond butter hits the spot. Sometimes the creaminess of cashews is just what you're craving. But what about when you hear the siren song of sweet, smooth, salted, and roasted peanut butter? Well, here's your answer: the perfect reproduction. This copycat counts on specific ingredients, so as much as possible try not to make substitutions. Peanut butter and jelly. In the raw. Amazing.*

### YIELDS 1 LARGE JAR OF NUT NUTTER AND A SMALL JAR OF JAM

1½ cups almonds
½ cup macadamia nuts
1 teaspoon coconut nectar
1 teaspoon sesame oil
1 scant teaspoon salt
8 prunes
1 cup water for soaking
1 cup blueberries
2 slices Simple Tasty Toast (recipe in Ch. 13) or other neutral-flavored bread

1. To make the "peanut butter" in a food processor combine the almonds and macadamia nuts. Allow the machine to run for a very long time, up to 5 minutes or more, until the nuts completely relax and release their oils, becoming a soft butter. Add the coconut nectar, sesame oil, and salt, and mix again until fully incorporated.

2. Store your "peanut butter" in a lidded glass jar in the fridge for up to a month.

3. To make the jelly, soak the pitted prunes in a cup of warm water for 4–8 hours. Transfer the prunes to a blender and purée with ½ to ¾ cup of the soak water, enough to make a smooth thick paste. Set aside.

4. Put the blueberries in a food processor and pulse to make a chunky slush. Pour through a mesh strainer or nut milk bag to separate the pulp from the juice. Save the juice to use in another recipe, or to drink.

5. In a mixing bowl, combine the blueberry pulp with the prune purée and mix to completely combine.

6. Store your jam in a lidded glass jar in the fridge for up to a week.

7. To make a sandwich, spread a thick layer of "peanut butter" over one slice of bread. Spread a thin layer of jam on another slice of bread. Sandwich together the halves, and enjoy!

*Chapter 12*

# Mix and Match for the Main Event

The purpose of food is to nourish our bodies, to provide energy in the form of calories and essential nutrients like lipids, vitamins, and minerals. But you know that food is about so much more than simple feeding. You live in a web of cuture and you interact within your community. In this world that you share, live in, and love in, food is a sacred ritual.

In the following pages you'll find dozens of recipes that will allow you to celebrate your raw vegan life. Whether you do that in solitude, in the company of your greatest confidant (that's you!), whether you're surrounded by your closest companions, or whether you're using these recipes to reach out and touch a brand new friend, know that these recipes will truly feed you. They feed the body because they are made from the healthiest ingredients on earth, and they feed the soul because they are made with mindfulness and intention. May you fill them with your love, and may they nourish you in return. How rawesome is that!

# Savory Spiced String Beans

*String beans are often treated as if they were vegetables, but they are in fact a legume. They're one of the few beans that can be eaten raw! Along with providing protein, string beans are high in vitamins A, C, K, and folate. They're also rich in potassium and manganese. Enjoy!*

SERVES 4

1 teaspoon savory herb seasoning blend, such as Herbamare, or Italian seasoning, or curry spice

2 tablespoons lemon juice

2 tablespoons olive oil, plus extra for garnish

¼ teaspoon salt

2 cups string beans

Sprig parsley, for garnish

1. Stir together the seasoning, lemon juice, olive oil, and salt.

2. Place the string beans in a large mixing bowl. Pour the sauce onto the beans and stir to coat the beans. Marinate for 3 hours at room temperature or overnight in the refrigerator.

3. Alternately, to speed up the marinating process, you can put the beans in a dehydrator for 2 hours at 110°F.

4. Serve at room temperature with a drizzle of olive oil and a sprig of parsley.

Swap It Out! In this simple recipe, you can play around with switching out the herbs, using different seasonal blends to keep things interesting. Variety ensures that you won't get bored, and that you'll continue to eat these health-promoting little pods.

# Open Sesame Asparagus and Mushrooms

*This is a simple and versatile dish, with an elegant marinade that marries well with myriad flavors. You just can't go wrong with the delicate grace of sesame oil, the slight saltiness of nama shoyu, and the sweet kiss of agave syrup. So feel free to add or substitute all your favorites. Switch out the asparagus for fiddleheads, or throw in some wild ramps for extra allium oomph. And of course, the "mushroom" title is nonspecific, so have it your way with any variety that pleases you. Buttons and criminis are widely available year-round, while shiitakes or maitakes also go well with this delicious delicacy.*

**SERVES 4**

2 teaspoons sesame oil

1 teaspoon nama shoyu

½ teaspoon agave syrup

1 pound fresh asparagus, trimmed and chopped

¾ cup chopped mushrooms

2 tablespoons sesame seeds, to garnish

1. In a small bowl, whisk together the sesame oil, nama shoyu, and agave syrup. Set aside.

2. In a large bowl, combine the asparagus with the mushrooms. Drizzle the sesame oil sauce over the vegetables and toss to completely coat.

3. This dish tastes best if allowed to marinate for at least 1 hour. You may also heat it up in the dehydrator, for a more warming meal.

4. Toss in the sesame seeds right before serving.

### Spotlight on Maitake Mushrooms

*Grifola frodosa* is the species known as maitake, a clustering mushroom native to Japan and North America. In Traditional Chinese Medicine, maitake is used as immune system support and to regulate balance in all systems. It's also rich in the minerals calcium, magnesium, and potassium, and it provides one of the few natural sources of vitamin D. So eat up!

# Curry Seasoning Spice Blend

*Curry seasoning is widely available for purchase, with a huge range of flavors, cost, and quality of ingredients. Of course, you can buy these blends off the store shelves, but it's almost as easy to mix them at home, yourself, to your own taste. This allows you full control over how much of which spices to include, and it allows you to choose exclusively organic herbs and ensure that your food is absolutely raw and free from processed ingredients. And what's better than that?*

**YIELDS ABOUT ½ CUP**

2 tablespoons ground cumin

2 tablespoons ground coriander

1 tablespoon cardamom seeds

2 teaspoons ground turmeric

½ teaspoon cayenne powder

½ teaspoon mustard seed

½ teaspoon ground ginger

1. In a spice grinder, coffee grinder, or blender, combine all the ingredients and process to a fine powder. You may have to do this in batches.

2. Store in a lidded glass spice jar in the pantry; will keep indefinitely.

### Curry Is Complicated

This recipe makes a basic curry seasoning. Once you've mixed and used it a bit, you'll get a feel for what you like and what you may want to change. Curry mixtures may include any great number of spices, depending on the region they originate from, their intended heat, and of course, preference. Some additional spices to consider for your curry blend include various other chili powders, fenugreek seeds, black peppercorns, dried curry leaves, dried garlic, fennel, caraway, cinnamon, cloves, nutmeg, and asafetida.

# Curried Cauliflower with Cashews

*This crackling curried veggie entrée works equally well as a chilled summer lunch or as a warm autumn supper. Full-flavored with the South Asian spices, the crunchy cauliflower and creamy, buttery cashews play well off of one another and are perfectly offset by the baby bok choy. Between the protein in the nut and the calcium in the greens, this recipe is perfect to serve on its own for lighter fare, or as a side dish if you're looking for an appetizer with a little more heft.*

**SERVES 4**

2 cups cauliflower florets

1 cup cashews, chopped

1 cup baby bok choy, sliced

½ cup sun-dried raisins

3 tablespoons coconut vinegar

3 tablespoons sesame oil

1 teaspoon Curry Seasoning Spice Blend (see recipe in this chapter)

¼ teaspoon garlic powder

⅛ teaspoon cloves

⅛ teaspoon sea salt

**1.** Break washed cauliflower florets into bite-size pieces and place in a large mixing bowl. Add cashews, baby bok choy, and raisins.

**2.** Whisk together the vinegar, sesame oil, Curry Seasoning Spice Blend, garlic powder, cloves, and sea salt in a small bowl.

**3.** Drizzle the dressing mixture over the vegetables and mix very well. Cover the bowl and place it in the refrigerator to marinate for at least 30 minutes. Mix well again before serving.

# Cajun Collard Greens

*Collards can be tough to prepare, but they're very nutritious, delicious, and well worth the extra work. First, tear the leaves away from the woody stem. Roll the leaves up together, then run a knife through them to cut thin long strips, like a chiffonade. A quick massage with some salt will get them wilting, and then you're good to go!*

**SERVES 4**

1 bunch collards, prepared as
   explained above
1 tablespoon olive oil
½ onion, diced
1 clove garlic, minced
2 medium tomatoes, diced
1½ teaspoons Cajun-spiced
   seasoning
Optional: raw hot sauce to taste

1. Massage the collards with the olive oil until they start to soften up. Add the onion and garlic and continue massaging.

2. Once collards are well-wilted, add the tomato, Cajun spice, and hot sauce. Toss well to completely mix, and serve.

■ **PRO'S TIP** Proper knife skills are almost as essential as a proper knife, so it's a good idea to take some time to practice different cuts (like julienne, dice, brunoise, etc). In this recipe you're asked to chiffonade, which is a technique traditionally used to cut herbs. To chiffonade, simply stack the leaves a few at a time, then roll them up, cutting along the roll to produce long thin strips.

# Lemon and Thyme Asparagus with Herbivore's Hollandaise

*Asparagus season is short-lived and well-loved. From mid-spring to early summer, you'll find this strange, alienesque stalk gracing the specials on every respectable menu across the city. And for good reason—asparagus is rich in a few very important minerals, namely, calcium, iron, selenium, and zinc. It also boasts a bevy of vitamins, from A, C, E, and K, all the way through to the many Bs. With such a narrow window when it's available, you can maximize your asparagus intake by pickling it in any number of the fermentation methods discussed in Chapter 1.*

**SERVES 4**

1 bunch of asparagus
¼ cup olive oil
¼ cup lemon juice
2 tablespoons red onion, finely
  minced
1 teaspoon dried thyme
½ teaspoon nama shoyu
½ cup Herbivore's Hollandaise Sauce
  (see recipe in Ch. 9)

1. Wash and trim the asparagus. Lay the spears in a shallow glass dish, like a small casserole dish.

2. In a small bowl, whisk together the olive oil, lemon juice, red onion, thyme, and nama shoyu. Pour over the asparagus.

3. Toss the asparagus in the marinade to coat completely. Cover and allow to marinate at room temperature for at least 2 hours, or overnight in the refrigerator.

4. Toss the asparagus again to recoat, and place the entire glass dish in the dehydrator. Dehydrate at 110°F for at least 2 hours, up to 4 hours. You may want to warm the hollandaise sauce in the dehydrator as well.

5. Remove from the dehydrator and lay the asparagus out on a serving platter. Spoon the hollandaise sauce over the asparagus and serve.

■ **PRO'S TIP** Don't waste that lemon peel after you've juiced the lemon! Take a few seconds to zest your rinds even when the recipe doesn't require it. The zest can be spread on a paper towel to dry, or even thrown in the dehydrator. Store dried zest in an old spice jar for use in all sorts of recipes, like adding excitement to salad, or sprucing up a soup, or sprinkling over sherbet.

# Corn on the Cob with Garlic Butter

*Let's be honest here. Perfectly fresh, just-off-the-stalk sweet summer corn really needs no embellishment; those big plump kernels popping their delicious juices are simply sublime all by themselves. Still, sometimes you want to fancy it up a bit, and pungent garlic is the perfect accompaniment to corn's natural candy-like quality. This is a simple recipe for a simple summer night. Simply healthy, simply delicious, simply rawesome!*

**SERVES 4**

1 cup young coconut meat
¼ cup coconut oil, warmed to liquid
1–2 cloves garlic
¼ teaspoon salt
4 fresh ears of organic corn

**1.** Place the coconut meat, coconut oil, garlic, and salt in a blender or food processor and blend together until smooth to create garlic butter.

**2.** Place the mixture in a lidded glass jar and refrigerate for 1 hour until it becomes solid.

**3.** Spread the garlic butter on the shucked ears of corn. There will be extra garlic butter, which will keep in the fridge for up to two weeks.

# "Mashed Potatoes" with Black Sesame Gravy

*Mmm, mashy taters, is there anything more quintessentially comfort food-y? And while this recipe may not actually use any potatoes, per se (shh, don't tell), it still offers all the same sensations. Especially warm out of the dehydrator. Smothered in dark gravy. Mmmm . . . .*

SERVES 4

For the gravy:
1 cup macadamia nuts
2 cups cauliflower, chopped
¼ cup olive oil
1 clove garlic
1 teaspoon sea salt, divided
1 teaspoon rosemary

For the "mashed potatoes":
½ cup black sesame seeds
1 cup chopped portobello mushrooms
2 tablespoons finely sliced scallions,
　or minced red or white onion
1 tablespoon nama shoyu
1 tablespoon lemon juice
1 clove garlic
Water for blending

1. In a food processor, purée the macadamia nuts until smooth. Add in the cauliflower, olive oil, garlic, ½ teaspoon sea salt, and rosemary. Continue processing until smooth to create the gravy. Set aside.

2. With a coffee grinder or spice mill, grind the sesame seeds into a powder.

3. Combine the sesame seed powder with the portobello, scallions, nama shoyu, lemon juice, and garlic in a blender. Process until smooth. Slowly pour in a little water until desired consistency is reached.

4. Spoon the "mashed potatoes" into individual bowls or a large serving bowl. Serve topped with or alongside the gravy.

# Hemp Heaven Stuffed Peppers

*Stuffed sweet peppers are an old Italian favorite, but this recipe takes this classic to a whole new level. This entrée is cold and crispy, refreshing and light, and is ready in under 15 minutes. It's easily portable, too, thanks to the cute little pepper vessel it's served in. Whether eaten on-the-go or enjoyed at the dinner table, you'll love this quick dish for its celebration of raw simplicity.*

SERVES 2

2 red bell peppers

½ cup pecans

¼ cup hempseed

¼ cup chopped red or white onion

1 tablespoon lime juice

1 teaspoon chopped jalapeño pepper

½ teaspoon Taco Seasoning Spice Blend (see recipe in this chapter)

¼ teaspoon salt

½ avocado, sliced

2 tablespoons cilantro, chopped

1. Cut the red bell peppers in half and remove the stems and seeds.

2. In a food processor, process the pecans, hempseed, onion, lime juice, jalapeño, Taco Seasoning Spice Blend, and salt.

3. Fill each red bell pepper half full with the prepared mixture and garnish with avocado slices and cilantro.

# NoLo's Jazzie Jammin' Beans and Rice

*Louisiana Creole cuisine is a culinary style that intermingles the influences of French, Spanish, Italian, Greek, Asian, and African flavors, all simmered together into a stew of down-home Southern cooking. Beans and Rice is standard fare, and this recipe makes good use of Creole's "Holy Trinity"—the combination of onions, celery, and bell pepper—but without the simmering. Best enjoyed while listening to jazz!*

**SERVES 2**

¼ cup sun-dried tomatoes, soaked
  and water reserved

2 tablespoons onion

1 clove garlic

2 tablespoons lemon juice, divided

1½ teaspoons fresh jalapeño pepper

1 teaspoon nama shoyu

¼ cup red bell peppers

¼ cup celery

1 teaspoon salt, divided

¼ teaspoon black pepper

1 teaspoon thyme

1 cup parsnips, peeled and chopped

1 cup sprouted lentils

1. To prepare the sauce, blend together the sun-dried tomatoes, onion, garlic, 1 tablespoon lemon juice, jalapeño, nama shoyu, red bell peppers, celery, ½ teaspoon salt, black pepper, and thyme. Add just enough sun-dried tomato soak water to create a thick sauce.

2. To make the rice, process the parsnips with ½ teaspoon salt and 1 tablespoon lemon juice in a food processor. Use the pulse function and process them just enough to make the mixture crumbly, like rice.

3. Put a scoop of parsnip rice on a plate with a scoop of sprouted lentils beside it. Spoon the sauce liberally on top of the "beans and rice."

# Protein Pesto Sprout Stacks

*This incredibly simple preparation results in a gorgeous and gourmet meal. With a reliance on fresh, ripe heirloom tomatoes, it's the perfect summer food. And if you already have pesto made, the whole shebang can be ready in under 10 minutes. No need to waste any extra time indoors!*

SERVES 2

1 cup sprouted lentils
¼ cup of your favorite pesto recipe
2 large heirloom tomatoes, in different colors if possible
1 small beet, peeled and grated
Olive oil to garnish

1. In a mixing bowl, toss the lentils with the pesto.

2. Slice each tomato into four very thick rounds. Stack one slice from each tomato on top of another, to make four stacks of two slices each, with each stack having two different colored slices.

3. Cover the two tomato stacks with a scoop of lentils. Top it all off with a sprinkle of grated beets, and garnish with a drizzle of olive oil to serve.

■ **PRO'S TIP** Perfect pesto at the ready! Homemade pesto is quick and easy—just check out the recipes in Chapter 9. But pesto tastes best when it's made with fresh herbs at the peak of their season, and that's only a few months out of the year. Your best bet is to make pesto in enormous batches, when the herbs are available and full of flavor. Freeze your pesto in ice cube trays. Then, once frozen, transfer the pesto cubes to glass jars for long-term storage. That way you'll always be able to grab a few cubes for a quick defrost, and you'll always have amazing pesto at the ready.

# Kung Pao Almonds with Raw Hoisin

*Kung Pao is a traditional dish in Szechuan-style Chinese cuisine. There's a lot of variation between the many classic and Westernized renditions, and Kung Pao is a dish that lends itself well to experimentation. This raw vegan version uses almond, sprouts, and seasonal veggies, all served up with a sweet, starchy dark hoisin-style sauce that lends this dish its earthy richness.*

### SERVES 4

¼ cup nama shoyu

¼ cup sesame oil

4 tablespoons chopped dates

½ tablespoon chopped fresh hot peppers (cayenne, jalapeño, chili)

1 clove garlic

1 tablespoon grated ginger

1 cup almonds, soaked 8–12 hours

1 cup mung bean sprouts

1 cup seasonal vegetables, chopped uniformly (asparagus tips, bell peppers, celery, cherry tomatoes, etc.)

¼ cup Jerusalem artichokes, sliced paper thin

1. In a food processor or blender, prepare the hoisin sauce by puréeing together the nama shoyu, sesame oil, dates, hot peppers, garlic, and ginger. Set aside.

2. Using a food processor, pulse the almonds until chunky.

3. In a mixing bowl, stir together the almonds, mung bean sprouts, seasonal veggies, artichokes, and prepared sauce.

4. Place the entire bowl in the dehydrator; dehydrate at 110°F for 3 hours and serve warm.

# Mushroom and Broccoli Stir-Dry

*This stir-dry is an easy, delicious dish that's reminiscent of Chinese beef with broc-coli. The sauce is simple and easy to whip up, making this a great go-to recipe any time you're in a pinch. It tastes a lot more complicated than it is, but don't worry. Chef's secrets stay in the kitchen.*

## SERVES 2

¼ cup nama shoyu

¼ cup sesame oil

2 tablespoons coconut vinegar

2 cloves garlic, crushed

1" knob of ginger, peeled and minced

2 medium portobello caps, gills removed and sliced

½ white onion, thinly sliced

1 medium bell pepper, chopped

2 cups broccoli florets

1 tablespoon sesame seeds, for garnish

1. In a small bowl, combine the nama shoyu, sesame oil, vinegar, garlic, and ginger. Set aside.

2. In a larger mixing bowl, toss together the vegetables. Pour the dressing over the veggies and mix well to completely coat.

3. Cover and allow to marinate at room temperature for 2 hours.

4. Toss again, then transfer the entire mixing bowl to the dehydrator and dehydrate at 110°F for 2–4 hours.

5. Garnish with sesame seeds and serve.

Swap It Out! If you want to bump up the satiety and protein, you could easily add in a handful of sprouted lentils, nuts or seeds of choice, or even some Completely Life-Changing Grain Crunchies (see recipe in Chapter 6), like buckwheat or quinoa.

# Orange and Ginger Stir-Dry

*This sweet stir-dry offers a tangy citrus sauce that's light and fresh and oh-so-lovely. It's a breeze to uncook and allows for endless versatility by simply swapping out the vegetables. Like salad, when it comes to stir-dry, it's really the sauce that makes or breaks it—luckily, this sauce is a big, bright, shining citrus star.*

SERVES 2

3 tablespoons orange juice

1 tablespoon apple-cider vinegar

2 tablespoons nama shoyu

1 tablespoon coconut oil, melted

1 tablespoon water

1 teaspoon agave syrup

1 teaspoon powdered ginger

2 cloves garlic, minced

1 bunch cauliflower, chopped

1 cup snap peas, trimmed and chopped

1 carrot, julienned

1 cup chopped bok choy

Orange segments, white membranes removed, for garnish

1. In a small bowl, combine the orange juice, apple-cider vinegar, nama shoyu, coconut oil, water, agave syrup, ginger, and garlic. Set aside.

2. In a larger mixing bowl, toss together the vegetables. Pour the dressing over the veggies and mix well to completely coat.

3. Cover and allow to marinate at room temperature for 2 hours.

4. Toss again, then transfer the entire mixing bowl to the dehydrator and dehydrate at 110°F for 2–4 hours.

5. Garnish with orange segments and serve.

---

*Fresh-Squeezed Calcium*

Oranges are notorious for their incredible vitamin C content, but these citrus superstars also boast an impressive cache of calcium. One orange contains about 50 milligrams of the mineral, making them an unexpected source of this precious mineral.

---

# Juicy Hues Stir-Dry

*This rainbow-bright medley is a beauty to behold. With sunny pops of orange, red, and yellow, intermingled with gorgeous green broccoli, it's a feast for the eyes as much as it is for the mouth. Well, maybe almost as much. These flavors just can't be beat, and hit the tongue from every angle: salty, sweet, spicy, and tart. Fix this up if you're ever feeling a little down. The prismatic colors and playful flavors are certain to turn your day around.*

## SERVES 2

3 tablespoons nama shoyu

2 tablespoons orange juice

1 tablespoon lime juice

1 tablespoon raw hot sauce (like Fearsome Fiery Green Hot Sauce or Fearsome Fiery Red Hot Sauce, both recipes in Ch. 9)

2 cloves garlic, minced

1 tablespoon olive oil

1 red bell pepper, chopped

1 yellow or orange bell pepper, chopped

1 bunch broccoli, chopped

1 mango, cubed

3 scallions, chopped

1. In a small bowl whisk together the nama shoyu, orange juice, lime juice, hot sauce, garlic, and olive oil. Set aside.

2. In a larger mixing bowl, toss together the bell peppers, broccoli, and mango. Pour the dressing over the veggies and mix well to completely coat.

3. Cover and allow to marinate at room temperature for 2 hours, or overnight in the refrigerator.

4. Toss again, then transfer the entire mixing bowl to the dehydrator and dehydrate at 110°F for 2–4 hours.

5. Garnish with scallions and serve.

# Totally Rawesome Sushi Rice

*Sushi rice is a specifically flavored, slightly sweet, slightly vinegared Japanese staple. Use this diverse recipe in many ways: in nori rolls, in a Deconstructed Sushi Bowl (see recipe in this chapter), or as a bed beneath any of the stir-drys (see recipes in this chapter). Easy to make and incredibly versatile, this rice stores very well, so it's a great asset to have on hand in the fridge. It's also great as a salad, tossed with your favorite dressing from Chapter 9!*

**SERVES 2**

2 cups cauliflower florets
1 tablespoon scallions, minced
1 tablespoon coconut vinegar
1 teaspoon agave syrup
¼ teaspoon salt

1. Place the cauliflower into a food processor and pulse until it becomes crumbly, like the consistency of rice.

2. Add the scallions, vinegar, agave syrup, and salt to the food processor. Pulse to combine.

3. Serve or store in a lidded class container in the refrigerator, where it will keep for 3–5 days.

# Deconstructed Sushi Bowls

*Rolling sushi can be fun and fancy, and makes for a great party presentation—but sometimes you want that great sushi flavor without the burden of bamboo mats and julienned vegetables. That's when this bowl is ideal: simple, straightforward, and with all the right tastes to hit the sushi soft spot. Enjoy!*

**SERVES 2**

3 sheets raw nori
1 batch Totally Rawesome Sushi Rice
  (see recipe in this chapter)
½ medium cucumber, diced
½ medium red bell pepper, diced
1 avocado, sliced
2 tablespoons green onions, diced
Nama shoyu, to taste

1. Cut 1 sheet of raw nori into small pieces. In a large mixing bowl, toss the Totally Rawesome Sushi Rice with the nori pieces, diced cucumber, and diced pepper.

2. Use the 2 nori sheets to line 2 soup bowls, laying the sheets in the bottom of the bowl (sheet may stick up over edge). Place ½ of the rice mixture in each bowl.

3. Top with the sliced avocado and green onions. Serve sprinkled with nama shoyu.

# Fruit Sushi Rainbow Roll

*In sushi culture, a rainbow roll is an inside-out roll that features various pieces of sashimi (raw fish) draped over the top. It's a colorful, beautiful dish, but it's certainly not raw vegan. Not to worry, we can easily adapt this look with the gorgeous gifts of vibrant fresh fruit! You can use whichever types you desire here, just remember that you're going for multiple hues and a soft texture that will lie down nicely.*

### SERVES 2

2 raw nori sheets
½ cup Totally Rawesome Sushi Rice
   (see recipe in this chapter)
½ cucumber, cut in long thin strips
Various fruits, cut into pieces
   roughly 1" × 2" × ¼"

1. Lay the nori sheets flat on a bamboo sushi mat or cutting board. Spread ¼ cup Totally Rawesome Sushi Rice along one edge. Place the cucumber on top of the rice.

2. Tightly roll up the nori roll using your fingers or the sushi mat. Use a little water to wet one edge of the nori to help create a seal.

3. Gently drape the fruit slices over the sushi roll, at a slight angle, alternating types and barely overlapping, to create a multicolored effect.

4. Let sit for 5 minutes and slice into 6 equal parts. Repeat with second piece of nori.

Swap It Out! Some fruits and veggies that are really rawesome in this dish include mango, papaya, avocado, passion fruit, thinly sliced melon, segmented oranges, and thinly sliced cucumber! Try them all!

# Ethiopian Almond Wat-a-Great-Dish!

*Ethiopian cuisine is gaining popularity in America, as we see a cultural shift towards more vegetarian-based dining. Naturally meat-free in many of its offerings, Ethiopian food is hearty, highly spiced fare that will fill you up and feed your soul. Wat is the Ethiopian word for stew, and berber is an amazing seasoning blend that you'll be able to find in any respectable spice shop. It is seriously delicious!*

### SERVES 4

1 cup sun-dried tomatoes, soaked at least 2 hours

½ cup pine nuts

2 tablespoons olive oil

1 teaspoon sea salt

½ tablespoon Berber spice

3 cups water

1 cup lentils, sprouted (refer to Soaking and Sprouting Chart in Ch. 1)

½ cup zucchini, chopped

¼ cup celery, minced

1 cup tomato, chopped

¼ cup almonds, soaked

2 tablespoons lemon juice

1. Prepare the stew base by blending together the sun-dried tomatoes, pine nuts, olive oil, salt, Berber spice, and water.

2. Mix the stew base, lentils, zucchini, celery, tomato, whole almonds, and lemon juice together in a large bowl to serve.

Swap It Out! Wat is usually eaten communally from a single plate in the center of the table. In place of utensils, the food is picked up with a sourdough pancakes called *injera*. In place of this spongy traditional flatbread, try eating this raw wat with collard greens or Swiss chard leaves.

# Curried Coconut Cream Noodles

*Another rawesomely unique creation! No nostalgia, no mimicking, no food play. This dish stands alone on its own creative concept, reliant on ingredients that are only available in the raw. So celebrate the healthy life, and dive into a plate of whipped young coconut cream and cool, crunchy kelp noodles. Trust me, you won't find anything quite like this in any other cuisine anywhere in the world!*

SERVES 2

1 cup young coconut meat

¼ cup dried coconut

½ cup young coconut water

1 teaspoon Curry Seasoning Spice Blend (see recipe in this chapter)

¼ teaspoon turmeric

2 tablespoons minced fresh basil

1 package kelp noodles, soaked in warm water

1. In a blender or food processor, blend together the young coconut meat, dried coconut, young coconut water, Curry Seasoning Spice Blend, and turmeric until smooth. Add the basil last and pulse.

2. Separate the soaked kelp noodles into serving bowls.

3. Pour the sauce over the noodles and stir to coat the noodles. Serve.

# Give-Me-More Moroccan Tajine

*Tajine is a North African dish, a type of stew that's slow-cooked in a special kind of cooking vessel. This version eschews the traditional tajine pot, and—of course— that whole cooking part. But with hearty sprouted lentils and a bold array of aromatic spices, this dish is definitely a nod towards its namesake. Serve this hearty meal straight from the dehydrator, with warm flatbreads to sop it all up.*

SERVES 2

½ cup sun-dried tomatoes, soaked

1 cup almonds, soaked

3 cups water

1 cup lentil sprouts (see Soaking and Sprouting Chart in Ch. 1)

¼ cup dulse

2 tablespoons lemon juice

1 teaspoon cinnamon

1 teaspoon cumin

Pinch of sea salt

½ teaspoon turmeric

1 cup portobello or crimini mushrooms, diced

Cilantro or parsley for garnish

1. Blend the soaked sun-dried tomatoes and almonds with water until smooth. Add in the lentil sprouts, dulse, lemon juice, cinnamon, cumin, sea salt, and turmeric and blend again until completely smooth. If you'd like a more textured stew, save out ½ cup of the sprouted lentils.

2. Pour the mixture into a large bowl and stir in the diced mushrooms (and/or reserved ½ cup whole lentil sprouts).

3. Warm in the dehydrator at 115°F for at least 1 hour.

4. Spoon into serving bowls and garnish with fresh herbs such as cilantro or parsley.

# Over-the-Top Tahini Pad Thai

*Pad thai is quintessential Thai street food: fried rice noodles in a sweet, tangy tamarind sauce. And while it's become an American favorite, it's rooted in centuries-old tradition and is one of Thailand's national dishes. This raw version nixes the egg and fish sauce, replaces peanuts with sesame tahini, and skips the fried noodles altogether—a lighter, fresher fare that's quintessential "raw revision"!*

**SERVES 2**

2 tablespoons lime juice

1 tablespoon tahini

1 tablespoon agave syrup

2 tablespoons nama shoyu

1 clove garlic, minced

½ tablespoon ginger

¼ cup sun-dried tomatoes, soaked

½ cup sun-dried tomato soak water

3 medium zucchinis

2 large carrots

½ cup mung bean sprouts

½ cup snow peas

¼ cup finely sliced scallions

2–4 tablespoons minced cilantro, for garnish

Lime wedges, for garnish

**1.** To make the pad thai sauce, place the lime juice, tahini, agave syrup, nama shoyu, garlic, ginger, and sun-dried tomatoes in a blender and blend until smooth. Gradually pour in the sun-dried tomato soak water until it blends into a thick sauce.

**2.** Using a spiral slicer or potato peeler or mandoline, make noodles with the zucchini and carrot. Alternatively, julienne or grate them.

**3.** Place the "noodles," mung bean sprouts, snow peas, and scallions on a large serving plate. Drizzle on the sauce and garnish with cilantro and slices of lime.

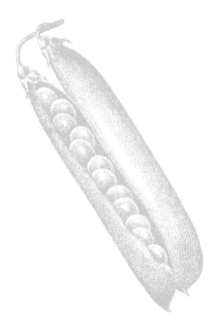

# Asian Noodles with Spicy Almond Sauce

*This sauce will rawk your world! Which is good, because you'll probably have quite a bit of leftovers. Which is really good, because then you'll have excellent sauce to sop up with all your best veggies, to smear into lettuce tacos, and to spread over crunchy crackers. Truly, this hearty, healthy almond sauce is exceptionally diverse, and it lasts for up to a week in the refrigerator. Which is good, because you'll want to put it on everything that you can.*

**SERVES 2**

1 cup almond butter

½ cup loosely packed cilantro

½ cup water, more if needed to thin

⅓ cup apple-cider vinegar

1 jalapeño pepper, seeded and chopped

3 tablespoons nama shoyu

1 tablespoon agave syrup or coconut nectar

1 tablespoon sesame oil

4 cloves garlic

1 package kelp noodles, soaked in warm water

¾ cup sprouted lentils (see Sprouting and Soaking Chart in Ch. 1)

1 cup snow or snap peas, trimmed and halved

1 large carrot, grated

2 tablespoons diced green onions

1 tablespoon sesame seeds

1. Place the almond butter, cilantro, water, vinegar, jalapeño, nama shoyu, agave syrup, sesame oil, and garlic in a food processor or blender and blend until smooth. Set aside.

2. In a large bowl, combine the soaked noodles with the lentils, peas, and carrot. Pour the desired amount of sauce over the noodles, about ½ to 1 cup, and toss well to thoroughly coat.

3. Garnish with green onions and sesame seeds before serving.

# Taco Seasoning Spice Blend

*"Taco seasoning" is a general term that refers to a mix of Latin spices that are often used when cooking ground meat, but the unfortunate fact is that most storebought mixes are loaded with sodium—or MSG! As with most things, it's best to just make your own at home. This rawesome spice mix is always handy to have around, as the flavor it imparts is surprisingly diverse. Try it sprinkled into a quick pâté, to add a little kick, or add a spoonful to cracker batter, for fiesta-flavored snackables. Even just a pinch of spice tossed with raw cucumber slices will take those veggies from dull to daring. So go ahead, have fun with it!*

### YIELDS ABOUT ¾ CUP

**4 tablespoons chili powder**

**2 tablespoons cumin**

**2 teaspoons garlic powder**

**2 teaspoons onion powder**

**2 teaspoons paprika**

**2 teaspoons sea salt**

**2 teaspoons black pepper**

**1 teaspoon red pepper flakes**

**1 teaspoon oregano**

**1 teaspoon cayenne pepper**

**1.** In a mixing bowl, combine all the ingredients and stir until uniform.

**2.** Store in a lidded glass spice jar in the pantry, where it will keep indefinitely.

### *Raw Powder?*

Most generic garlic and onion powder isn't going to be raw. You can buy really raw powders online, but you'll pay a pretty penny. Your other option, then, is to make them yourself. Sound daunting? It's not! All you need to do is thinly slice some garlic or onions, dehydrate them until they are completely crispy, and then blend them into powder using a spice or coffee grinder. Easy as pie!

# Tastes Over-the-Top-Amazing Taco Salad

*This is one mountain of Mexican-inspired flavor, exploding with savory spices and salty sensations, a veritable volcano of aesthetic variety. Not for the faint of tongue, and not for when you want something simple. This meal is fiery and fantastic and full of in-your-face flavors. So get your gear strapped on, and prepare to climb that mountain!*

### SERVES 2

1 cup sprouted lentils (see Soaking
and Sprouting Chart in Ch. 1)

2 tablespoons minced yellow onions

2 tablespoons olive oil, divided

½ teaspoon nama shoyu

1 clove garlic, crushed

2 teaspoons Taco Seasoning Spice
Blend (see recipe in this chapter)

Sea salt to taste

1 large head romaine lettuce,
shredded

1 cup cherry tomatoes, halved

4 green onions, diced

Juice of 1 lime

1 avocado, cubed

Optional: ¼ cup Soured Coconut
Cream (see recipe in Ch. 9)

Optional: ½ batch Crispy Corn Chips
(see recipe in Ch. 13)

1. To make the taco crumbles, combine the lentils, onions, 1 tablespoon olive oil, and nama shoyu in a food processor. Pulse until mixed but still textured, like taco filling. Transfer to a bowl and stir in the garlic and Taco Seasoning Spice Blend by hand. Add salt to taste and set aside.

2. In a very large mixing bowl, combine the shredded romaine, cut cherry tomatoes, and diced green onions. Drizzle with 1 tablespoon of olive oil and the lime juice. Toss to mix thoroughly.

3. Divide salad mix between 2 plates. Scoop half of the taco crumbles onto each salad. Top with the cubed avocado.

4. Garnish with the optional sour cream and chips.

# Cabbage Tacos with Walnut-Lentil Chorizo

*Chorizo is a red and spicy sausage, often eaten uncased, usually made of things you really wouldn't want to eat. But, as with almost all specialty products, it's so much more about the spice than it is about the base. So here, walnuts and sprouted lentils stand in for pork and who knows what else. With protein and fat for a rich, full flavor, this is one chorizo that your body will thank you for—and so will those sweet little piggies!*

SERVES 2

1 recipe lentil taco crumbles, from Tastes Over-the-Top-Amazing Taco Salad (see recipe in this chapter)
½ cup sprouted lentils (see Soaking and Sprouting Chart in Ch. 1)
½ cup walnuts, soaked 6–8 hours
2 tablespoons minced yellow onions
1 tablespoon olive oil
1 tablespoon apple-cider vinegar
½ teaspoon nama shoyu
2 teaspoons Taco Seasoning Spice Blend (see recipe in this chapter)
1 teaspoon paprika
1 teaspoon coriander
¼ teaspoon cloves
¼ teaspoon allspice
1 clove garlic, crushed
Sea salt to taste
1 avocado, cubed
1 mango, peeled, pitted, and chopped
2 tablespoons minced green onions
2 tablespoons chopped cilantro
2 large outer cabbage leaves, intact
Optional: 2 tablespoons Soured Coconut Cream (see recipe in Ch. 9)

1. To make the chorizo, combine the lentils, walnuts, onions, olive oil, vinegar, and nama shoyu in a food processor. Pulse until mixed but still crumbly. Transfer to a mixing bowl and stir in the Taco Seasoning Spice Blend, paprika, coriander, cloves, allspice, and garlic. Add sea salt to taste and set aside.

2. In a separate bowl, combine the avocado, mango, green onions, and cilantro. Gently toss to combine.

3. Spoon half of the chorizo mixture into each cabbage leaf. Top with half of the avocado mixture. If desired, garnish with Soured Coconut Cream before serving.

# Super-Charged Chilies Rellenos

*These stuffed peppers with a Latin twist are quick to make and absolutely delicious! And this beautiful dish makes a great centerpiece at the supper table, too. With classic south-of-the-border spices and a refreshingly sweet crunch factor, it's always sure to satisfy. And that sauce . . . unbelievable! Just try to keep from licking the spoon.*

SERVES 2

½ cup jicama, peeled and chopped

¼ cup red onion, chopped

1 tablespoon olive oil

½ cup tomato, chopped

¼ cup sun-dried tomatoes, soaked

1 teaspoon chili powder

½ tablespoon minced garlic

¼ teaspoon sea salt

½ teaspoon oregano

¼ teaspoon cumin

2 tablespoons lime juice

½ cup water

1 large yellow bell pepper

1 tablespoon minced cilantro, for garnish

1. To prepare the filling, add the jicama to a food processor and pulse until it becomes the consistency of rice. Transfer to a large bowl and stir in the red onion and olive oil.

2. To prepare the sauce, place the tomato, sun-dried tomato, chili powder, garlic, sea salt, oregano, cumin, lime juice, and water in a food processor or blender, and purée until smooth.

3. Slice the bell pepper in half. Remove the stems and seeds.

4. Fill each bell pepper half with a scoop of the filling. Pour the sauce over each bell pepper and garnish with fresh cilantro. Serve.

# In-Your-Face Italian Seasoning Spice Blend

*Italian seasoning is a basic blend of a few rather common herbs, and it can be purchased in any grocery store. However, it's hard to know the quality of the ingredients, and even organic gourmet brands may have gone through heat treatments and processing. By mixing your own spice blends at home, you can order bulk herbs from raw retailers, guaranteeing that what you're eating is always in line with your ideals and your intended lifestyle. This blend will come in handy on a very frequent basis, so it's best to make it in large batches. Once you've tried the original recipe, feel free to tweak it to your taste.*

**YIELDS A LITTLE OVER ½ CUP**

**2 tablespoons basil**
**2 tablespoons oregano**
**2 tablespoons thyme**
**2 tablespoons parsley**
**2 tablespoons marjoram**

1. In a mixing bowl, combine all the ingredients and stir until uniform.

2. Store in a lidded glass spice jar in the pantry, where it will keep indefinitely.

Swap It Out! The recipe offered above is for a very generalized Italian blend that will appeal to a wide swath. But there are other, more preference-specific spices that you may want to include in your own version. Some of these options are rosemary, garlic powder, onion powder, black pepper, red pepper, savory, or sage.

# Spiraled Spaghetti Marinara

*Some say the true test of a chef's skills is displayed in his or her marinara. So why not show off your own kitchen prowess, and make a big pile of pasta for somebody you love? After all, Italian food is totally conducive to courtship. For bonus love points, serve it up on a single plate,* Lady and the Tramp-*style. Then dig in and see if you end up nose-to-nose over a zucchini noodle. That's* amore!

**SERVES 2**

For the spiraled spaghetti:
3 large zucchinis
½ teaspoon sea salt

For the marinara sauce:
½ cup sun-dried tomatoes, soaked, soak water reserved
1 cup tomatoes, chopped
½ cup red bell pepper, chopped
1 tablespoon olive oil
1 clove garlic, minced
2 tablespoons raisins, currants, dates, or chopped apples
1½ teaspoons In-Your-Face Italian Seasoning Spice Blend (see recipe in this chapter) or other Italian seasoning

¼ teaspoon cayenne pepper powder

1. Using a spiralizer, process the zucchinis into long thin noodles. Alternately you may use a vegetable peeler, stopping when you get to the center with the seeds (see discussion in Chapter 2). Discard the zucchini centers.

2. Place the noodles in a big bowl. Sprinkle the sea salt on top and stir. Set aside.

3. In a blender or food processor, blend the soaked tomatoes and 1 cup of the soak water, along with the fresh tomatoes, bell pepper, olive oil, garlic, raisins, In-Your-Face Italian Seasoning Spice Blend, and cayenne pepper. Process until smooth.

4. Gently squeeze the noodles and discard any liquid. Toss the noodles with the sauce until completely covered. Serve on individual plates or on 1 big platter, with 2 forks.

# Tagliatelle with Rawesome Rose Sauce

*Tagliatelle is a ribbon-like, wide, and very flat pasta. Its width allows it to stand up well against thicker sauces, and here our zucchini tagliatelle clings to every creamy morsel of a rich, raw vodka sauce. Vodka sauce is essentially a blend of tomato marinara and a cream sauce. The best of both worlds! And it is, my friend. It really is.*

**SERVES 2**

3 large zucchinis

½ teaspoon sea salt

2 cups chopped tomatoes

½ cup cashews, soaked at least 2 hours

¼ cup extra-virgin olive oil

12 sun-dried tomato halves, soaked ½ hour only

1 teaspoon In-Your-Face Italian Seasoning Spice Blend (see recipe in this chapter) or other Italian seasoning

2 cloves garlic

Juice of ½ lemon

1. Using a vegetable peeler, peel the zucchini and set aside the skins. Peel the flesh into long, thin strips. Use a knife to cut each strip to the desired width (leaving wide, like tagliatelle). Stop peeling when you get to the center with the seeds, and discard the zucchini centers.

2. Place the noodles in a big bowl. Sprinkle the sea salt on top and stir. Set aside.

3. In a blender or food processor, blend the chopped tomatoes, cashews, olive oil, sun-dried tomatoes, In-Your-Face Italian Seasoning Spice Blend, garlic, and lemon juice. Process until smooth.

4. Gently squeeze the noodles and discard any liquid. Toss the noodles with the sauce until completely covered. Serve.

# Fabulous Fettuccini Alfredo

*Fettuccini Alfredo, the ultimate Italian comfort food, is a blessing to the taste buds but, alas, a burden on the body—until now! This rawesome recipe beats out unhealthy cholesterol and saturated dairy fats, and replaces them with equally rich plant oils that won't clog your arteries or hurt your heart. You want to stick around for a long time; after all, somebody's going to have to eat all this pasta.*

**SERVES 2**

**3 large zucchinis**
**½ teaspoon sea salt**
**¾ cup macadamia nuts**
**½ cup pine nuts**
**2 tablespoons lemon juice**
**2 teaspoons minced garlic**
**1 teaspoon agave syrup**
**½ teaspoon black pepper**
**½ cup water for blending**

1. Using a vegetable peeler, peel the zucchini and set aside the skins. Peel the flesh into long, thick strips. Use a knife to cut each strip to the desired width (leaving wide, like fettuccini). Stop peeling when you get to the center with the seeds, and discard the zucchini centers.

2. Place the noodles in a big bowl. Sprinkle the sea salt on top and stir. Set aside.

3. In a blender or food processor, blend the macadamias, pine nuts, lemon juice, garlic, agave syrup, and pepper. Gradually add the water as the sauce is blending. Add just enough water to help it blend into a thick, smooth sauce.

4. Gently squeeze the noodles and discard any liquid. Toss the noodles with the sauce until completely covered. Serve.

# Pesto-Packed Lasagna

*Raw lasagna is very popular in the raw gourmet culinary world, but if you're seeing it for the first time it may surprise you. Where some raw renditions of traditional cooked meals hit the nail on the head in terms of flavor and presentation, raw lasagnas are often more interpretive. This recipe takes on the layering of sauce and noodles that characterizes the classic casserole, but goes off on a rawesome tangent—which is a good thing! You don't want to simply mimic the cooked-food world. Instead, raw vegans aim to innovate—and we succeed!*

**SERVES 2**

2 medium zucchinis
¼ teaspoon sea salt
½ cup Cilantro Pumpkin Seed Pesto
   Perfection (see recipe in Ch. 9)
1 cup chopped spinach
2 large tomatoes, sliced
½ cup Simple Starter for Seed
   Cheese (see recipe in Ch. 10)
¼ cup raw olives, for garnish
Optional: ¼ cup Pine Nut Parmesan
   (see recipe in Ch. 10)

1. Create the lasagna noodles by slicing the zucchini on a mandoline or with a knife into long, very thin strips, as wide as possible. Sprinkle the strips with sea salt, and set aside to sweat.

2. In an 8" × 8" glass baking dish, lay out a thin layer of zucchini strips, slightly overlapping.

3. Spread a layer of Cilantro Pumpkin Seed Pesto Perfection over the zucchini strips, using a little less than half of the pesto. Top with a thin layer of spinach, about ½ cup, and then a layer using half the tomatoes. Finish with a layer of Simple Starter for Seed Cheese, using half the cheese (¼ cup). Repeat this process. The top layer should be zucchini noodles topped with pesto, which is why you'll use a bit less that half the pesto for each of the first 2 layers.

4. Sprinkle olives on top as a garnish. It is now ready to eat, or it can be warmed in the dehydrator at 145°F for 1 hour.

# Cheesy Rawvioli in Olio

*This is another interpretive dish, where the raw version is more of a nod in the general direction of the original inspiration—in this case, raviolis. The fundamentals are the same: thin pasta package stuffed with a savory, cheesy filling. But in this raw adaptation the ravioli "pasta" is actually made of jicama, and the "cheesy" filling is seed-based. It's lighter and healthier—and best of all it tastes amazing. Ravioli test: pass!*

**SERVES 2**

½ jicama, peeled
¼ cup Simple Starter for Seed
   Cheese (see recipe in Ch. 10)
1 tablespoon fresh basil, minced
2 tablespoons olive oil
½ cup cherry tomatoes, quartered
Optional: Pine Nut Parmesan (see
   recipe in Ch. 10), to garnish

1. Peel the jicama and slice it into very thin squares, about 2" × 2". A mandoline slicer works very well here. Set aside.

2. In a small mixing bowl, combine the Simple Starter for Seed Cheese with the basil and stir to mix well. Place ½ tablespoon of the mixture in the middle of a jicama slice. Place another jicama slice on top, gently pressing down, to create the ravioli. Repeat until all slices and cheese mixture are used.

3. Place the raviolis onto a plate. Drizzle olive oil and sprinkle with cherry tomatoes. Add Pine Nut Parmesan, if desired. Serve.

Swap It Out! Jicama makes a mean noodle, due to it's excellent texture and neutral taste. However, jicama can be hard to find. If you're unable to secure some jicama, never fear: there are plenty of other options. Beets, sweet potatoes, turnips, and other starchy root veggies can all stand in. These may change the flavor of the dish, but they'll all be delicious

# Raw Pizza Margherita

*Naples is regarded as the birthplace of modern pizza, although the tradition of piling toppings onto oiled bread is an ancient and cross-cultural phenomenon. This specific iteration—the Pizza Margherita—was created in honor of Queen Margherita Teresa Giovanni. It was 1889 and she was accompanying her king on a visit to Naples. She wanted something special, the chef and his wife conspired, and this elegant, timeless classic was conceived. The rest, as they say, is history.*

SERVES 2–4

1 batch Italian Pizza Crust (see recipe in Ch. 13)

1 cup Marinara Sauce (see recipe from Spiraled Spaghetti Marinara, in this chapter)

½ cup Simple Starter for Seed Cheese, divided (see recipe in Ch. 10)

2 medium tomatoes, sliced into rounds

Handful whole basil leaves

1. Prepare and dehydrate the Italian Pizza Crust as described in the recipe in Chapter 13.

2. Spread the Marinara Sauce onto the crust. Simple Starter for Seed Cheese onto the pizza and spread.

3. Lay tomato slices and basil leaves over the pizza. Dehydrate at 110°F for 2 hours or until warm.

# Barbecue Portobello Pizza

*As nontraditional as one can possibly get, this delicious dish takes a classic cooked favorite like pizza, then strips away its quintessential characteristics like red sauce and cheese. Processed through the postmodern food machine, and what you end up with is radical raw bliss: uncooked barbecue pizza! Enjoy!*

SERVES 2–4

1 batch Italian Pizza Crust (see recipe in Ch. 13)

1 cup Sweet and Savory Rawbecue Sauce (see recipe in Ch. 9), divided

1 large or 2 small portobello mushroom caps, cleaned, degilled, and sliced into short strips

½ cup red bell pepper strips

½ cup green bell pepper strips

½ sweet onion, sliced thin

1. Prepare and dehydrate the Italian Pizza Crust as described in the recipe in Chapter 13.

2. In a large mixing bowl, toss ½ of the barbecue sauce with the mushrooms, peppers, and onion.

3. When the Italian Pizza Crust has finished final dehydration, spread the other ½ cup barbecue sauce evenly over it. Top with the vegetable mixture.

4. Serve or return to the dehydrator at 110°F for 2 hours until warm.

SWAP IT OUT! There are so many ways to make a rawking nontraditional pizza. Start with a base of Italian Pizza Crust (see recipe in Chapter 13), then pick a theme. Maybe Curry Pizza! Mix curry seasoning into a cream sauce and use that as the pizza sauce, topped with tomatoes and Thai basil. Or . . . Mexican Pizza! With salsa, olives, and Walnut-Lentil Chorizo (see recipe in this chapter), and topped with guacamole. Or . . . Green Pizza! With pesto as the pizza sauce and all your favorite green veggies like kale shreds, asparagus tips, and scallions. Try adding a sprinkle of cilantro if you're really feeling feisty! You get the idea. So get creative!

# Horn of Plenty Ratatouille

*Ratatouille is an absolute celebration of vegetables. Such a pleasure, this naturally vegan creation that comes to us from the French region of Nice. What's that you say? A French dish that's already vegan? It's true! And that is truly something to celebrate. So raise a glass to fresh veggies and French cuisine.* Santé!

**SERVES 2**

½ medium eggplant
1½ teaspoons salt, divided
4 tablespoons olive oil
¼ cup red bell pepper
¼ cup sun-dried tomatoes, soaked
2 cloves garlic
4 tablespoons onion, diced
1 tablespoon herbes de Provence
1 cup tomatoes, thinly sliced
1 cup zucchini, thinly sliced
½ cup yellow or orange bell peppers, thinly sliced
½ cup yellow summer squash, thinly sliced

**1.** Slice the eggplant into thin round slices, sprinkle with 1 teaspoon salt, and brush with olive oil. Dehydrate at 115°F for 12 hours.

**2.** Prepare the sauce in a food processor with the S-blade by processing the red bell pepper, sun-dried tomatoes, garlic, onion, ½ teaspoon salt, and herbes de Provence until well-mixed but still chunky.

**3.** Toss the remaining ingredients and dehydrated eggplant together with the sauce and place into a casserole dish.

**4.** Serve as is, or dehydrate at 145°F for 2 hours and serve warm.

# Petite Beetloaf

*This miniature crimson cutie makes a great little meal for two, and it's a perfect choice when you want something grounding but don't need a lot of bulk. Between the walnuts and the sprouts, this delicious dish is very healthy—and it packs in a good dose of protein to boot! And, as an added bonus, this petite beetloaf is totally adorable, too!*

SERVES 2

¼ cup cabbage sprouts, mung sprouts, or other sprouts (see Soaking and Sprouting Chart in Ch. 1)

¼ cup alfalfa sprouts (see Soaking and Sprouting Chart in Ch. 1)

½ cup walnuts, soaked for 2–4 hours

2 teaspoons nama shoyu

¼ cup shredded beets

2 tablespoons of red or white onion, chopped

2 tablespoons celery hearts, chopped

Water for blending

1. Grind the sprouts and walnuts together with the nama shoyu in a food processor.

2. Add the beets, onion, and celery to the food processor. Briefly process with enough water to help the ingredients stick together.

3. Form the mixture into a little loaf, and dehydrate at 145°F for 2 hours. Then turn down the heat to 110°F and continue dehydrating for 12 hours. Serve.

***Passionate* Pairings** Serve this up with Kreative Ketchup or Sweet and Savory Rawbecue Sauce (see recipes in Chapter 9), or however else you used to enjoy your meatloaf!

# Savory Herbed Quinoa Crust

*Sometimes, nuts land heavy in the belly. They can be difficult to digest, and they're a caloric heavy-hitter for those who're watching their intake. But until recently, nuts were one of the only options when it came to uncooking and pastry-making. Well, no longer! When you're looking for something filling and delicious, but don't feel like feasting on another nut-centric course, this is the recipe that answers your prayers. Grain-based like a "real" pastry crust, this dish is a total game-changer. It's also adaptable: alter the spices however you see fit. Fill it with whatever you desire, or follow the recipes provided in the next few pages.*

YIELDS 1 QUICHE CRUST

1¼ cup quinoa flour, made from dehydrated sprouted quinoa (see recipe for Completely Life-Changing Grain Crunchies in Ch. 6)

½ cup Easy-Breezy Plant Milk (see recipe in Ch. 6)

2 tablespoons ground flaxseed

4 tablespoons water

2 tablespoons olive oil

1 clove garlic

½ teaspoon oregano

½ teaspoon thyme

½ teaspoon fennel

½ teaspoon sea salt

1. Use a spice or coffee grinder to make fine quinoa flour.

2. Place all ingredients in a large mixing bowl and stir well to mix thoroughly.

3. Turn out the dough onto a piece of wax paper. Top with additional sheet of wax paper and roll out the dough between the two pieces of wax paper. Dough should be about ¼" thick.

4. Transfer the dough to a tart pan, quiche dish, or other baking dish oiled with olive oil. Keep your fingers very wet when working with crust—it will be sticky. Use the overhang to repair any tears.

5. Dehydrate for 2 hours at 145°F. Use immediately or wrap in plastic and freeze. Will keep for months in the freezer.

# Shiitake and Asparagus Quiche

*What could be better than a melt-in-your-mouth delicious rich filling, all warm and encased in a flaky, light, subtly flavored pastry crust? Probably not much! This entrée is full of nutritious ingredients and it's utterly—indulgently!—satiating, but don't worry, it's not overly dense and it won't take you over your caloric edge.*

**SERVES 4–8**

2 cups shiitake mushrooms, diced

1 bunch asparagus, tips separated from stems

2 tablespoons olive oil

4 tablespoons lemon juice, divided

½ teaspoon salt

1 batch Savory Herbed Quinoa Crust (see recipe in this chapter)

½ cup macadamia nuts

1 clove garlic

¼ cup yellow onion

Water as needed

1. Combine the mushrooms, asparagus tips (not the stems), olive oil, 2 tablespoons lemon juice, and salt in a large mixing bowl. Toss to completely coat. Cover and let marinate for at least 2 hours, or overnight in the refrigerator.

2. Prepare the crust as directed in the recipe, drying it in a quiche pan.

3. In a food processor or blender, combine the asparagus stems (chopped, about 2 cups) with the macadamia nuts, 2 tablespoons lemon juice, garlic, and onion. Blend until smooth, adding water as needed to make a creamy thick sauce.

4. In a large bowl, mix the marinated mushrooms-and-asparagus-tips mixture with the asparagus sauce.

5. Transfer to the quiche crust and dehydrate at 110°F for 6 hours.

*Passionate* **Pairings** This dish is lovely when it's served up warm alongside a summer salad. Try the Totally Tasty Mediterranean Tomatoes, or the Sweetie Pie Scarlett Salad, both recipes in Chapter 7.

# Sorrel and Sun-Dried Tomato Quiche

*Another fancy and flavorful treat that's so much easier than it appears. Quiche is an elegant dish already, but filled with sorrel and sun-dried tomatoes, it becomes an instantly festive affair. Whether you're honoring a special occasion or simply celebrating another incredible day of this amazing life, you're sure to enjoy this delightful delicacy. Life is beautiful, no?*

**SERVES 4–8**

1 batch Savory Herbed Quinoa Crust (see recipe in this chapter)

1 cup macadamia nuts

1 avocado

2 tablespoons lemon juice

2 tablespoons sliced leeks

¼ teaspoon salt

1 cup chopped sun-dried tomatoes, soaked a least 2 hours, soak water reserved

1 bunch fresh sorrel, about 4 cups packed, shredded

1. Prepare the crust as directed in the recipe, in a quiche pan.

2. In a food processor or blender, combine the macadamia nuts, avocado, lemon juice, leeks, and salt. Blend together, adding just enough of the tomato soak water to make a thick chunky sauce. Do not overmix.

3. In a large bowl, mix the sauce with the sun-dried tomatoes and shredded sorrel.

4. Transfer to the quiche crust and dehydrate at 110°F for 6 hours.

# Fanciful Fennel Sprout Croquettes

*These unique little fritters will surprise and delight you, as the tangy interplay of fennel and mustard dances across your tongue. Cute as a button and tasty to boot, you can't go wrong with sprouted buckwheat and fresh aromatics like garlic, celery, and shallots. As an alternative to dinnertime fare, try these out as a savory breakfast. They'll be fine all night in the dehydrator, 8–12 hours, without a flip.*

SERVES 6

2 cups sprouted buckwheat (refer to Soaking and Sprouting Chart in Ch. 1)

1 tablespoon sprouted mustard seeds or 1 teaspoon mustard powder

½ cup ground flaxseed

1 clove garlic, minced

1 cup celery, diced

1 cup fennel, diced

2 shallots, minced

3 tablespoons fresh minced dill, or 1 tablespoon dried

¾ cup Marvelous Coconut Cashew Mayonnaise (see recipe in Ch. 9)

1. In a food processor, combine the buckwheat sprouts, mustard, flaxseed, and garlic and process until smooth.

2. In a large bowl, mix together all the ingredients except the mayonnaise. Form into small patties and dehydrate at 110°F for 6 hours. Flip over and dehydrate another 3–4 hours.

3. Serve warm out of the dehydrator, with a dollop of mayonnaise on each croquette.

# Shepherd's Sprout Pie

*Shepherd's pie is traditional peasants' food, a warm winter casserole that commonly includes mashed potatoes and vegetables. This raw version is slow-baked in the dehydrator to achieve a similar ambiance. It's hearty and homey and perfect for a cool night cuddled up beside the hearth. So snuggle up and dig right in!*

SERVES 2

**For the pie crust:**

1½ cups raw pecans

2 tablespoons liquid coconut oil

1 tablespoon In-Your-Face Italian Seasoning Spice Blend (see recipe in this chapter) or other Italian seasoning

2 teaspoons nama shoyu

½ clove garlic, minced

½ teaspoon sea salt

**For the filling:**

1 cup diced seasonal vegetable mix (for example, zucchini, red bell pepper, carrots, onion, or asparagus tips)

1 cup Black Sesame Gravy (from "Mashed Potatoes" with Black Sesame Gravy recipe in this chapter)

1 cup small sprouts (like fenugreek, alfalfa, clover, or lentil)

Few sprigs parsley, for garnish

1. Prepare the pie crust in a food processor. Blend the pecans until they break down and begin to stick to the walls.

2. Add the coconut oil, Italian seasoning, nama shoyu, minced garlic, and sea salt, and process until they are well-mixed.

3. Press the pecan mixture into 2 small casserole dishes to create a crust.

4. Mix the vegetables with ½ cup gravy. Fill each casserole dish with ½ cup diced vegetables. Top the vegetables with sprouts and then drizzle on the remaining ½ cup gravy.

5. Dehydrate at 110°F for 3–4 hours and serve warm. Garnish with fresh parsley.

# Wee Zucchini Hand Pies

*Hand pies are becoming something of a phenomenon, enjoyed in sweet or savory iterations and doled out by vendors from street carts to fancy establishments. This version is quick and easy and it makes for a small but memorable meal. The best part is the versatility: the recipe is written with the Zesty Italian Walnut Pâté (see recipe in Chapter 10) in mind, but the truth is that you can substitute just about any filling you can conceive of. From pâté to cheese spread to hummus to slaw, the options are as limitless as your own imagination!*

**SERVES 4**

3 medium zucchinis
1 cup warm water
1½ teaspoons sea salt, divided
1 cup spinach
2 tablespoons lemon juice
1 cup Zesty Italian Walnut Pâté (see recipe in Ch. 10)

1. Using a vegetable peeler, peel the zucchini into long, wide, and thin strips. Alternatively, use a knife to slice the zucchini into strips.

2. Mix warm water and 1 teaspoon sea salt in a large bowl. Soak the zucchini strips in the salt water for 5–10 minutes to soften.

3. Mince the spinach and place it into a small bowl. Wilt the spinach by massaging in ½ teaspoon sea salt and the lemon juice. Set aside.

4. Line each of 4 ramekins with the zucchini strips in a single layer, about 1" overlapping the edge of the ramekin.

5. Place a small layer of pâté into each ramekin. Top with a single layer of spinach and a second layer of pâté.

6. Fold the zucchini strips over the filling to cover. Serve.

# Tiny Tasty Mushroom Tartlets

*The name says it all, does it not? These tartlets are tiny, adorable, precious little pies. And they're tasty, dynamic, complex, and nuanced flavor combinations contained within a mini crust. With mushrooms and a mix of nuts providing protein and myriad micronutrients, these little tartlets have it all going on. And don't be intimidated by this long ingredients list! Supper will be ready to serve in under 30 minutes—promise.*

SERVES 4

For the crust:
1 cup walnuts
½ cup Brazil nuts
2 tablespoons liquid coconut oil
1 teaspoon sea salt

For the cashew sauce:
1 cup cashews
2 tablespoons olive oil
1 clove garlic, minced
2 tablespoons lemon juice
2 tablespoons nama shoyu
1 tablespoon chives, chopped
½ tablespoon rosemary, chopped
½ teaspoon black pepper

For the filling:
½ cup crimini mushrooms, sliced thin
½ cup hearts of celery, sliced thin

1. To prepare the crust, place the walnuts, Brazil nuts, liquid coconut oil (place container in warm water to melt), and salt in a food processor or blender and process until smooth.

2. Divide the crust into fourths and press into 4 small ramekins.

3. In a food processor, process the cashews until well-broken-down. Gradually add the olive oil, garlic, lemon juice, and nama shoyu. Blend until smooth. Add the chives, rosemary, and black pepper last and briefly pulse to mix. Set aside the cashew sauce.

4. Place a layer of sliced mushrooms and thinly sliced celery in the crust in each ramekin bowl. Fill with the blended cashew sauce and serve.

## Chapter 13

# Crackers, Breads, and Other Snacks

If there's anything that could possibly be difficult about the raw vegan lifestyle, it would be the lack of convenience foods. Sure there are always baby carrots for crunching, but baby carrots can get old fast. Success depends on an arsenal of spectacular snack foods that make it easy to eat on the go, or grab a quick munchy for in-between meals.

The following chapter is filled with ideas for just this sort of pantry staple. Try to keep a few choices on hand at all times; you can store excess items in the freezer to keep them from spoiling. From crackers to accompany your raw cheese or hummus, to flatbreads just waiting for a thick layer of guacamole, to fancified nuts that you'll barely be able to keep your hands off, this chapter has a recipe for every possible craving. Salty, sweet, savory, spicy, and any combination you can imagine—you're covered!

# Go-Go Granola Bars

*Once you get into a living foods groove, eating this way all the time can seem like second nature. However, when life gets busy, it can knock you off your game. When that happens you'll want to be prepared. That's where these Go-Go Granola Bars can make a big difference! Keep a container of these in the pantry for those hectic days that life can throw your way. When things get too busy to uncook or even to hit the grocery store, you can always grab one of these goodies and stay on the go-go-go!*

SERVES 8

1½ cups dry buckwheat

1 cup almonds, soaked (see Soaking and Sprouting Chart in Ch. 1)

½ cup dates or raisins, soaked for 1 hour

1 cup flaxseed, soaked (see Soaking and Sprouting Chart in Ch. 1)

½ cup young coconut meat

3 tablespoons agave syrup

1 tablespoon pumpkin pie spice

2 teaspoons cinnamon

1. Soak the raw buckwheat in 4 cups water for 30 minutes. Drain, rinse, and sprout for 24 hours.

2. Using a food processor or blender, process all the ingredients until well-mixed. Do not overprocess—mixture should still be chunky.

3. Form the resulting mixture into rectangle bar shapes and place on dehydrator trays with non-stick sheets. Dehydrate at 145°F for 2–3 hours. Flip over the bars and continue dehydrating at 110°F for another 12 hours or until dry.

4. Store in a tightly-lidded container in the cupboard. These will keep for a few months.

# Mini Monsters

*In health food circles, green smoothies are often affectionately referred to as "green monsters"—and these little nuggets of protein-packed goodness are like little green solid smoothies. They're another great asset to have around when life tosses you a curve ball. These little treats are energy-dense and full of important, invigorating nutrients. Try to keep a few on you at all times, but be careful—they're tasty and may tempt you into nibbling!*

**SERVES 8**

2 cups sprouted buckwheat (see Soaking and Sprouting Chart in Ch. 1)
1 cup dried coconut
1 cup pistachios
¼ cup dates, pitted and chopped
2 tablespoons agave syrup
1 tablespoon spirulina
1 tablespoon carob

1. Dehydrate the sprouted buckwheat until crunchy, about 6 hours at 110°F.

2. In a coffee grinder, grind the dried coconut to a flour.

3. In a food processor or blender, process all the ingredients together until well-combined and chunky. Form into little rectangle nuggets, about 1" × 1" × 2".

4. Dehydrate at 145°F for 2 hours. Turn down the temperature to 110°F and flip the nuggets. Continue dehydrating for 12 hours or until dry.

5. Store in a tight-lidded container in the refrigerator. These will keep for a few weeks.

# Unbaked Banana-rama

*This raw banana bread is a lovely, crumbly treat. It's easy to whip up and a good way to use your old and browning bananas. You know, bananas are a lot like love: sweeter and sweeter as time goes by! Just make sure you watch over them and use them before they spoil.*

SERVES 6

2 cups ripe bananas

3 cups almond flour (pulp from making milk, or ground whole almonds)

2 tablespoons liquid coconut oil

1 teaspoon vanilla extract

1 teaspoon cinnamon

¼ teaspoon sea salt

1 cup flaxseed

1. In a food processor or blender, cream the bananas. Pour in the almond flour, coconut oil, vanilla, cinnamon, and salt, and continue processing until well-mixed. Pour into a large bowl and set aside.

2. Grind the flaxseed into a coarse powder with a coffee grinder. Stir into the almond flour mixture.

3. Put ½ of the batter back into the food processor or blender and mix briefly. Then remove and repeat the process with the second ½ of the mixture.

4. Spread the batter about ¼" thick onto dehydrator trays with nonstick sheets. Use a spatula to score the batter into squares.

5. Dehydrate at 145°F. After 2 or 3 hours, flip the bread over. Turn heat down to 110°F and continue dehydrating for 8 hours.

*Passionate* Pairings This sweet bread works well as a breakfast or a quick on-the-go snack. Add a little flavored nut butter, like Very Vanilla Almond Butter or "Silk Chocolate" Hazelnut Spread (see recipes in Chapter 10) for protein and added satiety. You could even eat this as a dessert! Just drizzle with a little Unbelievable Raspberry Coulis (see recipe in Chapter 9). Delicious!

# Garlic Lover's Greatest Crackers

*These little crackers aren't for the faint of heart—or breath. Garlic is used in both culinary and medical applications, and, of course, wherever those two disciplines intersect—like right here in raw food living! Garlic boosts the immune system, cleanses the blood, fights off viruses, and helps to clear the digestive tract of harmful bacterial invaders. It's a true super food, recognized as such by the conventional as well as the alternative medical practices. Just one thing: don't serve these for date night!*

SERVES 6

2 cups sunflower seeds, soaked for 4 hours

½ cup ground flaxseed

½ cup young coconut meat

4–6 cloves garlic, sliced

1 teaspoon garlic powder

2 tablespoons water

2 tablespoons agave syrup

½ teaspoon salt

1. In a food processor or blender, process all the ingredients together until well-mixed but still chunky.

2. Spread the resulting mixture onto dehydrator trays with nonstick sheets. Score the crackers into desired size using a spatula.

3. Dehydrate at 145°F for 2 hours. Flip the crackers and continue dehydrating at 115°F for 12 hours until crunchy. Store in an airtight container in the pantry; will keep for weeks.

# Good Earth Crackers

*Straight from the ground and filled with hearty cereal grains, energy-dense seeds, plants and sap, and fruit and juice, these uncomplicated crackers work well with any savory dip or spread—and they merge their flavors to match their accompaniment. Solid, unrefined, natural flavors speak to simple meals and unfussy preparations, which is part of what being raw vegan is all about! Such practical players are helpful to have on hand in the cupboard, where they'll keep for up to two months in an airtight container.*

SERVES 6

1 cup buckwheat
1 cup sunflower seeds
½ cup flaxseed
4 tablespoons agave syrup
1 teaspoon sea salt
2 tablespoons lemon juice
½ jalapeño pepper

1. Soak the buckwheat for 30 minutes. Rinse and drain. Soak the sunflower seeds for 1 hour. Rinse and drain. Soak the flaxseed for 30 minutes in ½ cup water. Do not drain.

2. Place all the ingredients into a food processor or blender and process until well-mixed and chunky.

3. Spread the cracker batter on dehydrator trays with nonstick sheets and use a spatula to score into desired size. Dehydrate at 145°F for 2 hours. Turn down heat to 110°F and dehydrate for 12 hours or until crunchy.

# Tomato, Basil, and Flax Crackers

*Nuts and seeds are delicious in crackers, and those staples certainly make an appearance in this recipe. But these crackers kick things up a notch by including the phytonutrients and antoxidants from a variety of vegetables as well. How rawesome is that?*

SERVES 6

1 cup sunflower seeds
½ cup sun-dried tomatoes
2 cups flaxseed
½ cup celery, finely chopped
¼ cup dates, pitted and chopped
1 tablespoon jalapeño pepper,
  seeded and minced
2 tablespoons olive oil
2 teaspoons sea salt
1 cup chopped fresh tomatoes
4 tablespoons fresh basil, chopped

1. Soak the sunflower seeds in water for 4 hours. Soak the sun-dried tomatoes for 3 hours.

2. Grind the flaxseed into a coarse powder using a high-speed blender or spice or coffee grinder. You may have to do this in batches. Set aside.

3. Process sunflower seeds, sun-dried tomatoes, celery, dates, jalapeño pepper, olive oil, and sea salt in a food processor or blender.

4. Add the fresh tomatoes, basil, and ground flaxseeds and pulse until all ingredients are well-mixed.

5. Spread the mixture about ¼" thick onto dehydrator trays with nonstick sheets. Use a spatula to score the batter into cracker shapes.

6. Dehydrate at 145°F for 2 hours. Turn over the crackers and continue dehydrating at 115°F for an additional 8 hours. Store in an airtight container in the pantry for up to 2 months.

# Seriously, Sauerkraut Crackers!

*These crackers are a seriously efficient, sneaky way to smuggle sauerkraut into unsuspecting diners. Use these innocent-seeming snacks to slip your friends and family a healthy dose of live, active, healing probiotics. Or, just eat the whole batch yourself as a supplement to your already beautiful, bountiful diet. No one will ever be the wiser!*

**SERVES 6**

2 cups sunflower seeds, soaked for 4 hours

1 cup You Won't Believe How Simple Sauerkraut (see recipe in Ch. 10) or storebought unpasteurized sauerkraut

2 cloves garlic

¼ teaspoon sea salt

½ cup ground flaxseed

1 cup water

1. Process sunflower seeds, sauerkraut, garlic, and sea salt in a food processor or blender.

2. Add the ground flaxseed and water, and pulse until all ingredients are well-mixed.

3. Spread the mixture onto 2 dehydrator trays with nonstick sheets. Use a spatula to score the batter into desired sizes.

4. Dehydrate at 145°F for 2 hours. Turn over the crackers and continue dehydrating at 115°F for an additional 8 hours.

***Passionate* Pairings** These are mild, neutral crackers that work especially well as open-faced sandwiches. Try them in any number of recipes such as the Practically Perfect Puttanesca Bruschetta or the Open-Faced Avo-Smash (see recipes in Chapter 11), or any other spectacular sandwich you can conceive of!

# Hoppin' Poppin' Pumpkin Curry Crackers

*Pepitas, or green pumpkin seeds, are a superstar in the nutrition scene, with high levels of protein, iron, zinc, and omega-3 fats. Zinc can be somewhat cumbersome to procure in an entirely raw diet, which makes these crunchy gems quite the asset. Here they're paired with curry for a pleasantly spicy, totally flavorful cracker. Eat up!*

**SERVES 6**

1 cup flaxseed

2 cups green pumpkin seeds

1 cup sunflower seeds, soaked at least 2 hours

1 cup orange juice

¼ cup chopped onion

¼ cup dates, pitted and chopped

2 garlic cloves

1 tablespoon Curry Seasoning Spice Blend (see recipe in Ch. 12) or other curry powder

1 teaspoon sea salt

1. Grind the flaxseed into a powder using a coffee or spice grinder, or a high-speed blender.

2. In a food processor or blender, process together all the ingredients into a smooth batter.

3. Spread the batter ¼" thick onto dehydrator trays lined with nonstick sheets. Score the batter with a spatula into square or triangle shapes.

4. Start dehydrating at 145°F. After 2 hours, turn the dehydrator down to 110°F.

5. After 4 hours, remove the nonstick sheet and flip the crackers. Continue dehydrating for an additional 8–12 hours. Store in an airtight container, will keep for up to 2 months.

***Passionate* Pairings** Serve these as tasty flatbread along with a simple spring salad, such as the Lettuce Lover's Little Slice of Heaven or the Good, Clean Green Eats (recipes in Chapter 7). You can also use them as a dipper for your favorite chilled soup, like the Chunky Cherry Walnut Gazpacho or the Farmer's Harvest Hearty Gazpacho (recipes in Chapter 8).

# Traditional Sprouted Essene Bread

*Essene bread is named after an ancient, desert-dwelling religious group, the Essenes. This band of Jewish people was one of the first cultures to sprout their grains before using them, which as you now know is an important part of digestion and nutrient absorption. The Essenes would "bake" their bread at low temperatures in the desert sun—you don't have to try this, but your dehydrator is a perfect substitute. So give this millennia-old raw foods recipe a try!*

**SERVES 4**

2 cups wheat berries, soaked and then sprouted 2 days
1½ cups water
2 tablespoons agave syrup
1 tablespoon olive oil
1 teaspoon sea salt

**1.** In a food processor or blender, grind the sprouted wheat and water together until a dough forms.

**2.** Mix in the agave syrup, olive oil, and sea salt. Briefly process until all the ingredients are mixed together.

**3.** Spread the mixture with a spatula onto dehydrator trays with nonstick sheets. Spread the mixture evenly, about ½" thick, and score into squares.

**4.** Dehydrate at 145°F for 3 hours. Flip the bread over and continue dehydrating at 110°F for 8 hours. Will keep in an airtight container for up to 4 weeks.

Swap It Out! This template adapts well to most any grain, so feel free to swap out the wheat for rye, barley, kamut, or any other that you prefer.

# Simple Tasty Toast

*May I introduce: raw toast! This food is not quite a crispy cracker, but it has too much crunch to be called a bread so toast it is! But no matter what you call it, this is a recipe to make again and again. Its endless versatility, delightfully nutty yet neutral flavor, and high nutrient content make this recipe the toast of the town!*

**SERVES 6**

2 cups hulless oats, soaked and sprouted for 12–24 hours
½ cup macadamia nuts
½ cup sunflower seeds, soaked at least 2 hours
1 cup ground flaxseed
1 cup tomato purée
1½ cups Irish Moss Paste (see recipe in Ch. 14)
1 tablespoon olive oil

1. In a food processor or blender, process together the oats, macadamia nuts, and sunflower seeds to make a mash. Do not overprocess.

2. Transfer this mixture to a large bowl and add the rest of the ingredients, mixing well to incorporate. Using your hands works best here.

3. Spread the batter ¼" thick onto dehydrator trays lined with nonstick sheets. Score the batter with a spatula into the desired shape.

4. Start dehydrating at 145°F. After 2 hours, turn the dehydrator down to 110°F.

5. After 4 hours, remove the nonstick sheet and flip the crackers. Continue dehydrating for an additional 8–10 hours. Store in an airtight container for up to 2 months.

### Spotlight on Hulless Oats

Almost all oats sold in the grocery store, and even in specialty shops, are not raw. They must be mechanically hulled and in the case of rolled oats flattened, and this is a hot process. But hulless oats are a specific variety that is grown without a hull at all, which means that they don't need to be processed and can be sold raw. You can order hulless oats—the only truly raw oat—from raw foods retailers online such as: *www.sproutpeople.com.*

# Onion Bread or Buns

*At first glance this may seem like a not-so-good idea, what with the pungency of raw onion and the quantity called for in this recipe. Are you nervous? Never fear! After lengthy dehydration the onions really mellow out—almost as though they've been caramelized—and become soft and chewy and sweet and, well, pretty dang amazing! These onion buns make a lovely sandwich bread, and can also be formed into little rolls to serve as burger buns.*

**SERVES 6**

**2 cups flaxseed**
**2 cups sunflower seeds**
**4 cups sweet onion**
**½ cup olive oil**
**¼ cup nama shoyu**
**2 teaspoons fresh thyme**

1. Grind the flaxseed to a powder in a coffee or spice grinder. Set aside.

2. Grind the sunflower seeds in a food processor. Pour into a large mixing bowl and set aside.

3. Process the sweet onions in a food processor until they are small pieces.

4. Stir and mix all ingredients together in the mixing bowl.

5. Spread the mixture onto 2 dehydrator trays lined with nonstick sheets. Using a spatula, score the sheets into desired cracker shape. Dehydrate at 145°F for 2 hours. Lower the temperature to 110°F and continue dehydrating 4 hours, then flip the crackers onto mesh sheets and remove the nonstick sheets. Continue dehydrating for another 4 hours, but watch to make sure they do not overdry (the edges will curl if they get too dry). Store in an airtight container in the pantry for up to 2 months.

# New York Rye

*Rye bread is characterized less by the taste of the rye itself and more by the inclusion of the uniquely flavored caraway fruit. These minuscule fruits, which many people call caraway seeds, have a pungent flavor unlike any other spice. It tastes, well, just like rye bread—in the raw!*

SERVES 6

2 cups rye berries, soaked and sprouted (see Soaking and Sprouting Chart in Ch. 1)

2½ cups zucchini roughly chopped, about 2 medium zucchinis

1 cup ground flaxseed

1 cup water

2 tablespoons caraway seeds

1. Grind the rye berries seeds in a high-speed blender (if possible) or a food processor or regular blender. Pour into a large mixing bowl and set aside.

2. Process the zucchinis in a food processor until they are small pieces.

3. Stir and mix all ingredients together in the mixing bowl.

4. Spread the mixture onto 2 dehydrator trays lined with nonstick sheets. Using a spatula, score the sheets into desired cracker shape. Dehydrate at 145°F for 2 hours. Lower the temperature to 110°F and continue dehydrating 8–12 hours. After 4 hours, flip the crackers onto mesh sheets and remove the nonstick sheets. Watch to make sure they do not overdry (the edges will curl if they get too dry). Store in an airtight container in the pantry for up to 2 months.

### Watch Your Teeth

Rye berries are very tough, even after soaking. Make sure you process them completely, breaking each kernel into bits. Otherwise, you're liable to end up breaking something else!

# Sweet Portuguese Bread

*Sweet Portuguese Bread is a treat often served for Christmas or Easter, but you can enjoy it any time of year—or any time of day—that you please. It makes a great breakfast, especially when it's smeared with a little almond butter or coconut butter or fruit compote. It's also delicious when it's served with something savory, such as a soup or supersized salad. Sounds diverse, right? Well, it is, so give it a whirl and see how you like it. You may just be surprised!*

## SERVES 4

1 cup almonds

2 cups flaxseed

1 cup grated apple

2 tablespoons agave syrup

2 tablespoons orange juice

2 teaspoons cardamom

½ teaspoon sea salt

½ cup Easy-Breezy Plant Milk (see recipe in Ch. 6)

1. Soak the almonds in water for 12 hours. Drain and rinse the almonds.

2. Grind the flaxseed into a coarse powder with a coffee grinder.

3. Place all ingredients in a food processor or blender, adding the flaxseed last, and process until well-mixed. Mixture should be slightly thick and chunky.

4. Form the mixture into an oval-shaped loaf and slice into round, toast-sized pieces.

5. Place the round slices onto dehydrator trays with nonstick sheets. Dehydrate at 145°F for 3 hours. Flip the bread over and continue dehydrating at 110°F for 2 hours or until the desired texture is reached. Do not overdry (edges will curl if it gets too dry). Store in an airtight container in the pantry for up to 2 months.

# Italian Pizza Crust

*This savory, herb-infused sprouted grain crust is the perfect platter for any pizza topping you can conjure up. But feel free to be creative: roll it out into long strips and braid it into bread sticks, or create a little hollow pocket and stuff it before dehydrating for a fantastic raw calzone. The flavor of the dough carries the recipe all on its own, so it also works well as a cracker or flatbreads.*

**SERVES 4**

2 cups buckwheat, sprouted (refer to Soaking and Sprouting Chart in Ch. 1)

1 cup sunflower seeds, soaked

½ cup sun-dried tomatoes, soaked

1 tablespoon olive oil

1 tablespoon agave syrup

¼ teaspoon cayenne pepper powder

1 tablespoon In-Your-Face Italian Seasoning Spice Blend (see recipe in Ch. 12) or other Italian seasoning

½ teaspoon sea salt

1. In a food processor, combine all ingredients and process until well-mixed with small chunks. They should be mixed long enough to form a batter-like consistency.

2. Form the dough into 4 circles, about ¼" thick. Make the edges a little thicker to form a crust. Dehydrate at 145°F for 2 hours. Flip over the dough and continue dehydrating at 110°F for 4 hours. Serve immediately or store in an airtight container in the fridge for up to a week.

# Not Your Typical Tortillas

*Authentic Mexican tortillas are pressed from hand-ground maize flour, called masa. And these delicious raw versions are . . . not. There's no corn, no wheat, no flour, and no cooking! The resulting wrap is soft and pliable, suitable for creating the best of burritos, enchiladas, or whatever else you'd like to create! After all, variety is the spice of life, so feel free to have some fun!*

SERVES 4

2 cups young coconut meat
¼ cup red bell pepper, chopped
1 tablespoon beet juice
¼ teaspoon salt

1. Blend together all the ingredients in a food processor or blender until completely smooth.

2. Spread the burrito wrap mixture onto 2 dehydrator trays lined with nonstick sheets. Dehydrate at 115°F for 4 hours.

3. Cut the burrito wraps into 4 round tortilla shapes. Fill with your favorite veggies or pâté.

Swap It Out! This recipe uses red bell pepper and beet juice to give the wrapper a lovely reddish hue, but you can substitute other veggies to change the color: try spinach juice to make them green, or golden beet juice and turmeric for a yellow cast. Food tastes so much better when it's beautiful!

# Crispy Corn Chips

*Remember that lip-smacking saltiness that hovered at the corners of your mouth? That crunchy chip that was so satisfying to bite down on? Well, it's time to regain that long-lost memory. Celebrate for salsa's sake! Three cheers for lonely hummus everywhere! The corn chip has returned, and it's catching up with all its old friends—and this recipe is your invitation to the party!*

SERVES 4

½ cup ground flaxseed
½ cup water
6 cups sweet corn
½ cup medium red bell pepper
Juice from 1 lime
½ teaspoon sea salt, more to sprinkle on top

1. Combine the ground flaxseed with the water and set aside.

2. In a food processor or blender, purée the corn, bell pepper, lime juice, and salt. You may have to do this in batches. Transfer to a large bowl, add in the flaxseed mixture, and stir to completely combine.

3. Spread the batter over 3 dehydrator trays lined with nonstick sheets. Sprinkle with extra salt, if desired, and use a spatula to score the sheets into chip shapes. Dehydrate 2 hours at 145°F, then turn the temperature down to 115°F and continue dehydrating for 8 hours. Flip the chips and peel away the nonstick sheets, and continue dehydrating until very crispy, up to 4 hours. Store in an airtight container in the pantry for up to 2 weeks.

# Groovy Green Corn Chips

*Now that we've successfully conquered the corn chip, it's time to put your own special spin on the dish, right? And naturally, in the world of raw and healthy foods, your own little spin looks a little green! Would you expect anything else? Of course not. Adding green elements to unsuspecting foods is what raw enthusiasts do best!*

SERVES 4

½ cup ground flaxseed
½ cup water
6 cups sweet corn
2 cups dark leafy greens, like kale, collards, or chard
½ teaspoon sea salt, more to sprinkle on top
¼ teaspoon cayenne pepper

1. Combine the ground flaxseed with the water and set aside.

2. In a food processor or blender, purée the corn, greens, ½ teaspoon of sea salt, and cayenne pepper. You may have to do this in batches. Transfer to a large bowl, add in the flaxseed mixture, and stir to completely combine.

3. Spread the batter over 3 dehydrator trays lined with nonstick sheets. Sprinkle with extra salt, if desired, and use a spatula to score the sheets into chip shapes. Dehydrate 2 hours at 145°F, then turn the temperature down to 115°F and continue dehydrating for 8 hours. Flip the chips and peel away the nonstick sheets, and continue dehydrating until very crispy, up to 4 hours. Store in an airtight container in the pantry for up to 2 weeks.

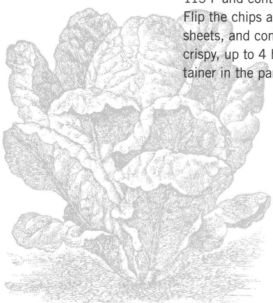

# Sweet and Spicy Zucchini Jerky

*This is an amazingly savory treat, earthy and salty and just a little bit spicy. It comes out tough, which can be just the thing you're craving when you're in a jerky mood. It also dances around a distinctly "meaty" flavor, making this a great addition to soups, sandwiches, salads, and any other spot where bacon would traditionally fit. But don't be afraid to just eat it out of your hand, either on-the-go or as a great workplace snack. After all, all that chewing facilitates heavy thinking!*

**SERVES 4**

¼ cup olive oil

¼ cup apple-cider vinegar

3 tablespoons agave syrup

2 tablespoons lucuma powder

¼ teaspoon salt, more to taste

¼ teaspoon paprika

⅛ teaspoon cayenne pepper

⅛ teaspoon black pepper

3 large zucchinis sliced into rounds

1. In a large mixing bowl, whisk together the oil, vinegar, agave syrup, lucuma powder, salt, paprika, cayenne pepper, and black pepper. Add the zucchini rounds and toss thoroughly to coat.

2. Lay out rounds on unlined dehydrator trays and dehydrate at 145°F for 2 hours, then continue dehydrating at 110°F for 2–6 more hours, until jerky is completely dried out but still pliable. Store in an airtight container in the pantry, for up to a month.

# BBQ Babies

*Little League games? Summer at the river? Backyard barbecues? Weekend camping trips? Picnics and potato salad? What's the memory that you associate with the strong, distinctive flavor and feeling of BBQ-flavored chips? Most likely it involves sun, and childhood, and lots and lots of fun. This is exactly what BBQ should be—and it's exactly how this raw manifestation of those pleasure-soaked memories will make you feel, like a kid all over again!*

### SERVES 4

4 cups zucchini

½ cup sun-dried tomatoes, soaked at least 2 hours

1 clove garlic

2 tablespoons olive oil

1 tablespoon apple-cider vinegar

1 tablespoon yacon syrup

1 tablespoon agave syrup

½ tablespoon chili powder

2 teaspoons onion powder

1 teaspoon paprika

1. Slice the zucchini thinly and set it aside. Place all the remaining ingredients in a blender and blend together until smooth.

2. Place the zucchini into a casserole dish or large bowl and marinate in the prepared sauce for 2 hours.

3. Lay out rounds on unlined dehydrator trays and dehydrate at 145°F for 2 hours, then continue dehydrating at 110°F for 2–6 more hours, until the zucchini is crunchy. Store in a sealed container in the pantry for up to 4 weeks.

Swap It Out! Zucchini is the most common type of summer squash, and its relatively neutral flavor makes it a frequent player in the raw chef's kitchen. However, zucchini isn't the only summer squash that can make an appearance. In this recipe you can substitute green or yellow crooknecks, or any other soft-skinned heirloom variety that's available.

# Sweet Tater French Drys

*If you can take greasy fried street food like falafel and make it raw, if you can take an American classic like meaty burgers and mimic them raw, if you can find a raw approximation of tuna fish and grilled cheese and sloppy Ruebens, than you must, you simply must, make something to go along with them. Enter the rawesome french fry. This is a super-easy recipe and it "cooks" up quickly as well. Pop it in the dehydrator when you're finishing up your lunch, and you'll have warm fries waiting come dinnertime.*

**SERVES 2**

2 medium sweet potatoes, peeled
1 tablespoon olive oil
1 teaspoon paprika
Sea salt to taste

1. Peel each potato and slice them into very thin, long strips, like fries.

2. In a large mixing bowl, place all ingredients and toss well to coat. Tongs work well here.

3. Lay the fries on unlined dehydrator trays. Dehydrate at 145°F for 2 hours, then turn down to 115°F and continue dehydrating for another 3 hours. Do not overdry. Eat immediately; these do not store well.

# Spicy Marinated Nuts

*Plain raw nuts are great on their own, popped into your mouth for a quick and easy snack, but sometimes you want something extra special. And why not? Don't those awesome nuts deserve it? Shouldn't they get to play dress-up once in a while, too?*

**SERVES 4**

3 cups mixed nuts (Brazil nuts, cashews, walnuts, pecans, or almonds)
4 tablespoons agave syrup
2 tablespoons nama shoyu
1 tablespoon cinnamon
¼ teaspoon cayenne pepper powder

1. Mix all ingredients together in a bowl until the nuts are covered.

2. Let the nuts marinate for 3 hours at room temperature.

3. Pour off excess liquid and store nuts in an airtight container in the refrigerator.

# "Roasted" Sunflower Seeds

*This is a simple recipe that's open to many possible directions. On its own it's distinctly reminiscent of traditional roasted sunflower seeds, with the nama shoyu lending its salty, "browned" flavor. From this template you can customize as you see fit. Try adding fresh herbs and spicy elements, like garlic, red onions, or jalapeño blended into the marinade. Or, throw in a teaspoon of any of the spice blends that appear in Chapter 12. If you really want to get crazy, you could drizzle in some agave syrup for a surprising sweet twist!*

SERVES 4

4 cups sunflower seeds, soaked for
  6–8 hours
½ cup olive oil
½ cup nama shoyu
¼ cup water
4 tablespoons lemon juice

1. Drain and rinse the sunflower seeds. Set aside.

2. In a blender, blend all remaining ingredients together until smooth.

3. Place the sunflower seeds into a large bowl. Pour in the prepared marinade and let the seeds soak for 3 hours.

4. Drain the marinade. Spread the seeds in a single layer on dehydrator trays. Dehydrate at 145°F for 2 hours. Turn down heat to 110°F and continue dehydrating for 24 hours or until desired dryness is reached (should be nice and crunchy). Store in an airtight container in the pantry for up to a month.

# Oiled Rosemary Cashews

*There's just something indescribable about that flavor pairing of rosemary and sea salt, isn't there? Magic happens. As far as taste sensations go, these rich and hearty cashews are similar to crusty chunks of fresh-baked rosemary sea salt bread. Enjoy a handful (or two) with your next bowl of soup, and capture that old familiar feeling.*

SERVES 4

3 cups cashews
¼ cup extra-virgin olive oil
1 tablespoon dried rosemary
½ teaspoon sea salt

1. Soak the cashews for 6–8 hours. Rinse and drain.

2. In a large mixing bowl, stir all ingredients together.

3. Spread the cashews onto dehydrator trays.

4. Dehydrate at 110°F for 24 hours or until the desired dry, crunchy texture is reached. Store in an airtight container in the pantry for up to a month.

# Cucumber Crunchies

*These unique Cucumber Crunchies are a great way to add a little texture to your life. Try them crumbled on top of salads, stirred into soups, or slide them between the layers of soft veggies in your favorite sandwich. But be aware: dehydrating will intensify the bitterness in cucumber skin. Some people don't mind (and even enjoy) this flavor, but others find it off-putting. If you're not a fan of bitterness, take the time to peel your cukes as part of your recipe prep.*

SERVES 4

1 tablespoon olive oil
1 teaspoon apple-cider vinegar
1 teaspoon dried dill
1 clove garlic, crushed
Dash of sea salt
2 extra-large cucumbers, the bigger around the better, sliced into rounds

1. In a large mixing bowl, whisk together the oil, vinegar, dill, garlic, and salt. Add the cucumber rounds and toss thoroughly to coat.

2. Lay out the rounds on unlined dehydrator trays and dehydrate at 145°F for 2 hours, then continue dehydrating at 110°F for 2–6 more hours, until cucumbers are crispy. Store in a sealed container in the pantry for up to a month.

# French Kale Chips

*Kale chips are a gift given to the world by industrious raw fooders. That's right, this is an entirely raw-inspired, raw-conceived, raw-centric snack. No mimicry, no nostalgia. Nothing pretending to be anything else. Just kale—delightful, abundant, beautiful kale—shining in all of its health-giving glory. Thank you, raw foods movement!*

**SERVES 4**

6 cups kale
¼ cup olive oil
¼ cup apple-cider vinegar
½ teaspoon sea salt
2 tablespoons lemon juice
1 clove garlic
2 tablespoons herbes de Provence

1. Remove the stems from the kale and discard. Tear the leaves into big pieces. Place into a very large bowl and set aside.

2. Place all the remaining ingredients, except the herbes de Provence, in a blender or food processor and blend until smooth. Add the herbes de Provence last and briefly pulse until well-mixed.

3. Mix the sauce with the kale in a bowl. Use your hands to ensure the kale is well-coated with the sauce.

4. Place the kale on dehydrator trays. Dehydrate at 115°F for 4–8 hours or until dry. Store in a sealed container in the pantry for up to a month.

Swap It Out! These particular French kale chips make use of the spice blend herbes de Provence, but you can easily make your own Italian kale chips using the In-Your-Face Italian Seasoning Spice Blend, or Indian kale chips using the Curry Seasoning Spice Blend, or south-of-the-border kale chips using the Taco Seasoning Spice Blend (all spice blend recipes in Chapter 12).

# Garlic Kale Chips

*You won't be able to eat just one of these truly spectacular, totally addictive and delicious little morsels. Flavored with tangy tahini, pungent garlic, and just enough salt to bring out all the subtleties, these fabulous flavors conspire to keep you reaching for more. Of course, you're eating kale, so there's really nothing wrong with that!*

**SERVES 4**

6 cups kale
¼ cup tahini
2 tablespoons apple-cider vinegar
2 tablespoons water
1 tablespoon nama shoyu
½ teaspoon salt
4 large cloves garlic
2 tablespoons sesame seeds

1. Remove the stems from the kale and discard. Tear the leaves into big pieces. Place into a very large bowl and set aside.

2. Place all the remaining ingredients, except the sesame seeds, in a blender or food processor and blend until smooth.

3. Mix the sauce with the kale and sesame seeds in the large bowl. Use your hands to ensure the kale is well-coated with the sauce.

4. Place the kale on dehydrator trays. Dehydrate at 115°F for 4–8 hours or until dry. Store in a sealed container in the pantry for up to a month.

# Chili Kale Chips

*Spicy, but not too spicy. Salty, but not too salty. A little tangy, a little acid, but certainly nothing that's too tart. As you can see, these chips have got a whole lot going on, so it's a good thing they're balanced so beautifully. With a full bouquet of a flavor profile, they bloom again and again as they reach each region of your tongue. They're seriously stimulating, and seriously fun—so enjoy!*

SERVES 4

6 cups kale
¼ cup tahini
¼ cup apple-cider vinegar
1 tablespoon lemon juice
1 tablespoon nama shoyu
½ teaspoon salt
½ teaspoon garlic powder
½ teaspoon cumin
½ teaspoon chili powder

1. Remove the stems from the kale and discard. Tear the leaves into big pieces. Place into a very large bowl and set aside.

2. Place all the remaining ingredients into a blender or food processor and blend until smooth.

3. Mix the sauce with the kale in a bowl. Use your hands to ensure the kale is well-coated with the sauce.

4. Place the kale on dehydrator trays. Dehydrate at 115°F for 4–8 hours or until dry. Store in a sealed container in the pantry for up to a month.

# Juice Pulp Fruit Nuggets

*This is a wonderful way to make use of your extra juice pulp, to maximize both the nutrients and the economics of your produce. If you don't juice very often, you can save your pulp in the freezer and make these snacks once you've collected enough. This recipe works best with sweet and starchy pulp, like that from carrots, apples, bell peppers, sweet potatoes, etc. A little green pulp (from spinach, kale, etc.) would be okay, but avoid the more intensely vegetable-like vegetables, such as cucumbers, celery, and green herbs.*

SERVES 4

2 cups juicer pulp
1 small, or ½ large, ripe banana
½ cup ground flaxseed
½ cup raisins
¼ cup agave syrup
½ teaspoon vanilla
½ teaspoon cinnamon
Optional: chopped almonds, walnuts, pecans, diced apricots, goji berries, hempseed, cacao nibs, shredded coconut, etc. to taste

1. In a a large mixing bowl, add all ingredients (including optional items) and mix well to combine.

2. Form the batter into small nuggets roughly the size of a golf ball, slightly flattened. Place on dehydrator trays lined with nonstick sheets. Dehydrate at 145°F for 2 hours. Turn down the temperature to 110°F and flip the nuggets. Continue dehydrating for 12 hours or until dry. Store in a sealed container in the refrigerator for up to a week

# Early Trekkin' Trail Mix

*Trail mix is an old standby, originally designed to facilitate easy eating on a hike—hence the "trail" part of the name. It has since become the fuel of choice for those on the go. Trail mix is portable, easy to eat, and totally customizable, which is great because here you're making it raw. This recipe stores well and will last in an airtight container in the pantry for up to 2 months. Keep a small container in your bag and in your glove box, in case of emergencies!*

SERVES 4

¾ cup dry buckwheat

1 cup almonds

1 cup green pumpkin seeds

3 tablespoons agave syrup

1 tablespoon carob powder

1 teaspoon cinnamon

1 cup dried fruit of choice, like goji berries, cherries, currants, and/or raisins

**1.** Soak the buckwheat for 6 hours and sprout for 1 day. At the same time, soak the almonds for 12 hours. Soak the pumpkin seeds for 4 hours.

**2.** Mix the buckwheat, almonds, and pumpkin seeds together and add the agave syrup, carob powder, and cinnamon.

**3.** Spread the mixture onto dehydrator trays and dehydrate at 145°F for 2 hours. Lower temperature to 115°F and continue dehydrating for another 8 hours.

**4.** Add the dried fruit and mix well.

Swap It Out! In this recipe you can replace the pumpkin seeds with sunflower seeds, or any other nut or seed you like. Walnuts stand in well for almonds, and of course the dried fruit is totally up to you.

*Chapter 14*

# Drinks and Desserts

For so many people the amazing, unparalleled, incomprehensibly incredible raw desserts made their transition to raw veganism possible. Raw desserts are in a class all their own, with mass appeal that even standard-American-diet-eating omnivores can recognize. Yeah, raw desserts definitely have it going on!

In the following pages you'll find a fabulous collection of some of the greatest special occasion drinks, mocktails, warm beverages, sweet treats, cookies, cakes, pies, ice creams, and so much more. Made only of the simplest and finest all-natural ingredients, flavored with wholesome and unrefined sweeteners, enhanced with seasonal fruits and elegant, exotic ingredients, this chapter has everything you need to round out—and finish off—your most excellent raw vegan life. So plop a big, fat cherry on top. You deserve it!

# Cultured Coconut Kefir

*Kefir is a fizzy fermented drink that's full of beneficial bacteria. It's easy to make at home, but it does require a starter colony, which come as kefir grains. Look for grains in your local health food store, or from online vendors like www.kefirlady. com, or on websites like Craigslist and Freecycle. Once you've secured some grains, start brewing up healthy, probiotic beverages at home! Yum!*

**YIELDS 2–3 CUPS**

**Water kefir grains, at least 2
  tablespoons
2 cups fresh young coconut water, at
  room temperature
Optional: 1 cup fresh fruit juice**

1. For the first round of fermentation, add the kefir grains to the coconut water in a glass container. (It's important to use glass, not plastic, metal, or wood, which may interfere with the fermentation process.)

2. Cover the container with a rag or a few layers of cheesecloth, secured with a rubber band or string. You want a semibreathable barrier. A paper coffee filter works well here, too.

3. Allow to sit undisturbed at room temperature for 48 hours.

4. At this point the first ferment is finished. It should be fizzy and slightly soured. You can either drink the kefir as it is, or you can do a second round of fermentation to flavor it.

5. Strain the kefir grains from the kefir. You can use these again immediately to begin another batch, or you can store them in a glass jar in the fridge, covered with just a bit of kefir water.

6. For the second round of fermentation, add the kefir to the fresh fruit juice in a glass container. (As above, it's important not to use metal, plastic, or wood.)

7. Once more, cover the container with a semibreathable barrier.

8. Allow to sit undisturbed at room temperature for another 24–48 hours, depending on how fizzy you like it.

9. The kefir will break down the sugars in the juice and become even more fizzy. It's probiotic soda! Store in a lidded glass jar in the refrigerator for up to 2 weeks.

# Rawesome Rejuvelac

*Rejuvelac, a fermented beverage, is made from grains—most often wheat berries—and tastes a bit like sour lemonade. But unlike other fermented beverages, this recipe doesn't require any starter cultures. Once it's made, Rawesome Rejuvelac contains a bounty of beneficial bacteria and can be drunk on its own as a health tonic or used as a starter culture for totally rawesome cheeses. How's that for multipurpose?*

### YIELDS 3 CUPS

**1 cup hard wheat or rye berries**
**3 cups unchlorinated water**

1. Soak the wheat or rye berries and sprout them for 1–2 days.

2. Drain and rinse the sprouts. Place them into a ½-gallon glass jar and fill the jar with water.

3. Fasten a rag or cheesecloth over the opening of the jar with a rubber band or string. Let the jar sit at room temperature for 2 days.

4. Pour the Rawesome Rejuvelac into a new jar, straining out the grains. The beverage will keep in the refrigerator for 2 or 3 days, but ideally it should be consumed within 24 hours.

5. The same grains can be used to make a second batch. Fill the jar with fresh water and let it sit for 24 hours. Pour into a new container and discard the seeds.

# Sparkling Ginger Limeade

*Limeade is lemonade's sassy cousin, and ginger limeade is just plain fun. This recipe gets its carbonation from coconut kefir, which combines with the ginger to become a powerful digestive tonic. It's like soda that's good for you. Serve this on a hot summer day and enjoy its delicious flavor. The taste alone is to live for—and never mind the health effects!*

### YIELDS 2½ CUPS

½ cup lime juice
½" knob of ginger, peeled
2–4 tablespoons agave syrup, depending on your preference
1½ cups Cultured Coconut Kefir (see recipe in this chapter) or sparkling mineral water
½ cup ice cubes
Fresh mint for garnish

1. Place the lime juice, ginger, agave syrup, and Cultured Coconut Kefir into blender and blend until smooth.

2. Add the ice cubes to the blender and briefly pulse until slightly chunky. Serve in tall glasses with a garnish of fresh mint.

# Festive Fresh Mint Mimosas

*Brunch just got a whole lot better! Mimosas are such a symbol of celebration. How else can you ever get away with drinking a cocktail—or mocktail—before noon? So whether your heading out to a romantic Sunday morning, a fancy summer garden party, or some sort of family fun time, these virgin versions of everyone's favorite fizzy breakfast beverage are sure to make your celebration extra special.*

### YIELDS 3 CUPS

1 orange
2 cups fresh orange juice
1 cup Cultured Coconut Kefir or Rawesome Rejuvelac (see recipes in this chapter) or plain sparkling mineral water
Fresh mint leaves, for garnish

1. Slice orange in half. Cut thin slices of the orange (shaped like a wheel) and save them to use as a garnish.

2. Stir orange juice together with the sparkling beverage.

3. Serve in champagne flutes and garnish each glass with mint leaves and one thin orange wheel slice.

# Bloody 'Bucha

*This mocktail makes a play on the classic vodka, V-8, and Tabasco-infused concoction, the Bloody Mary! Another cocktail considered suitable for any time of day, this virgin version relies on delicious and healthy kombucha, an ancient fermented tea, as a base. Kombucha is widely available at health food stores; try to use a non-fruit-flavored variety in this recipe.*

YIELDS 4 CUPS

1 cup kombucha
1 cup chopped tomatoes
½ jalapeño pepper
1 small garlic clove
¼ teaspoon black pepper
2 cups ice cubes
Celery sticks, to garnish
Optional: raw pitted olives, to garnish

1. In a blender, add the kombucha, tomatoes, jalapeño, garlic, and pepper, and blend until smooth.

2. Add the ice cubes to the blender and blend to mix. Serve in tall glasses with a celery stick and olives.

# Sweet Boba Milk Tea

*Boba, or bubble tea, is a sweet drink that's popular throughout Asia, most notably in Taiwan and Hong Kong. More recently it has become something of a food phenomenon in America. The milk tea is served with large tapioca pearls and an extra wide straw for sucking them up. It's a fun drink, and delicious, too, and now there's a raw rendition for your enjoyment!*

## YIELDS 3 CUPS

¼ cup chia seeds

1½ cups Easy-Breezy Plant Milk (see recipe in Ch. 6)

1 cup tea (see sidebar "Brewing Raw Tea")

½ cup ice

1 tablespoon agave syrup

2 tablespoons blueberries

1. In a small bowl, soak the chia seeds in the Easy-Breezy Plant Milk. Stir the seeds occasionally during the first 10 minutes. Cover the bowl and continue soaking in the refrigerator for 6–8 hours.

2. In a large shaker cup with a lid, place chia-seed mix, the brewed tea, ice, and agave syrup. Tighten the lid and shake vigorously. Alternatively, use a Tupperware container with lid to shake the ingredients. The shaking motion creates the air bubbles.

3. Place the blueberry "pearls" at the bottom of a pint glass. Pour the mixture from the shaker over the blueberries and serve.

### Brewing Raw Tea

Although boiling water and brewing tea the old-fashioned way is a no-no for raw foodists, you can still whip up a cup of your favorite tea. You can keep this raw by starting with sun-dried tea leaves (available online, or you can grow your own) and steeping them, 1 tablespoon per cup of water, in the dehydrator for 4–8 hours at 115°F. Strain and allow to cool to room temperature.

# Coconut Horchata

*Horchata is a sweetly spiced milky drink popular throughout Spain and Latin America. Though the details vary by region, traditionally horchata "milk" is made by boiling and blending rice or nuts with cane sugar and spice. This raw adaptation, which is based on classic Mexican horchata, uses rich creamy coconut combined with cinnamon and vanilla. Horchata is often served over ice, so save this treat for your next lazy, warm afternoon.*

**YIELDS 3½ CUPS**

**1 cup dried shredded coconut**
**3 cups water**
**1 tablespoon agave syrup**
**1 tablespoon cinnamon**
**Optional: 1 teaspoon vanilla**

1. First make the coconut milk. In a blender, combine the coconut with the water and blend on high for 2 minutes. Place a nut milk bag or fine mesh strainer in a large bowl and pour the contents of the blender into the bowl. This will strain the milk from the pulp. Use your hands to press and squeeze all the liquid out. Reserve the pulp for another use.

2. Now, make the horchata. Place the milk back into the blender and add the rest of the ingredients. Blend until well-combined.

3. Strain and serve in tall glasses, over ice.

# Mexican Not-Hot Chocolate

*The mention of cocoa conjures to mind all sorts of sweet and comforting images. Piping hot mug on a cold winter night, quickly melting marshmallows, and sticky chocolate mustaches, to name a few. Clearly, cocoa is child's play. But this is a drink that's designed for adults. Refined, well-balanced, and of course, made of the healthiest ingredients on earth.*

### YIELDS 2¼ CUPS

**2 cups Easy-Breezy Plant Milk (see recipe in Ch. 6)**

**3 tablespoons raw cacao**

**1 tablespoon cinnamon**

**1 teaspoon to 1 tablespoon agave syrup, to taste**

1. Whisk together all the ingredients in a bowl until well-combined.

2. Warm the bowl of liquid in the dehydrator set at 115°F, until it is nicely heated.

3. Transfer contents to a blender, quickly blend to completely mix, and then serve immediately.

Swap It Out! American hot chocolate is simply made from cocoa, milk, and sugar. The Mexican version is much the same, but includes a touch of cinnamon. You're welcome to leave it out if you wish, but it sure does make for a lovely addition.

# Ooey-Gooey Chunky Chewy Raw Fudge

*This fudge gives new meaning to the term* rich. *Truly, it's a chocolate lover's dream come true. A little bit nutty, a little bit sticky, a whole lot of creamy and more chocolate than should be legal. It's everything you want in fudge, and it's vegan, and it's raw, and most of the ingredients are actually good for you! So feel free to indulge. You deserve it!*

SERVES 8

1½ cups pecans
1½ cups pitted dates
½ cup cacao powder
¼ cup coconut oil
¼ cup agave syrup
½ teaspoon sea salt

1. Place all the ingredients in a food processor and pulse until well-combined but still chunky.

2. Transfer to a 8" × 8" glass dish that has been greased with coconut oil. Press the fudge into place to fit the pan, and refrigerate to set, about 3 hours. Store in a sealed container in the fridge (about a month) or freezer (up to 6 months).

# Quick Choco-Bites

*These bites are so easy, in so many ways. Easy to make, these treats contain only five ingredients and come together in no time at all—under 10 minutes between the first thought, "I should have some dessert," and the final thought, "Oh my god these taste amazing!" They're also easy to transport. Just wrap a few in plastic and throw them in your bag. They're great to sneak into parties and other social events, so you can thoroughly enjoy yourself right along with all your cooked-cake-and-ice-cream-eating companions. Never be the odd man out again!*

SERVES 8

1 cup pitted dates, chopped and
   soaked for 10 minutes
1 cup walnuts or cashews
¼ cup cacao or carob powder
1 tablespoon almond butter
¼ cup dried shredded coconut, more
   for rolling if desired

1. Process all ingredients in a food processor or blender. Leave some texture; do not overmix.

2. Shape into little golf-ball-sized balls. If desired, roll in coconut flakes. Place on a tray and chill in the refrigerator.

3. Store in a covered container in the fridge (up to a month) or freezer (up to 6 months).

# Chewy Chocolate Nib Cookies

*It can be really fun to whip up decadent cheesecakes, silky sorbets, and delicate, elegant truffles. Raw gourmet is so exciting! But then again, sometimes you just want a cookie. A warm chocolate chip cookie, to be exact, with a cold glass of almond milk. And you should have it. Here's how!*

SERVES 6

1 cup soaked, sprouted, and dehydrated buckwheat, as described in Completely Life-Changing Grain Crunchies (see recipe in Ch. 6)
¼ cup flaxseed
2 cups macadamia nuts
½ cup dried dates
½ cup liquid coconut oil
1 teaspoon vanilla extract
½ cup raw cacao nibs

1. Grind the buckwheat and flaxseed into a powder using a coffee grinder. Set aside.

2. Process the macadamia nuts in a food processor until they become a powder. Do not overprocess.

3. To the food processor, add in the buckwheat and flaxseed powder, dates, coconut oil, and vanilla, and process until you achieve a creamy texture comparable to smooth peanut butter.

4. Stir in the cacao nibs by hand.

5. Form into cookie shapes and lay them out on dehydrator trays fitted with nonstick sheets. Dehydrate at 145°F for 2 hours, then reduce heat to 110°F and continue dehydrating for an additional 6–8 hours. Store in a sealed container in the refrigerator for up to 2 weeks.

# Oatmeal Cinnamon Raisin Cookies

*Traditional oatmeal cookies rely on rolled oats, which cook up quickly and absorb a lot of moisture while providing an amazing, unmatched flavor. This recipe uses raw, hulless oats, which require a bit of advanced prep. But the labor is well worth the gain, however, when you bite in and taste that perfect, signature oatey flavor. Riding on hints of cinnamon and sugar, and punctuated with pops of candy-sweet raisins, these are cookies that taste like tradition.*

**SERVES 6**

2 tablespoons chia seeds

½ cup water

2 cups hulless oats, soaked and sprouted (see Soaking and Sprouting Chart in Ch. 1)

½ cup Easy-Breezy Plant Milk (see recipe in Ch. 6)

⅔ cup agave syrup

2 tablespoons coconut oil

2 tablespoons lucuma powder

½ teaspoon vanilla

¼ teaspoon salt

½ cup raisins

1. In a spice or coffee grinder, grind chia seeds to a fine powder. Whisk the chia powder with the water and set aside.

2. In a food processor, process the oats to a fine chunky mixture. Transfer to a large mixing bowl.

3. Add in the chia mix and the Easy-Breezy Plant Milk, agave syrup, coconut oil, lucuma powder, vanilla, and salt. Mix well. Fold in raisins and mix.

4. Form into cookie shapes and lay them out on dehydrator trays fitted with nonstick sheets. Dehydrate at 145°F for 2 hours, then reduce heat to 110°F and continue dehydrating for an additional 6–8 hours. Store in a sealed container in the refrigerator for up to 2 weeks.

### Hulless Oats for Health

Everybody knows that oats are great for your heart, because they're high in fiber and naturally act to lower cholesterol. But oats, hulless oats in this case, are also high in the vitamins A, C, E, and many of the Bs, as well as the minerals calcium, iron, magnesium, phosphorous, and potassium. Finally, oats include significant quantities of all nine essential amino acids, making them an excellent source of protein. How's that for a powerful cookie?

# Healthy Wholesome Thumbprint Cookies

*Is the name of this cookie an intrinsic redundancy? I mean, aren't all of these recipes "healthy" and "wholesome"? Well, yes! But the case could be made that some are more so than others, and if we're making that case, then these cookies come down squarely on the side of "more so." Perhaps it's just because they're a cookie and therefore expected to be naughty. But that's not true here. Nope, these little treats are oh so nice.*

SERVES 6

¼ cup flaxseed

1 cup hulless oats, soaked and sprouted (see Soaking and Sprouting Chart in Ch. 1)

1 cup dried figs

½ cup dried cranberries, more for topping

¼ cup almond butter

¼ cup orange juice

1. Grind the flaxseed into a powder using a coffee grinder or heavy-duty blender. Set aside.

2. Grind the oats into a fine meal using a food processor or heavy-duty blender. Set aside.

3. Soak the figs in water for 20 minutes. Chop off and discard the stems.

4. In a food processor, process the ground flaxseed, the powdered oats, the soaked figs, dried cranberries, and almond butter until well-mixed. Gradually add the orange juice.

5. Form the mixture into cookie patties about 2 inches across and make an indent in the center of each cookie with your thumb. Place a cranberry or three in the impression. Dehydrate for 2 hours at 145°F. The cookies taste good both after dehydrating for 2 hours or after dehydrating for another 12 hours at 115°F. Store in a sealed container in the refrigerator for up to 2 weeks.

# Charming Apricot Jam Bars

*There's no way these bars are raw! They couldn't be, not with that pastry that tastes just like a buttery, flaky, slightly-sweet-and-oh-so-crumbly crust that's been made with white flour, shortening, and a warm stove. Not with that sticky saccharine apricot jam topping that must have been reduced over heat. No, these perfect pastry treats, at home in any gourmet bakery, just couldn't possibly be raw. Could they? The answer, of course, is yes! So eat up raw vegans—and enjoy!*

**SERVES 8**

⅓ cup coconut oil, more for greasing

1 cup coconut flour

½ cup Easy-Breezy Plant Milk (see recipe in Ch. 6)

¼ cup agave syrup

½ teaspoon vanilla extract

½ teaspoon sea salt

2 cups dried apricots, soaked, reserving the soak water

1. Melt the coconut oil by floating it in a small bowl within a larger bowl of hot water. Use a little coconut oil to grease an 8" baking tray.

2. To make the pastry, combine the coconut flour, plant milk, melted coconut oil, agave syrup, vanilla, and sea salt in a mixing bowl and stir to completely combine.

3. Once the batter is mixed, press it into the bottom of the oiled baking tray.

4. Place all the soaked apricots in a blender or food processor. Add enough of the soak water to form a thick but smooth paste, probably just over 1 cup. When the apricots are fully blended, spread them evenly on top of the crust.

5. Refrigerate to set for a few hours before serving. Store in a sealed container in the fridge for up to a week.

# Lemon Bars Like You Remember

*The pastry crust of these perfectly textured lemon bars is, of course, unbelievably flaky for not containing butter or flour. But the real anomaly of these beautiful bars is the lemon topping, which seems impossibly jelled, achieving that incredible clear-custard consistency while eschewing eggs and heat. The secret is in the Irish moss, a specialty product that's used to give raw puddings that certain light, firm, "mousse-y" feeling. Who knew moss could be oh-so-amazing?*

**SERVES 8**

1 cup coconut oil, divided, more for greasing

1 cup coconut flour

½ cup Easy-Breezy Plant Milk (see recipe in Ch. 6)

¾ cup agave syrup, divided

½ teaspoon vanilla extract

½ teaspoon sea salt

½ cup Irish Moss Paste (see recipe in this chapter)

Juice and zest from 3 lemons

**1.** Melt the coconut oil by floating it in a small bowl within a larger bowl of hot water. Use a little coconut oil to grease an 8" baking tray.

**2.** To make the pastry, combine ⅓ cup of the melted coconut oil, coconut flour, Easy-Breezy Plant Milk, ¼ cup of the agave syrup, vanilla, and sea salt in a mixing bowl and stir to completely combine.

**3.** Once the batter is mixed, press it into the bottom of the oiled baking tray.

**4.** In a blender or food processor, combine the Irish Moss Paste, ⅔ cup melted coconut oil, ½ cup agave syrup, lemon juice, and zest. Blend to completely combine. Pour topping over pastry crust.

**5.** Refrigerate to set for a few hours before serving. Store in a sealed container in the fridge for up to a week.

# Irish Moss Paste

*Irish moss is an incredibly nutritious seaweed that happens to have some super special properties. When properly prepared, this delicious ingredient becomes a light and fluffy gel-like substance that can be used to make amazing desserts like custards, mousses, cheesecake fillings, and more. Irish moss also provides an excellent, low-calorie alternative to nuts and coconut oil.*

**MAKES ABOUT 3 CUPS**

**1 cup Irish moss**
**1–2 cups water**

1. Irish moss is a seaweed that will come in dried (not powdered) form. First you'll need to wash it well. In a strainer over the sink, rinse and scrub the Irish moss to remove any hard bits or ocean grit.

2. Place the moss in a glass jar and fill the jar with cold water. Soak the moss in the refrigerator—it's important to keep it cold. Rinse and replace the water every 4–6 hours. Continue for 12–36 hours, until the moss loses its ocean odor. It will also lighten in color, becoming almost translucent.

3. When the moss is finished soaking and has no more odor, measure it in a measuring cup and then put it into a blender (works best) or food processor. Add an equal amount of cold water.

4. Blend the moss with water, between 1–2 cups, until it is silky smooth, stopping as needed to scrape down the sides. This may take a long time, up to 10 minutes, so watch that it doesn't overheat. You may need to take a break. If you need to add more water, add a little at a time. Your final paste should be just thin enough to run, but essentially thick and viscous.

5. Irish Moss Paste will store in the refrigerator for 2 weeks, but will continue to gel. If you use stored Irish Moss Paste, you may have to adjust the amount for the recipe, using a little less.

# Indian Almond Chai Bars

*This healthy recipe doubles as a dessert or a snack bar, and either way the warming spices and sweet flavor will leave you satisfied. This is an especially great goody to make in winter. Raw can become harder when the weather cools down, and one great way to combat cooked-food cravings is by using warming spices and eating plenty of comforting treats! This decadent recipe offers a bit of both.*

SERVES 4

2 cups almonds
½ cup flaxseed
1 cup water
1 teaspoon chai spice blend
1 cup goji berries
½ cup date paste
4 tablespoons agave nectar

1. Soak the almonds for 12 hours in water. Grind the flaxseed to a powder.

2. To make the tea, bring 1 cup water to a boil. Let it cool for a few minutes and then steep the chai spice blend in the water for 5 minutes. Strain and discard the spice blend but reserve the liquid. Alternatively, you can use chai tea bags instead of the dried chai spice blend.

3. In a food processor, process all ingredients with the chai tea liquid until well-mixed but still chunky.

4. Form the mixture into rectangular bar shapes.

5. Dehydrate the bars at 145°F for 2 hours. Flip over the bars and continue dehydrating at 115°F for 12 hours. Store in a sealed container in the refrigerator for up to 2 weeks.

### Chai Spice

Chai is a traditional black tea brewed in India. It combines the flavors of cardamom, cinnamon, ginger, star anise, peppercorn, and cloves to create a strong, aromatic, spicy blend. Chai is popular in ayurvedic medicine, enjoyed for it's flavor but also reputed to have important health-promoting properties.

# Orange and Almond Macaroons

*Macaroons are a classic raw food recipe favorite. They center around one of the most beloved ingredients in raw cuisine—the coconut—in its dried and shredded form. These cookies are great to have on hand for when you need a little something-something, so make these cookies when you have time and store them in the freezer for anytime a cookie craving hits.*

**SERVES 6**

**1 cup almonds**
**½ cup cashews**
**½ cup pine nuts**
**¼ teaspoon salt**
**¼ cup orange juice**
**1 teaspoon vanilla extract**
**½ cup liquid coconut oil, for blending**
**2 cups dried coconut**

1. Process the almonds in a food processor until they are ground into small chunks. Set them aside.

2. In a food processor, process the cashews, pine nuts, and salt until combined. Gradually add the orange juice and vanilla extract. Gradually pour in the melted coconut oil as its blending until the batter takes on the consistency of almond butter or chunky peanut butter.

3. Pour the dried coconut and ground almonds into the batter and pulse until it is well-mixed and chunky.

4. Form into rounded shapes roughly the size of golf balls. Serve the macaroons as is, or dehydrate at 145°F for 3 hours. Store in a sealed container in the refrigerator for up to 2 weeks.

# Black Forest Custard

*The term "Black Forest" in this recipe title refers to the German region that originated the Black Forest Cherry Cake. Here, the traditional cake's combination of chocolate and cherries, that dynamic duo, that impeccable partnership, that exquisite marriage of sweet chocolate and tart cherries, manifests as a charming custard. Once you've cracked the coconuts, it all comes together easily, and those coconuts make for such a light and fluffy pudding. However, if coconuts are hard to find, you can substitute macadamia nuts in their place.*

SERVES 4

¼ cup dates, loosely chopped
¾ cup young coconut meat
½ cup young coconut water
2 tablespoons raw cacao powder
1 cup fresh cherries

1. In a blender or food processor, blend all the ingredients together, except the cherries.

2. Add the cherries last and briefly pulse until they are mixed in but still chunky. Pour into bowls and serve.

### *Spotlight on Cherries*

There are two distinct types of cherries: sweet ones and tart ones. Sweet cherries include Black Bing, Lambert, and Royal Anne. Tart varieties are the familiar dark red cherries often found in pies. Popular species are Montmorency and Morello. All cherries are extremely alkaline and reduce acidity in the blood.

# Can't Get Enough Chocolate Pots

*Pudding, custard, crema, flan . . . it's hard to effectively encapsulate this dessert in a single descriptor. Mousse comes close, but even that seems to fall short. Descriptive words aside, this recipe is cacao at its finest, impossibly rich in flavor considering how light the texture is. Uncomplicated and straightforward, this dish is about allowing chocolate to shine bright, unhindered by additional sauces or fruity accoutrements. So one word to describe it? How about: masterpiece.*

SERVES 4

1 cup coconut milk, made as instructed in Coconut Horchata (see recipe in this chapter)

½ cup Irish Moss Paste (see recipe in this chapter)

½ cup agave syrup

¾ cup raw cacao powder

½ teaspoon vanilla extract

1. Combine all ingredients in a high-speed blender (or food processor or blender, though it may change the consistency) and purée on high until completely smooth and whipped, about 2 minutes.

2. Pour into small serving bowls or "pots" (hence the recipe title) and refrigerate for at least 4 hours to set.

# Sweet Cream and Strawberries Ice Cream

*The secret to a sublimely silky nondairy dessert is simple: don't skimp. It's dessert, after all, and enjoying it should be a sensuous experience. This ice cream takes full advantage of the most luscious epicurean offerings: rich young coconut meat, sticky sweet agave syrup, and plump ripe berries. It's a no-holds barred celebration of pleasure. So let the celebration begin!*

SERVES 4

1½ cups frozen strawberries

1½ cups young coconut meat

½ young coconut water

⅓ cup agave syrup

2 teaspoons vanilla

¼ teaspoon sea salt

1. In a food processor or blender, purée all ingredients together until smooth and creamy.

2. Transfer the mixture to a large freezer-proof glass dish, and freeze.

3. Stir every 30 minutes until a smooth ice cream forms, about 4 hours. If the mixture gets too firm, transfer to a blender, process until smooth, and then return to freezer. Store in a covered container in the freezer for up to 4 weeks.

# Iced Apricot Ginger Sorbet

*Sorbet is a naturally nondairy dessert that's made from fruit-flavored frozen water, and this recipe takes that idea to heart and infuses the landscape of gentle apricot with pert and perky ginger. It's also almost entirely fat-free, so enjoy it without a worry. Feeling like something cool on a summer morning? Sorbet for breakfast! Need an afternoon sweet treat to pick you up? Sorbet as a snack! How about a little something to top off an elegant dinner. Sorbet for dessert! Any way, any time of day. Have at it!*

SERVES 4

⅔ cups water
½ cup agave
2 teaspoons fresh minced ginger
5 cups chopped fresh apricots
3 tablespoons lemon juice

1. In a food processor or blender, purée all ingredients together until completely smooth.

2. Transfer the mixture to a large freezer-proof casserole dish, and freeze.

3. Stir every 30 minutes until a smooth sorbet forms, about 4 hours. If the mixture gets too firm, transfer to a blender, process until smooth, and then return to freezer. Store in a covered container in the freezer for up to 4 weeks.

# Fresh Mint and Nib Gelato

*Mint is such a refreshing flavor, and the herb itself is a powerful medicinal. Mint is a digestive aid that fights indigestion—a great reason to top off a meal with a big bowl of gelato! What are you waiting for? Dig in!*

SERVES 4

2 tablespoons coconut oil
1 cup cashews
⅓ cup dates
1 tablespoon cacao nibs
2 tablespoons fresh chopped mint

1. Warm the coconut oil to a liquid by placing the container in a bowl of warm water for a few minutes.

2. Place all the ingredients in a blender and blend until smooth.

3. Pour mixture into ice cream trays or molds. Freeze for 3 hours or until mixture becomes solid. Serve or store in a covered container in the freezer for up to 4 weeks.

# Chocolate "Magic Shell" Sauce

*"Magic Shell" is a super-fun product designed by "food science" laboratories that relies on strange processing to produce a sauce that's liquid at room temperature and solid when it gets cold. The concept is simple enough, but it creates quite a fun effect when poured over a scoop of ice cream, effectively creating a hard coating that encases the sweet iced treat inside. And now raw foodists can experience the same sort of delightful dessert with this mock magic shell!*

SERVES 2

3 tablespoons coconut oil
1 tablespoon cacao powder
1 teaspoon to 1 tablespoon agave
  syrup, to taste

1. Melt the coconut oil by placing it in a small bowl and floating that in a larger bowl of hot water.

2. Mix all ingredients in a bowl and whisk together.

3. Use immediately, pouring over ice cream or other cold dessert, such as cheesecake fresh from the fridge.

# Perfect Pumpkin Pie

*Kiddies in costumes. Piles of bronzed leaves. Scarfs and mittens making their way into rotation. Oh, autumn! Whether you love the season or dread its approach, you can't deny that that brisk wind and falling leaves makes you long for an autumnal favorite: pumpkin pie! If you said goodbye to pumpkin pie in the past, it's time to renew your relationship. Say hello to this incredibly authentic autumn dessert!*

**SERVES 8**

**For the crust:**

2 cups almond pulp (from Easy-
Breeze Plant Milk recipe in Ch. 6)
or soaked almonds

1 cup pitted dates, soaked at least 1
hour

½ cup melted coconut oil, more for
greasing

¼ cup cacao nibs

2 teaspoons cinnamon

½ teaspoon sea salt

**For the filling:**

2 cups cashews, soaked at least 2
hours

1 cup fresh pumpkin juice

½ cup agave syrup

½ cup coconut oil, melted

2 teaspoons cinnamon

1 teaspoon turmeric

½ teaspoon nutmeg

½ teaspoon ginger

¼ teaspoon cloves

**1.** To make the crust, combine in a food processor the almond pulp, dates, coconut oil, cacao nibs, 2 teaspoons of the cinnamon, and salt, and pulse to blend. You want it well-combined but not completely smooth. Press it into a pie pan that's been greased with coconut oil. Put the crust in the freezer and allow it to set up for at least 1 hour.

**2.** To make the filling, combine in a food processor or blender the cashews, pumpkin juice, agave syrup, coconut oil, cinnamon, turmeric, nutmeg, ginger, and cloves, and blend thoroughly, pausing every so often to scrape down the sides. You want it as smooth as possible.

**3.** Remove the crust from the freezer and pour in the filling. Freeze a minimum of 2 hours before serving. After initial freeze, the pie can be stored in the refrigerator for up to a week.

### Edible Peel?

In many cases you can leave the skin on the fruits and veggies that you blend or juice. Common options include cucumber, carrot, lemon, apple, pear, zucchini/soft squash, and in this case, pumpkin. The peels are often a valuable source of antioxidants and other nutrients. However, if you're going to eat the skins, you need to be certain that the produce is organic. If you can't secure an organic supply, it's better to discard the peel after all.

# Chocolate Torte with Berry Cheesecake Filling

*Ultracreamy berry cheesecake in an ultradark bittersweet chocolate crust. Do you really need to know anything else about this recipe? Basically it's an unbelievable dessert with rich flavors and luxurious tastes that really needs to speak for itself. So get unbaking!*

### SERVES 8

**For the crust:**

2 cups walnuts or pecans

1½ cups pitted dates

¼ shredded coconut

¼ cup cacao nibs

¼ cup melted coconut oil, more for greasing

½ cup cacao powder

½ teaspoon sea salt

**For the filling:**

2 cups cashews, soaked

1 cup berries, fresh or frozen (raspberry, blueberry, blackberry, or blend)

¼ cup melted coconut oil

⅓ cup agave syrup

1 teaspoon vanilla

**1.** To make the crust, in a food processor, combine the walnuts, dates, shredded coconut, cacao nibs, coconut oil, cacao powder, and sea salt, and pulse to blend. You want it well-combined but not completely smooth. Press it into a pie pan that's been greased with coconut oil. Put the crust in the freezer and allow it to set up for at least 1 hour.

**2.** To make the filling, in a food processor or blender, combine the cashews, berries, coconut oil, agave syrup, and vanilla, and blend thoroughly, pausing every so often to scrape down the sides. You want it as smooth as possible.

**3.** Remove the crust from the freezer and pour in the filling. Freeze a minimum of 2 hours before serving. After initial freeze, the pie can be stored in the refrigerator for up to a week.

***Passionate* Pairings** If you want to take this cheesecake from "oh my goodness amazing" straight into the realm of "OH MY GOODNESS AMAZING," try it with a liberal drizzling of Unbelievable Raspberry Coulis (see recipe in Chapter 9). Now that needs no further explanation!

# Midcentury Revival Grasshopper Pie

*Grasshopper pie is a special dessert that was popular in the 1950s, so named for the cocktail that shares its moniker. But it wasn't just any old frozen cheesecake. Grasshopper pie was made with gelatin and whipped egg whites, which bestowed a specific mousse-like character to the creamy green filling. It was also served up in a cookie crust—Oreo most often—with Cool Whip on top. Wow, right? This recipe captures all that deliciousness while making sure your dessert rings of rawesomeness. What are you waiting for? Give it a try!*

**SERVES 4**

1 batch Ooey-Gooey Chunky Chewy Raw Fudge (see recipe in this chapter)

2 cups packed fresh mint leaves

½ cup Irish Moss Paste (see recipe in this chapter)

½ cup cashews, soaked at least 2 hours

½ cup agave syrup

3 tablespoons melted coconut oil, more for greasing

2 tablespoons spinach juice

½ teaspoon vanilla

1. Make the Ooey-Gooey Chunky Chewy Raw Fudge as instructed, but press it into a pie pan that's been greased with coconut oil. Put this crust in the freezer and allow it to set up for at least 1 hour.

2. In a food processor or blender, combine the fresh mint leaves, Irish Moss Paste, cashews, agave syrup, coconut oil, spinach juice, and vanilla, and blend thoroughly, pausing every so often to scrape down the sides. You want it as smooth as possible.

3. Remove the crust from the freezer and pour in the filling. Freeze a minimum of 2 hours before serving. After initial freeze, the pie can be stored in the refrigerator for up to a week.

Swap It Out! This raw pie takes a different, natural approach. The texture is spot-on. However, the use of real, fresh mint imparts a distinctly earthy flavor. Many healthy eaters actually enjoy this, but if you'd like to you can replace the fresh mint with a mint extract or oil.

# Basically Amazing Shortcake with Lemon Icing

*This simple recipe is super-easy to make, and with a bit of tweaking you can spice or spruce it up however you please. Add fruit purée for a flavored cake, or chopped dried fruit for a sort of raw stollen. Carob or chocolate takes it in a different direction, or you could just add cinnamon, ginger, and nutmeg for a standard spice cake. Clearly, there's lots of wiggle room. So wiggle!*

**SERVES 4**

2 cups almonds, soaked

1 cup dates

½ teaspoon salt

½ cup cashews, soaked at least 2 hours

4 tablespoons agave syrup

3 tablespoons lemon juice

½ teaspoon lemon zest

1. In a food processor, process the almonds, dates, and salt until well-mixed into a batter.

2. Form the batter into a round cake shape, on a serving dish. Set aside.

3. In a blender, blend together the cashews, agave syrup, lemon juice, and lemon zest until smooth. Spread the frosting over the cake. Freeze the cake for 1 hour to help the frosting set. At this point, it is ready to serve. It can be stored, covered, in the fridge for 3–5 days.

***Passionate* Pairings** Here the cake base is presented with a coating of delicious lemon frosting. As with the cake itself, the frosting is highly adaptable. As written, this cake and lemon frosting are amazing when served with a drizzle of Unbelievable Raspberry Coulis (see recipe in Chapter 9).

### Let Them Eat Cakes!

There are literally hundreds of different, distinct types of cakes. Some common varietals include: Angel Food, Battenberg, Bundt, Coffee Cake, Cupcakes, Depression-Style, Devil's Food, Fairy Cake, Gingerbread, Opera, Panettone, Pavlova, Pineapple Upside Down Cake, Pound Cake, Red Velvet, Sponge, Sun Cake, Tea Loaf, Tiramisu, and Wedding Cake, just as a start. Why not try your hand at trying to raw-volutionize a few of your favorites?

# Index

## About the Author

Mike Snyder is the president of TheRawDiet.com and an expert on vegetarian and vegan raw foods nutrition. He has been active in the raw foods community for more than ten years. He has studied with Viktoras Kulvinskas, the founder of the modern raw foods movement, and with Gabriel Cousens, one of its best-known proponents. As a health coach, Snyder assists clients worldwide in transitioning to raw foods. He provides keynote addresses and presentations, food prep demonstrations, seminars, and teleseminars across the country. He recently coauthored *The Everything® Raw Food Recipe Book*. He lives in Portland, OR.